RESURRECTING THE JEW

PRINCETON STUDIES IN CULTURAL SOCIOLOGY

Paul J. DiMaggio, Michèle Lamont,
Robert J. Wuthnow, and Viviana A. Zelizer,
Series Editors

Resurrecting the Jew

NATIONALISM, PHILOSEMITISM, AND POLAND'S JEWISH REVIVAL

GENEVIÈVE ZUBRZYCKI

PRINCETON UNIVERSITY PRESS

PRINCETON AND OXFORD

Published by Princeton University Press
41 William Street, Princeton, New Jersey 08540
99 Banbury Road, Oxford OX2 6JX

press.princeton.edu

Library of Congress Cataloging-in-Publication Data

Names: Zubrzycki, Geneviève, author.
Title: Resurrecting the Jew : nationalism, philosemitism, and Poland's Jewish revival / Geneviève Zubrzycki.
Description: Princeton ; Oxford : Princeton University Press, [2022] | Series: Princeton studies in cultural sociology | Includes bibliographical references and index.
Identifiers: LCCN 2021059569 (print) | LCCN 2021059570 (ebook) | ISBN 9780691237220 (hardback) | ISBN 9780691237237 (paperback) | ISBN 9780691237244 (ebook)
Subjects: LCSH: Jews—Poland—History—21st century. | Jews—Poland—Social conditions—21st century. | Jews—Poland—Social life and customs—21st century. | Nationalism—Poland—Religious aspects. | National characteristics, Polish. | Poland—Religious life and customs—21st century. | Judaism—Relations—Catholic Church. | Catholic Church—Relations—Judaism. | BISAC: SOCIAL SCIENCE / Sociology of Religion | SOCIAL SCIENCE / Jewish Studies
Classification: LCC DS134.56 .Z83 2022 (print) | LCC DS134.56 (ebook) | DDC 305.892/40438—dc23/eng/20220208
LC record available at https://lccn.loc.gov/2021059569
LC ebook record available at https://lccn.loc.gov/2021059570

British Library Cataloging-in-Publication Data is available

Editorial: Fred Appel and James Collier
Production Editorial: Natalie Baan
Text and Cover Design: Chris Ferrante
Production: Lauren Reese and Erin Suydam
Publicity: Charlotte Coyne and Kate Hensley
Copyeditor: P. David Hornik

Cover image: Mural in Bawół Square, Kazimierz, the historical district of Kraków, 2019. Photograph by kgbo.

This book has been composed in Source Serif 4 and Futura PT

10 9 8 7 6 5 4 3 2 1

Pour ma fille, et mon père

CONTENTS

ILLUSTRATIONS

Figures

Tables

Maps

Graphs

Every spring since 2013, tens of thousands of Poles have pinned a yellow paper daffodil to their lapels in commemoration of the Warsaw Ghetto Uprising and the victims of the Holocaust. Opened, the flower metamorphoses into a Star of David, transforming a commemorative gesture into an act of performative solidarity, perhaps even of contrition. Initiated by the Polin Museum of the History of Polish Jews in Warsaw, the "daffodil campaign" now reaches the four corners of Poland. For weeks after the official commemorative ceremonies, thousands of Poles go about their daily activities wearing yellow stars on their jackets and coats.

This act of posthumous solidarity can be puzzling and perhaps shocking to outside observers. It seems almost unimaginable in North America or Western Europe. What makes it thinkable and desirable, even virtuous, for large numbers of non-Jewish Poles in Poland? How can we make sense of such a commemorative practice, and of the passion of numerous non-Jewish Poles for all things Jewish, in the twenty-first century? These are the empirical questions this book answers. But it also raises questions relevant well beyond Poland, questions at the core of cultural sociology and at the center of roiling public debates: How do we distinguish between types and degrees of engagement with the history and the culture of the Other? What are the limits of performative solidarity and empathetic forms of cultural appropriation, especially when that Other has been violently erased and continues to be oppressed?

Resurrecting the Jew is the culmination of ten years of field research in multiple Polish cities and towns, but it has much deeper roots. In *The Crosses of Auschwitz: Nationalism and Religion in Post-Communist Poland* (2006), I investigated the questioning of the relationship between Polishness and Catholicism after the fall of communism, and why and how national identity is given form in specific symbols, transmitted in stories and rituals, and potentially transformed in specific events. My window into these sociological issues was the "war of the crosses" in 1998–99, when self-defined Poles-Catholics erected hundreds of crosses in the immediate proximity of Auschwitz to mark the site as one of *Polish* martyrdom and to underline Poles' fundamentally Catholic identity. Even beyond the conflict between Poles-Catholics and Jews over the memory of Auschwitz, the controversy became a signal event to debate Polishness and its relation to Catholicism.

During a later phase of the fieldwork at the Auschwitz-Birkenau Museum, in 2001, I met and befriended high school teachers enrolled in a special course at the museum on how to teach the Holocaust. As we carpooled between Kraków and Oświęcim, I learned how they came to be interested in the Holocaust and Polish-Jewish relations. Some of them were evangelical Christians who had discovered the Hebrew Bible in their Bible study groups, spent time as domestic workers in Israel, and volunteered to help Holocaust survivors in Poland. They observed Jewish holidays and gave biblical Hebrew names to their children.

It was in the course of that research that I first interviewed leaders of the Jewish community, began to meet with memory activists, and participated in commemorative marches like the international March of the Living at Auschwitz and the local March of Memory in Kraków, an event that commemorates the 1943 liquidation of the Kraków Ghetto. That fieldwork unfolded in the context of the watershed public debate over Jan Tomasz Gross's book *Neighbors: The Destruction of the Jewish Community in Jedwabne, Poland* (2000, 2001). *Neighbors* described how ethnic Poles murdered their Jewish neighbors in the small town of Jedwabne during the summer of 1941, provoking public soul-searching about Poles' role in the Holocaust and Polish-Jewish relations. Jedwabne was on everyone's lips—in stores, buses, radio talk shows, café discussions, public seminars, and churches. That year turned out to be a pivotal one for Polish memory and identity. For a scholar of nationalism, it was a riveting period.

Living in Poland for several years in the 1990s, and again in the early 2000s, enabled me to witness the growing interest in a variety of Jewish-related themes as an active historical process. It was evident in the gentrification of Kraków's Jewish Quarter, Kazimierz; the slow but steady growth and increased visibility of that city's festival of Jewish culture; and the creation of local "Jewish Days" throughout the country. In that sense, then, even before *The Crosses of Auschwitz* appeared in bookstores, the seeds for the present work, *Resurrecting the Jew*, were already sown.

The seeds germinated while I worked on my second book, *Beheading the Saint: Nationalism, Religion, and Secularism in Quebec* (2016). Even though it focused on a society an ocean away on a different continent, *Beheading the Saint* pushed me to think about the broader meaning and challenges of secularism. How is it defined and enacted in different national contexts? Why had Catholic Québec secularized so quickly after its political transition in the 1960s, but Poland had not after 1989? How is the secular project articulated in Poland, where 95 percent of the population is nominally Catholic and most people are practicing Catholics?

Conducting field research in Poland while completing a book on Québec added complexity and nuance to the research for *Resurrecting the Jew*. Visiting Poland several times a year over many years was conducive to interpreting the long chains of events and actions that constitute something as otherwise abstract as a "revival." It allowed me to track the evolution of the Jewish turn's many dimensions, observe multiple iterations of annual festivals, attend the same religious festivities in different cities, and build long-term working relationships. Such "longitudinal" research enabled me to witness the personal journeys of some of my subjects: those who completed conversions and those who decided not to; those who immigrated to Israel, then stayed or returned; those who started attending cultural events and eventually discovered Jewish origins and decided to embrace them and reconstruct a Jewish identity.

My own identity often served as a gateway for interlocutors to discuss what constitutes Polishness. Whereas in the United States many assume that I am Polish because of an accent in English that they can't quite place, together with my hard-to-pronounce last name, in Poland, because of my family name and because I speak Polish better than most foreigners, people often think I was born there and then emigrated in my youth. For French speakers, my given name and accent leave no doubt as to where I'm from: I was born in Québec and raised in a francophone family. I identify as Québécoise. My mother is Québécoise, and my father was born in France during the Second World War, the son of Polish refugees. His family emigrated to Canada before the war's end, when he was a small child. In my late teens I became curious about the country of my paternal grandparents and visited Poland for the first time in the summer of 1989.

In my previous fieldwork in Poland, right-wing Polish Catholics often took it for granted that I was Polish. Even when I explained that my link to Poland and Polishness was tenuous, the fact that I managed "to learn Polish so well" served not only to confirm my Polishness to my interlocutors but to give proof that Polishness was "in my blood." In my fieldwork for *Resurrecting the Jew*, most non-Jewish Poles continued to read me as Polish, but my Jewish interlocutors, Polish and non-Polish, often assumed I had Polish Jewish roots. This is perhaps not surprising, since many people presuppose that social scientists' research projects are directly or indirectly related to the researcher's personal identity. Some asked in blunt terms whether or "how" I was Jewish (i.e., which side of my family might be Jewish, and how far back). When I responded that I was not, my interlocutor often insisted: "Are you sure?" quickly followed by "Have you looked [for Jewish roots]??" Some ventured further comments like "Well, you seem pretty Jewish to me!" These occasions provided fruitful opportunities to puzzle out the criteria they applied to gauging Jewishness.

Other interlocutors inquired about my origins with more generic leads: "So what's your story?" Typically, I would start by telling them what I do, where I live, and where I'm originally from, and they would, in turn, follow with questions about my family. I would then tell them about my mother's side and move on to the narrative of how my paternal grandparents made their way separately to France during the war, that my father was born there in August 1940, and that after reuniting a couple of years later, the family came to Canada through Spain and Portugal. This family history was sometimes heard as a Jewish one by Jews (especially by non-Polish Jews with limited knowledge of Polish history). On one uncomfortable occasion I was introduced to a senior rabbi as the "granddaughter of survivors." My heart sank. I had to correct this interpretation without embarrassing the speaker. And so I followed up by saying, "Oh, my grandparents had it tough, but it was nothing compared to the fate of Polish Jews."

For other interlocutors, the mere fact that I was studying the Jewish revival led them to infer that I must have Jewish origins. Once, after a public lecture in a North American city, an elderly couple asked me to settle a wager: the husband bet I was Jewish, the wife that I wasn't. When I told them I was not, the gentleman sputtered, "Unbelievable! But you understand the issues so well and pronounced Jewish terms just like my mom did!"

These personal experiences show, first, how unscripted moments like these are instrumental in the way identities are assumed, made, declared, and attributed in myriad social interactions; and, second, how complex and uncertain "being Jewish" can be for new participants in the Jewish revival. The hazy borders of Jewishness in Poland made the fieldwork easier in one sense: because many of the participants were not conversant in Jewish rituals, my own inexperience did not stand out. Someone would typically walk me through a ceremony and explain what I was supposed to do (and, more often, not do). Likewise, asking about people's identity seemed easy in social contexts where the topic was on everyone's minds, and where most participants had either already made a journey of self-discovery or were in the process of "figuring things out." That process often took place in supportive, small-group settings: in meetings at community centers like Kraków's Jewish Community Centre (JCC), Hillel, or cafés. If my questions did not cause discomfort in my interviewees, then, it was because such questions were routinely discussed in safe and supportive environments.

Yet that context posed some methodological challenges. Because many Jewish interviewees had already organized the various pieces of their identity—messy, fluid, layered, incomplete—into a streamlined and coherent narrative, the challenge for me was to uncover the formation of that narrative. To that end, I relied less on questions like "Did you grow up Jewish?" or "When did you find out you were Jewish?" than on general prompts like "Tell me a bit about yourself, where you're from, what your family does," and asked them to describe their life now and how they envisioned the next five or ten years. This less direct approach left space for interviewees themselves to narrate the emergence of their ethnic and religious identities, outside the framework of rehearsed identity narratives.

In interviews with non-Jews involved in the Jewish revival, the problem of avoiding an already-cemented storyline was less at issue. At sites like the JCC, the Kraków Jewish Culture Festival, a museum, or other Jewish or Jewish-related events or organizations, responses to my generic "Tell me about yourself and what brought you here?" varied greatly. In talking about themselves in relation to the Jewish revival, individuals rarely seemed to adhere to scripts. In fact, these conversations often seemed to be the first time that my interviewees had reflected on the meaning of their involvement and what it implied for their life trajectories. Although certain themes recurred in these conversations, responses seemed spontaneous, and my conversation partners were not infrequently surprised at themselves.

One reason for the lack of a familiar script might be that I conducted most of those interviews in 2011–12, before the work of non-Jewish volunteers at places like the JCC, the Jewish Culture Festival in Kraków, museums, and other cultural institutions began to be publicized. More recently, interviews, vignettes, and profiles of volunteers have been posted on these organizations' websites and in publications, making volunteers more self-aware and generating more standardized terms for articulating their experiences. As a result, participants' narratives explaining their participation in the Jewish revival now tend to converge.

A number of caveats apply to this study. What is called the "Jewish revival" in Poland is characterized by a whirlwind of Jewish-related commercial activities, public discourse, and academic production. I focused on the elements that appeared to have the most resonance, that exemplified key issues or processes, and were accessible to me. I visited more sites, observed more events, and interviewed more people than could possibly be discussed or cited in these pages. All these encounters informed my understanding of the factors propelling the evolving Jewish turn and the processes giving it form.

While *Resurrecting the Jew* is a sociological study of an empirical phenomenon, it also provides an analysis of key issues that have shaped public life in the last three decades in Poland: struggles over the definition of Polish national identity and attempts at secularizing it; reckonings with the past and the reshaping of collective memory; of cleavages, many old, some new. I hope this book contributes to a finer understanding of both the dynamics of Polish nationalism and the role of cultural processes in shaping politics in other societies.

Paris, July 11, 2021

ACKNOWLEDGMENTS

If setting words on paper is a deeply solitary act, the labor of writing a book is richly communal. Here I name some of those who contributed their knowledge, time, and effort to this work.

I am most in debt to all those who shared their life stories, hopes, fears, and frustrations, and invited me to join them in the discovery of Jewish life in Poland. Jonathan Ornstein opened the doors of Kraków's JCC to me in 2010, and he and his wife Kasia Leonardi made the JCC community into a home away from home while I carried out research for this book. Thanks to Jonathan, I met dozens of members of the Jewish community throughout Poland and dozens of non-Jewish Poles supporting the renewal of Jewish life in the country. Many shared their personal journeys into Jewishness, and non-Jewish staff and volunteers explained their motivations for supporting the Jewish revival in Poland. Thanks are due also to Rabbis Michael Schudrich, Tyson Herberger, Boaz Pash, and Avi Baumol for allowing me to observe ritual events in Kraków and Warsaw and to participate in communal celebrations. Monika Elliott and the staff at the Joint Distribution Committee in Warsaw facilitated my participation at a Limmud Polska workshop, for which I am also grateful.

Next, I am grateful to Birthright Israel and its international vice-president of education, Zohar Raviv, for granting me permission to join a Polish group. Hillel Polska director Magda Dorosz, Matylda Jonas-Kowal, and Tosia Grynberg offered a warm welcome in Warsaw and provided invaluable insights on the trip's educational goals and pedagogical process. My heartfelt thanks also go to the group of young Jewish Poles who allowed me to witness their discovery of Israel, and shared with me the impact of the trip on their Polish Jewish identity, struggles, and life plans upon our return to Poland. They were kind in not making me feel too ancient.

I am indebted to Janusz Makuch for many conversations over the years, and to his team for giving me a behind-the-scenes look at the Jewish Culture Festival in Kraków. Thanks also are due to Robert Gądek and Paweł Kowalewski, who shared unpublished data on the festival that allowed me to follow its growth and evolving mission.

Dariusz Stola invited me to the grand opening festivities of the Polin Museum of the History of Polish Jews in October 2014, and facilitated access to unpublished data on the number of visitors at the museum. The museum staff also generously tracked down photographs and provided permission to use them in the book. A heartfelt thank-you.

Sławek Sierakowski discussed at length with me his involvement in the Jewish Renaissance Movement in Poland and introduced me to Yael Bartana. Yael generously shared her trilogy *And Europe Will Be Stunned* with me and made time to talk in person, even though she had already given multiple lectures and interviews on the films. I learned much about the origins of the project, her creative process, and her own interpretation of each film through meetings in her home in Berlin, in pubs in Amsterdam, and on campus in Ann Arbor. Yael sparked new ideas for this book and for possible future projects.

Back in Ann Arbor, I worked closely with multiple research assistants whose help was indispensable at different stages of the project. Natalie Smolenski prepared a preliminary bibliography; Jessica Zychowicz compiled data on the Kraków Jewish Culture Festival and coded reviews of the festival published in the Polish press; Anna Woźny prepared the data for maps and graphs, coded testimonies, filled in the many holes in the timeline of Jewish life in postwar Poland that appears in appendix B, and tracked down hard-to-find references. Most importantly, Jessica and Anna became conversation partners as the project evolved, and I am forever grateful for their contributions. In Warsaw, I was fortunate to gain the help of Magdalena Zatorska and Agata Rybus, who documented their observations of visits to the Polin Museum. The maps of festivals of Jewish culture in chapter 5 were designed by the wonderfully resourceful cartographer Waldemar Spallek.

I also learned from more general conversations with colleagues, students, and public audiences who helped sharpen the arguments presented here. These many brilliant interlocutors pushed me to dig deeper into the empirical materials and to widen my horizon beyond Poland. The insights, critiques, and suggestions of Doris Bergen, Rogers Brubaker, Kathleen Canning, Yolande Cohen, Jess Dubow, Elizabeth Dyson Branch, Jacques Ehrenfreund, Kriszti Fehérváry, Zvi Gitelman, Phil Gorski, Agnieszka Graff, Fiona Greenland, Irena Grudzińska-Gross, Anna Grzymała-Busse, Rita Hermon-Belot, Rob Jansen, Jan Kubik, Krishan Kumar, Morgane Labbé, Joanna Niżyńska, Jeff Olick, Atalia Omer, Gosia Pakier, Ewa Pasek, Aga Pasieka, Emmanuel Peddler, Brian Porter-Szűcs, Agnieszka Rudzińska, Bożena Shallcross, Andrew Shryock, Scott Spector, Dariusz Stola, Ron Suny,

Karen Underhill, Jeff Veidlinger, Marcin Wodziński, Piotr Wróbel, Tomek Zarycki, Natalie Zemon-Davis, Eviatar Zerubavel, Yael Zerubavel, and Agata Zysiak were tremendously helpful. Marcin Napiórkowski, Paweł Dobrosielski, Olga Kaczmarek, and the members of the Vernacular Culture research group in Poland, as well as Robert van der Laarse and the Terrorscape research group in the Netherlands, provided different frameworks to think about the Jewish revival in Poland, disrupting my habits of thought and expanding my approach. For thirty years now, Irena Borowik has been a crucial intellectual sounding board. I first met Irena when I was an MA student, when she agreed to guide my research on the Catholic Church in Poland. She has remained my mentor ever since, a dear friend who makes my trips to Kraków always feel like homecomings.

I am especially grateful to Erika Büky, Irena Grudzińska-Gross, Paul Christopher Johnson, Aga Pasieka, Ewa Tartakowsky, Anna Woźny, and anonymous reviewers for reading the manuscript once it had acquired its full shape and pushing me to refine and clarify my arguments, even when I thought I could go no further. Thanks also to Fred Appel at Princeton University Press for nudging me about the book these last few years and for helping me tell a bigger story. The copyediting of P. David Hornik, as well as PUP's production team under the expert supervision of Natalie Baan, made the transformation from manuscript to printed book as painless as an author could hope.

Public lectures—both delivering them and responding to questions—have been critical in the honing of this work. Earlier versions of most of the chapters were presented at many institutions over the years, and I wish to acknowledge these gracious institutional hosts, including the University of Chicago, the University of Virginia, the University of Illinois Chicago, the University of Wisconsin, Notre Dame, Princeton, Harvard, Rutgers, the New School for Social Research, Northwestern, UCLA, the University of Toronto, the Université de Montréal, the University of Warsaw, the University of Łódź, the University of Vienna, the Higher School of Economics in Saint Petersburg, the European University Institute in Florence, the Université de Lausanne, and multiple research centers at the École des Hautes Études en Sciences Sociales and the École Pratique des Hautes Études in Paris.

And Paris is where I completed the manuscript, during a sabbatical in 2020–21. Although the city was on partial or full lockdown for most of the year, its beauty and quiet energy during the pandemic nourished, gave comfort, and provided the élan I needed to cross the finish line. I owe a special thanks to my colleague and dear friend Morgane Labbé for arranging an appointment at the École des Hautes Études en Sciences Sociales. A monthlong visiting professorship at the École Pratique des Hautes Études and chances to present the book in a series of lectures in Philippe Portier's and Alfonsina Bello's seminars were also valuable, and a welcome respite from the lonely work of writing. Thanks, too, to Ewa Tartakowsky and Catherine Goussef for meeting me at the Jardins du Luxembourg on cold winter days to help me work through some challenging passages.

A book's publication is also the occasion to thank other people in our lives who make our work possible. My husband, intellectual partner, and best friend Paul Christopher Johnson deserves a medal for putting up with my many absences while I was conducting research in Poland and Israel, for calming my anxieties during the writing phase, and for his patient reading and careful editing of the full manuscript. I could not have written this book without him. I depended on Elaheh Sadeghnia and Jeanene Lyson for helping at home with Anaïs when she was little and I was away. Thank you both for being members of our extended family.

When I began this project in 2010, I had just assumed the directorship of the Copernicus Center for Polish Studies (CCPS) at the University of Michigan. With time, I added a few other centers to my administrative portfolio. I'm grateful to my colleagues and staff at the CCPS, the Center for European Studies, the Center for Russian, East European and Eurasian Studies, and the Weiser Center for Europe and Eurasia for their support and friendship, and for their tremendous dedication to Eastern European studies: Susan Barrera, Derek Bloom, Rachel Brichta, Gitta Kohler, Małgorzata Kowalczyk, Liz Malinkin, and Marysia Ostafin.

Finally, field-based research depends on material support. I've been privileged to receive grants from the Society for the Scientific Study of Religion, as well as from the University of Michigan's Office of Research; the College of Literature, Science and the Arts; and the Weiser Center for Emerging Democracies. Time is also essential, and I was fortunate to hold a fellowship at Michigan's Frankel Institute for Advanced Judaic Studies in 2015–16. I had the honor to finalize this book under the auspices of a Guggenheim Foundation Fellowship. I'm deeply grateful to all these organizations for their financial support and the trust they have shown in this project.

I dedicate this book to my daughter, Anaïs Zubrzycki-Johnson, who has spent over two-thirds of her life watching her mother at work on this project; and to my father, Pierre Zubrzycki, who encouraged me to discover the country of his parents at nineteen, setting me on a life-changing path.

The following provides a guide to the pronunciation of Polish words and names.

a   is pronounced as in *nap*
ą   as French on in *avion*
c   as ts in *cats*
ch as in *loch*
cz as hard ch in *church*
ć   as soft ch
ę   as French ain in *bain*
g   always hard, as in *girl*
i   as ee
j   as y in *yes*
ł   as w
ń   as Spanish ñ in *año*
u   and ó as oo in *boot*
w   as v
sz as hard sh in *ship*
ś   as soft sh
ż   and rz as zh in *Zhivago*
ź   as softer zh

CHAPTER 1

Contemporary Poland and "the Jews"

What Poland is and "should be" has been at the center of public debates and political fights since the fall of state socialism. That battle is fiercer now than ever. Polish society has become even more divided with the rise of populism in recent years. One faction favors a traditional vision of Polish identity crystallized around Catholicism, conservative family values, and a national narrative emphasizing Polish martyrdom and heroism. Another promotes progressive values and secularism and questions key tenets of Polish national mythology. It's a fight for the heart of Polish national identity.

In that contest over Poland and Polishness, history and memory occupy center stage, and no other aspect of Polish history has been more disputed than that of Polish-Jewish relations. In the past two decades, Poles have engaged in a divisive debate about the participation of ethnic Poles in violent crimes against Polish Jews before, during, and after the Second World War. That difficult process of soul-searching and reckoning with the past is described by the Right as anti-Polish defamation, which the current government, led by the far-Right populist Law and Justice Party, attempts to short-circuit, using every weapon in its arsenal.[1] At the same time, though, Poland's small Jewish community is undergoing a significant renewal, and a substantial number of institutions, public figures, memory activists, and ordinary citizens are engaged in a multifaceted resurrection of Jewish culture.

How can we make sense of these seemingly contradictory phenomena; right-wing populism, antisemitism, and denial on the one hand, and a "Jewish turn" on the other? One might be tempted to see that Jewish turn

---

[1] Law and Justice is a far-Right, national-Catholic, Euroskeptic, populist party that has held the parliament and the presidency since 2015. For extracts of the party platform, in English, see http://porterszucs.pl/2016/02/05/pis-in-their-own-words.

as simply a move to counter right-wing populism or antisemitism, but this rather stunted interpretation sidesteps the internal logic of each of the movements. I argue that both anti- and philosemitism—non-Jews' support of, and even identification with, Jews—are part of a single struggle to define what constitutes Polishness. Polish philosemitism is a dynamic, unfolding movement that, in its most introspective form, challenges the narrow ethnocultural association of Polishness with Catholicism. It strives to articulate a civic and secular definition of national identity and to build a modern polity. *Resurrecting the Jew* shows why and how this project has arisen and examines its challenges and limitations.

Collective Memory and Culture Wars

On January 26, 2018, the Polish parliament voted to approve an amendment to its Institute of National Remembrance Act, which was originally ratified in 1999 to enable the investigation and prosecution of crimes against the Polish nation committed during the Second World War and the communist period.[2] The amendment added to the Institute's mission "protecting the reputation of the Republic of Poland and the Polish Nation." It threatened up to three years' imprisonment for "anyone claiming publicly and against the facts" that "the Polish Nation or the Republic of Poland is responsible or co-responsible for Nazi crimes committed by the Third German Reich."[3]

---

2 The full and official name of the institute is *Instytut Pamięci Narodowej–Komisja Ścigania Zbrodni przeciwko Narodowi Polskiemu*. It is, however, commonly referred to as *IPN*. The official English translation is "Institute of National Remembrance—Commission for the Prosecution of Crimes against the Polish Nation."

3 All translations from Polish are mine unless otherwise noted. The full text of the law is available at https://dziennikustaw.gov.pl/DU/rok/2018/pozycja/369. Similar laws had previously been adopted specifically to target academic publications considered in right-wing milieus as "defamation" of the Polish nation. I detail these memory laws in appendix B. The timing of the vote was no accident. The government used the occasion of International Holocaust Remembrance Day, observed on January 27 to commemorate the liberation of Auschwitz-Birkenau on that day in 1945, as a platform to denounce the use of the term *Polish death camps* with reference to Nazi concentration camps in occupied Poland or in Polish land annexed to the Third Reich. Multiple Polish governments have also fought the use of that expression in foreign media, with considerable success—for example, after President Barack Obama referred to Nazi death camps as Polish camps at the ceremony awarding the Presidential Medal of Freedom to the late Jan Karski. See https://www.youtube.com/watch?time_continue=2&v=Rd-v24pAg7s. Most American newspapers and other major media outlets have updated their stylebooks to stop that phrase being used (https://www.imediaethics.org/ap-updates-its-stylebook-on-concentration-camps-polish-foundations-petition-for-change-has-300000k-names).

Numerous organizations and public figures in Poland immediately and forcefully denounced the amendment in official statements, public letters, and petitions.[4] Widely panned in global media as the "Holocaust speech law," the bill was described by the Israeli prime minister Benjamin Netanyahu as "distortion of the truth, the rewriting of history and the denial of the Holocaust."[5] Law and Justice's propaganda machine mounted a vigorous response. In an astounding statement posted on the government's official YouTube channel, Prime Minister Mateusz Morawiecki asserted that Poland was a victim of both the Second World War and now also of Holocaust denial, because "Holocaust denial is not only the denial of German crimes, but also [arises] when someone diminishes the responsibility of [the] real perpetrators and attributes that responsibility to their victims." The new amendment arose from Poland's determination to "fight against this lie," Morawiecki explained. In that discursive reframing, the law—and Poland—was serving to protect historical truth: "Today, as the world must once again fight against a new wave of antisemitism, the government of Poland states its position clearly: there is no room for hatred or the distortion of history."[6] Despite the international outcry and domestic protests, ten days after the Polish parliament voted for the bill, President Andrzej Duda—from Law and Justice—signed it into law.[7]

The Holocaust speech law was but one episode in the Law and Justice Party's application of its "historical policy," which aims at shaping collective memory by either repressing or promoting specific interpretations

4 See, for example, the statements issued by the Polin Museum of the History of Polish Jews (http://www.polin.pl/en/news/2018/01/29/statement-of-the-director-of-polin-museum-concerning -a-proposed); by former ambassadors (http://www.tokfm.pl/Tokfm/7,103085,22984827,list-polskich -ambasadorow-obecna-polityka-jaroslawa-kaczynskiego.html); and by scholars, journalists, artists, and politicians (https://oko.press/apel-stu-naukowcow-dziennikarzy-artystow-politykow -o-wycofanie-zmian-ustawie-o-ipn-tedy-droga-odzyskania-zbiorowej-godnosci).

5 See https://www.timesofisrael.com/netanyahu-polish-pm-talk-agree-to-iron-out-row -over-holocaust-legislation.

6 The official English-language speech can be watched at https://www.youtube.com /watch?v=R9bS9z5OiWY&t=147s. The following day, the video was transformed to include a dramatic soundtrack, colorful images of modern-day Poland and flyover shots of the Polish landscape, interlaced with archival footage of World War II showing German soldiers' boots on cobblestoned streets and in concentration camps. It concluded with the striking label "#GERMANDEATHCAMPS" superposed on a grim black-and-white shot of the infamous tower gate of Birkenau (https://www.youtube.com/watch?v=GXcm7k3FpJc).

7 Under international pressure, the government later softened the law, removing the threat of jail time. The announcement of that decision was made in a joint declaration by the Polish and Israeli prime ministers, Morawiecki and Netanyahu. That declaration was vigorously condemned by Yad Vashem, the World Holocaust Remembrance Center in Israel (https://www .yadvashem.org/press-release/05-july-2018-07-34.html?utm_source=social&utm_medium=tw).

of the past.[8] Targets of the policy include assessments of World War II, the communist period, and the postcommunist transition, as well as of more recent events, such as the 2010 plane crash in Smolensk, Ukraine, that killed the president of Poland Lech Kaczyński, his wife, the crew, and eighty-seven dignitaries—a tragedy presented and commemorated as an attack on the Polish state by Russia with the aid of Polish traitors. What these events have in common is a specific representation of Poland and Poles as martyrs, in line with tropes of national mythology developed in the nineteenth century, when the disappearance of Poland from the map of Europe was represented in literature as its crucifixion. The poetic metaphor of Poland as Christ among nations was enshrined and reproduced in the arts, popular culture, religious rituals, and commemorative practices. It was later solidified by the devastation caused by the Second World War and the imposition of communism in its aftermath (Zubrzycki 2006, 2010; Porter-Szűcs 2014).

The Holocaust speech law was deployed to stall an important process of national reckoning with the role of ethnic Poles in the Holocaust, initiated in the early 2000s. Polish indifference toward the genocide of Polish Jews had been discussed in the mid-1980s following the broadcasting on Polish television of Claude Lanzmann's 1985 documentary film *Shoah* and the 1987 publication of Jan Błoński's essay "Poor Poles Look at the Ghetto" in the prominent Catholic weekly *Tygodnik Powszechny* (Universal Weekly). But it was the publication in 2000 of *Neighbors: The Destruction of the Jewish Community in Jedwabne, Poland* by the Polish-born, US-based historian Jan Tomasz Gross that burst the dam and led to extended public debate and soul-searching about Polish violence against Jews during and after World War II. The short book described in painful detail how in the summer of 1941 ethnic Poles tormented and murdered their Jewish neighbors in

8 In Polish, *polityka historyczna* means both a broad "politics of history" and a more specific "historical policy." The expression derives from the German *Geschichtspolitik*. While *Geschichtspolitik* specifically describes Germans' reckoning with their Nazi past, the English expression "politics of memory" more generally concerns debates about the past, and how the past should be recorded, remembered, and disseminated or else silenced and forgotten. The politics of memory can involve *historical policies*, policies that distinguish between "true" and "correct" histories and "false/falsified" ones; specify how history should be narrated; or even legally regulate specific interpretations of the past (Noiriel 2012; Gensburger and Lefranc 2017; Belavusau and Gliszczyńska-Grabias 2017). Revisionist historical policies are especially salient following regime change; they range from place-name alterations and the removal of monuments to the literal rewriting of history in official documents and textbooks. For a discussion of that literature and a typology of reckonings with difficult pasts, see Zubrzycki and Woźny (2020). For analyses of the politics of memory and commemoration in postsocialist societies, see Bernhard and Kubik (2014).

the small town of Jedwabne in northeastern Poland.[9] The newly founded Institute of National Remembrance opened an official investigation of the murders described by Gross, and on July 10, 2001, on the sixtieth anniversary of the pogrom, the government officially acknowledged Polish responsibility and erected a monument at the site where several hundred Jews were forcibly brought to a barn and burned alive.[10] Although the monument's inscription fails to explicitly indicate that it was Poles and not Germans who committed the crime, the official apology by then-president Aleksander Kwaśniewski was unequivocal: "Here in Jedwabne," he declared, "citizens of the Republic of Poland died at the hands of other citizens of the Republic of Poland." He called it a "fratricide."[11]

Neighbors' *Narrative Shock*

Neighbors created such a rupture that one could speak of Poland "before" and "after" its publication. Not only were Poles no longer cast as the main victims of the war; they were now perpetrators of some of its horror. By disrupting the narrative of martyrdom—for one cannot be both a sacrificial victim and a willing executioner—*Neighbors* provoked what I have

9 Pronounced Yed-WAB-neh. The book was first published in Polish under the title *Sąsiedzi: Historia zagłady żydowskiego miasteczka* in 2000. The English translation appeared in 2001. It was important to Gross for the book to appear in Polish first so that the interested public had a chance to discuss the issue (personal communication, January 13, 2020). The book's impact in Poland was immediate and far-reaching. In addition to public discussions and an official investigation, it prompted an important debate among historians in the form of lengthy editorials in the Polish press: see *Jedwabne: Spór historyków wokół książki Jana T. Grossa "Sąsiedzi"* (Warsaw: Biblioteka Frondy, 2002). Gross's own responses to the debates appeared in a collection of essays published in 2003.

10 The party in power then was the Alliance of the Democratic Left (*Sojusz Lewicy Demokratycznej*, or *SLD*). The findings of the investigation by the Institute of National Remembrance were published in two volumes (Machcewicz and Persak 2002a, 2002b) and included the partial exhumation of the mass grave. (The mass grave was opened so that investigators could see what it contained, but the bodies were left untouched to respect Jewish law, Chief Rabbi of Poland Michael Schudrich told me [Warsaw, September 28, 2012].) The remains of up to three hundred Jewish victims were found, along with approximately one hundred German rifle bullets and cartridge cases. The remains of some forty other men and the head of a concrete statue of Lenin were found in a secondary mass grave (Stola 2003: 139–52, Persak 2011: 429). Those remains were most likely of the men forced to dismantle a statue of Lenin installed in the village square during the Soviet occupation of Eastern Poland (1939–41) and executed as punishment for their alleged collaboration with the Soviets.

11 The monument's inscription reads "To the memory of the Jews from Jedwabne and environs; men, women, and children who shared dominion over this land, murdered, burned alive at this place on July 10, 1941." An English translation of President Kwaśniewski's speech can be found at http://www.radzilow.com/jedwabne-ceremony.htm.

called *narrative shock* (2006, 2010, 2013b), a questioning of a key story of the nation, shaking its identity to its core.[12] It also engendered important scholarship demonstrating that crimes committed by ethnic Poles against Jews before, during, and after the war were much more widespread than the dominant Polish narrative had allowed.[13]

The shock was so great that many turned to denial and counteraccusations: "It was not Poles who killed the Jews, but the Germans," "There were far fewer Jews murdered than Gross claimed," or even "The Jews had it coming after all, since they collaborated with the Soviets." Such opinions were frequently expressed in newspaper editorials and letters to the editor, academic panels, public roundtables, and church sermons. A countermemorial to Polish victims of the war, monumentalizing that perspective, was dedicated in Jedwabne's main square in 2003.[14] Almost predictably, in 2011, neofascist vandals defaced the Jedwabne memorial to the Jews who were murdered by spray-painting on stones surrounding the monument the statements "They were flammable" and "I do not apologize for Jedwabne."[15]

Among groups on the Right, any attempt at discussing Poles' participation in the Holocaust is perceived as defamation and a profanation of the Polish nation, which is held sacred.[16] It is to counter what they call the "politics of shame," and to protect the nation at home and its "good name" abroad, that the Law and Justice government, supported by the hierarchy of the Catholic Church, the right-wing Radio Maryja, conservative public

---

12 I coined the expression *narrative shock* in *The Crosses of Auschwitz* to refer to the shock to Poles' historical consciousness and national identity created by the narrative reconfiguration of Auschwitz after the fall of state socialism, and the debate surrounding *Neighbors* in the early 2000s. I further developed the concept in subsequent publications (2010, 2013b). The phrase has since been adopted by many other scholars, though not always with proper attribution (Janicka and Żukowski 2021).

13 See, to cite only the most prominent texts on the topic, Jan Tomasz Gross and Irena Grudzińska-Gross, *Złote żniwa: Rzecz o tym, co się działo na obrzeżach zagłady Żydów* (2011), translated as *Golden Harvest: Events at the Periphery of the Holocaust* (2012); Jan Grabowski, *Judenjagd: Polowanie na Żydów, 1942–1945* (2011), published in English in 2013 as *Hunt for the Jews: Betrayal and Murder in German-Occupied Poland*; Barbara Engelking and Jan Grabowski, eds., *Dalej jest noc: Losy Żydów w wybranych powiatach okupowanej Polski* (2018).

14 The monument was dedicated by the bishops of Łomża, Stanisław Stefanek and Tadeusz Zawistowski, on May 3, 2003, on the feast day of Our Lady of Częstochowa, Queen of Poland. May 3 is also a secular national holiday—the anniversary of the Constitution of May 3, 1791. For a detailed analysis of the countermemorial, see Zubrzycki (2013b).

15 https://wyborcza.pl/7,75398,10209838,atak-neofaszystow-na-pomnik-w-jedwabnem.html?disableRedirects=true.

16 For contributions on contested Jewish and Polish memories in the postwar and post-socialist periods, see Zimmerman (2003), Zubrzycki (2006, 2013b), Gebert (2008), Polonsky (2009), Forecki (2010).

FIGURE 1. Cartoon mocking the Right's ongoing campaign to promote Polish Righteous Among the Nations, which appeared on the leftist collective *Krytyka Polityczna*'s website on March 31, 2018. The placard nailed on the cross reads "The King of Jews was to be crucified here, but Poles saved him" (Plawgo / Pyrka for krytykapolityczna.pl, reprinted with permission of Krytyka Polityczna.)

figures, and various nationalist organizations are engaged in a process of remythologization ranging from outright denial to the promotion of new narratives of Polish-Jewish relations.[17] In recent years, for example, attention has been redirected toward Poles who rescued Jews and who are honored by Israel as Righteous Among the Nations. Their actions have been commemorated in numerous museums, monuments, murals, and movies (see chapter 4). The historian Jan Grabowski has nicknamed that rhetorical strategy the "Righteous Defense" (2016:19), a strategy that has been critiqued by many on the Left (figure 1). Public attention has also been redirected toward other Polish stories of Polish martyrdom.[18]

17 The Roman Catholic Church in Poland is a diverse and vibrant institution, but its hierarchy and the majority of the clergy are primarily constituted by what I call "traditional conservatives," for whom national identity is tightly intertwined with the Catholic faith. Radio Maryja is even more nationalist: founded in Toruń in 1991 by Father Tadeusz Rydzyk, the station is the voice of anticommunism, anti-EU sentiment, and antisemitism. In recent years it has added vociferous antirefugee, antifeminist, and anti-LGBT propaganda to its arsenal. Its charismatic leader has managed to create a quasi-social movement around the station's right-wing politics—the Family of Radio Maryja—consistently mobilizing followers devoted to the cause of protecting or restoring a "true Poland" (Krzemiński 2009, 2017; Sekerdej and Pasieka 2013: 61–65). In 2011 the Family of Radio Maryja was estimated to comprise a million members. While Radio Maryja is not the dominant face of Catholicism in Poland, it is the most vocal, and occupies public space with immense semiotic force.

18 The most significant are the cases of Katyń, where some twenty thousand Polish army officers, intellectuals, and civilian prisoners were murdered in 1940 by the Soviet NKVD (see

Poland's Jewish Turn

Denial and deflection constitute only half the story. With equal fervor and conviction, scholars and public intellectuals continue to unearth the participation of ethnic Poles in the Holocaust (e.g., Grabowski 2020). They refuse to allow the recognition of Polish Righteous to dilute or diminish the process of national soul-searching initiated with the publication of *Neighbors*. This activity is part of an important process of recovering and reclaiming Poland's Jewish past.

It is as part of this mnemonic awakening that various Jewish festivals have mushroomed in Poland since the mid-2000s. Today there are about forty such festivals held annually in more than a dozen Polish cities and towns. In addition, the interest in Jewish culture is now observable all year round in the renewed popularity of klezmer music; the proliferation of Judaica bookstores and Jewish-style restaurants; the inauguration of new museums, memorials, and memory spaces; the engagement of artists and public intellectuals with Poland's Jewish past and Polish-Jewish relations; and the emergence and development of Jewish and Holocaust studies programs in universities. The historian and Jewish studies scholar Marcin Wodziński (2021) found that between 2011 and 2021, approximately one hundred books and several hundred articles on Jewish topics were published *every year*, many written to be accessible to a broader public.[19] A last indicator of the Jewish revival, for which there are no official statistics, is a modest but steady number of conversions to Judaism.[20]

Philosemitism is not unique to Poland, of course.[21] As Daniel Cohen (2017) notes in an essay on the phenomenon in postwar Europe, it has had

---

Etkind et al. 2012; Kosicki 2015); the massacre of Polish civilians by Ukrainian nationalists in Volhynia in 1943; the stories of the "doomed soldiers" (*żołnierze wyklęci*), anti-Soviet and anti-communist soldiers during and after the war who were later persecuted by the communist regime; and the 2010 plane crash in Smoleńsk (Zubrzycki 2013a; Golonka-Czajkowska 2018).

19 Those numbers are similar to those for the previous decade: Wodziński (2011) noted, for example, that between 2006 and 2009, 365 books on Jewish themes were published in Poland.

20 Interviews with Rabbis Michael Schudrich, Boaz Pash, Tyson Herberger, Itzak Horovitz, and Tanya Segal in 2012 and 2013; personal interviews with converts, March 2011, March 2013. Throughout this book, I name individuals when they spoke to me as representatives of institutions, but use pseudonyms to preserve the anonymity of private individuals.

21 For a discussion of the history and theoretical underpinnings of the terms *antisemitism*, *anti-antisemitism*, and *philosemitism*, see Bauman (1998), Alteflix (2000), and Judaken (2008). On philosemitism in history, see Lassner and Trubowitz (2008) and Karp and Sutcliffe (2011); in postwar Germany, see Stern (1991); in post-1989 Germany, see Gilman and Remmler (1994); in postwar Poland, see Mushkat (1992). On philosephardism in Spain, see Rohr (2007) and McDonald (2021).

different significations at various times and places. In imperial Germany, philosemitism was primarily articulated as a "defense of Jews against the rising popularity of anti-Semitism." The term was in fact coined by self-acknowledged antisemites in Germany in the 1880s to denigrate those opposing antisemitism and defending Jews (Karp and Sutcliffe 2011:1). In England, on the other hand, admiration for Jews drew on early modern Christian polemic and Victorian morals, while in postrevolutionary France the positive image of the Jew became "a touchstone of French Republican universalism" (Cohen 2017).

Diana Pinto observes that in 1990s Europe, Jewish history and culture served as "spaces" in which individual societies could work through their national histories (1996; see also J. E. Young 1993). Ruth Ellen Gruber's (2002) pioneering work documents and analyzes these spaces, coining the expression "virtual Jewishness" to capture various Jewish cultural initiatives primarily enacted by and for non-Jews. Virtual Jewishness, she showed, transpired across multiple domains of public life, from the discovery and restoration of material heritage to the production and consumption of cultural goods. This raised difficult questions of authenticity and cultural appropriation, eliciting feelings and discourses ranging from confusion and discomfort to indignation for some Jewish observers.

In the German context, Bodemann refers to a new guild of "German experts on Jewish culture and religion . . . enacting Jewish culture" from biographical, historical, and museological perspectives as "professional almost-Jews" (1996:57). Such experts exist in Poland as well, and Henryk Hałkowski, a native of Kraków's Jewish Quarter, community activist, and writer, cynically used the more direct expression "professional Jews" (za-wodowi Żydzi) to describe a similar group of experts (2003:151–52).

Magdalena Waligórska (2013) prefers instead the term *Jewish stand-ins* in her ethnography of klezmer musicians in Kraków and Berlin in the early 2000s. She describes the klezmer scenes she studied as "contact zone[s] where Jews and non-Jews enter into conversation about the painful Polish Jewish or German Jewish past, exchange ideas, and work together, but also challenge each other, compete, and articulate their (sometimes conflicting) interests" (12). Inspired by Naomi Seidman's "(Jewish) politics of vicarious identity," Erica Lehrer adopts the term *vicarious Jewishness* in Poland to describe "Jewish-identifying Poles" involved in the revival of Kazimierz, Kraków's historic Jewish Quarter. Vicarious Jewishness in Poland, she argues, serves—among other purposes—as a cultural critique of Polish antisemitism (2013, esp. 188 passim).

I adopt the term *philosemitism* to denote a wide spectrum of practices guided by a curiosity and desire to learn about Judaism, Jewishness, and Jewish history; to uncover and preserve the remnants of Jewish life; and to memorialize the death of millions of Jews (Polish and non-Polish) murdered on Polish soil. As with antisemitism, that process implies various degrees of objectification and instrumentalization of Jews (conscious or not). This is why the cultural critics Elżbieta Janicka and Tomasz Żukowski characterize philosemitism as violent (2021).

Even within a single society, however, philosemitism is far from uniform. To provide a nuanced, fine-grained, and comprehensive portrait of the phenomenon requires examination of a variety of empirical materials. Public discourses, performances, monumental productions, and artistic creations are certainly important, but they offer little purchase on the different meanings philosemitic practices have for those engaging in them. In this work, I therefore also investigate the motivations of individual Poles, of different generations, social horizons, and political leanings, for participating in the Jewish turn. I analyze how they imagine the Jew in their discourses and everyday practices, how they represent Poland's Jewish past, and how they imagine a future Poland. I pay attention to how they understand and explain the Jewish turn, and how they articulate the relationship between this phenomenon and their personal journeys and life goals. This approach allows for the identification of various "registers" of engagement with things Jewish, ranging from crude cultural appropriation to critical-introspective or political engagement (see chapter 5). Further, I investigate how Polish Jews themselves participate in the Jewish turn, how they feel about non-Jewish Poles' fascination with Jews and Jewish culture, and how the revival of Jewish communal life intersects with Polish philosemitism (see chapter 6). The ethnographic approach furnishes a more complete picture of Poland's Jewish turn and situates the phenomenon in the broader problematic of nationalism.

This discussion inevitably raises the question of how one defines Poles, Jews, Polishness, and Jewishness in opposition and in conjunction. Although I use the terms "Poles" and "Jews" in this book, I do not imply that these are homogeneous groups, nor that they are separate or mutually exclusive. Group identity is always constituted dialectically in relation to an "Other," and an individual's identity within a group is typically defined along a spectrum, with different markers coming into play such as gender, class, and sexual identity. "Poles" and "Jews" are therefore categories that make sense insofar as they are distinct from each other in a specific context. I use the term "Polish Jews" to denote Poles currently living in

Poland who identify as Jewish, as well as those who may have emigrated from Poland at any time during and after World War II. In the context of the Jewish turn more specifically, I use the terms "Jews" or "Jewish Poles," and "non-Jewish Poles" to denote an individual or group of persons' relationships to Judaism or Jewishness (ancestry, conversion, personal convictions). I use "Jewishness" to refer to Jewish cultural identity, and "Judaism" to refer more narrowly to the Jewish faith. In all instances I recognize that identities are complex, fluid, and contested.

Renewing Jewish Life in Poland

While philosemitism and Jewish revivals exist in other European societies, their intensity and territorial spread in Poland are remarkable. This phenomenon is sociologically puzzling precisely because it is enacted almost entirely by non-Jews. In postwar Germany, the carving out of Jewish space in the public sphere was initially performed by converts to Judaism, members of Jewish/Israeli and German associations, and a cadre of academics. The arrival of some eighty thousand Soviet Jews after the collapse of the Soviet Union in 1991, however, injected new energy into German Jewish communal life (Bodemann 1996). In Hungary the process has been led by Hungarian Jews, and it is facilitated by their relatively high number in that country (between 75,000 and 100,000, representing 7–10 percent of Hungary's population), their concentration in Budapest, and the extent of surviving material heritage in that country, including some twenty active synagogues in Budapest alone.[22]

In contrast, little remains of Poland's once large, vibrant, and diverse Jewish communities. Before World War II, Poland had the largest Jewish population in Europe (about 3.5 million), representing approximately 10 percent of its total population. Ninety percent of Polish Jewry was exterminated in the Holocaust, and many survivors chose to rebuild their lives elsewhere. Postwar pogroms, personal attacks and intimidation, and the loss of property—destroyed in the war or stolen by former neighbors—pushed others to leave (Aleksiun 2003; Gross 2006; Cichopek-Gajraj 2014).

---

22 https://www.worldjewishcongress.org/en/about/communities/HU. Sergio DellaPergola (2020) estimates Hungary's core population of Jews, which "includes all persons who, when asked in a sociodemographic survey, identify themselves as Jews, *or* who are identified as Jews by a respondent in the same household, *and* do not profess another monotheistic religion" to be 47,300. On Hungary's Jewish revival, see Gruber (2002), Kovács (2010), and Monterescu and Zorándy (2020).

Antisemitic purges in 1968 forced the departure of approximately fifteen thousand more Polish Jews (Stola 2000, 2010; Plocker 2022). As a result, the number of Jews living in Poland today is estimated to be between 4,500 and 13,000 (the wide variation hinging on how Jewishness is determined: halacha [Jewish law], formal membership in Jewish organizations, meeting the criteria for Israel's Law of Return, or self-identification in the 2011 census).[23]

Jewish leaders, however, estimate that between forty thousand and a hundred thousand Poles have some Jewish ancestry, representing significant potential for community and religious growth.[24] And the community has grown in both number and vitality since the fall of state socialism. Beginning in 1989, after the socialist narrative had effaced difficult topics of Polish history, it became possible (and even necessary) to examine and discuss the past. In filling that vacuum, many Poles discovered their Jewish ancestry. Others knew they were Jewish but had not felt they could speak about their identity freely. The opening of the Eastern Bloc enabled foreign institutional support and funding for the renewal of Jewish life. New Jewish schools were opened, associations were established, and magazines, cultural and community centers were founded. The development of Holocaust and Jewish-heritage tourism, along with the infrastructures to support that sector, facilitated the revitalization of Jewish spaces such as Kraków's Kazimierz district.[25] Most of what remained of Jewish communal property was also eventually returned to the official Jewish communities, or *Gminy*.[26]

23 In the Polish census of 2011, approximately two thousand individuals indicated "Jewish" as their only ethnicity; an additional five thousand indicated it as their second ethnicity (with Polish as their primary one) (Główny Urząd Statystyczny 2015). (The census does not have a question on religious affiliation.)

24 Based on interviews with Rabbi Schudrich in 2012 and Jonathan Ornstein in 2021.

25 Like most of Kraków, Kazimierz was not destroyed during the war, but it remained in a pitiful state of disrepair until the 1990s. Its proximity to Auschwitz, only an hour away, facilitated the development of hotels and restaurants, as tourists visit the museum on day trips but return to the city for the night. Kazimierz has also benefited from a tourism boom following the popularity of the movie *Schindler's List*, released in 1993. Numerous agencies started offering *Schindler's List* tours, showing both historical sites and the locations where movie scenes were shot, blending history and fiction in a single narrative. In 2010 Oskar Schindler's former enamel factory was converted into the Museum on the Occupation of Kraków during the Second World War. On domestic and foreign tourism to Kazimierz, see Jochnowitz (1998), Kugelmass and Orla-Bukowska (2008), Gruber (2002), Lehrer (2013), Waligórska (2013); on urban development and gentrification more specifically, see Murzyn (2004, 2006).

26 *Gmina* (plural *Gminy*) has both administrative and religious significations in Polish. It may refer to a territorially based self-governing unit or to a specific denominational community. The *Gmina Wyznaniowa Żydowska*—the Jewish denominational community—combines

Aspirational Multiculturalism

As significant as the process of Jewish community and religious renewal is, the activities generally lumped under the term "Jewish revival" remain primarily driven by non-Jewish social actors. What motivates their efforts? One key motivation is to recover what has been lost and erased so as to recreate Poland's multicultural past and thereby build and promote a plural, secular society in and against an ethnically and religiously homogeneous nation-state.

For most of its history Poland was indeed quite diverse, inhabited by a variety of ethnic, linguistic, and religious communities. After World War II and the Holocaust, and with the postwar redrawing of Poland's borders along with pogroms, state-sponsored ethnic cleansing, and antisemitic purges, this picture abruptly changed.[27] On the eve of the war, ethnic Poles constituted 65 percent of the Second Republic's population; by the late 1940s they accounted for about 95 percent of the population of the new People's Republic. The religious makeup of the population changed in a similar fashion (table 1).

Poland's current ethnic and religious homogeneity is therefore the result of relatively recent and very violent historical events and political

---

both significations. Because the English translation of the term *Gmina*—community—does not capture the administrative aspect of the Polish original, I use the original *Gmina/Gminy* in Polish, capitalized, when referring to the official, legally recognized, administrative organizations that oversee religious life, communal property, and cemeteries, and the English "community" to refer to social, cultural, and informal Jewish groups. The February 20, 1997, law on the relations between the state and the Jewish denominations in the Republic of Poland specified the legal status of the *Gmina* and returned communal property—synagogues, cemeteries, and religious objects—to local *Gminy*. The issue of *private*-property restitution remained unsettled and hotly contested both in Poland and abroad. In 2021 Poland's restitution law was amended to set a thirty-year time limit to appeal administrative decisions resulting in property seizure, de facto prohibiting the descendants of Jews whose property was seized during the Second World War and retained during the communist era from receiving restitution. That decision led to diplomatic tensions with Israel. For an insightful discussion of the issues impeding the restitution of so-called formerly Jewish private property and the context shaping that debate in Poland, see Stola (2008). For the full text of the law, "Ustawa z dnia 20 lutego 1997 r. o stosunku Państwa do gmin wyznaniowych żydowskich w Rzeczypospolitej Polskiej," see http://isap .sejm.gov.pl/isap.nsf/DocDetails.xsp?id=WDU19970410251. For a brief history, in English, of the restitution process and its legal underpinnings, consult the webpage of the *Gmina Wyznaniowa Żydowska w Polsce*, https://warszawa.jewish.org.pl/en/heritage/restitution.

27 As a result of the Second World War and the peace agreements, Poland ceded to the USSR 170,000 km² of its eastern territory, divided up between the Ukrainian and Belarusian Socialist Republics. In exchange, Poland received 100,000 km² of former German territory in the west, cutting off Germany from Silesia and Eastern Pomerania as well as a part of Brandenburg. German populations were deported; ethnic Poles in the east were "repatriated," often relocated westward to the so-called recovered territories.

TABLE 1. *Ethnic and Religious Composition of the Second Republic of Poland and of the Popular Republic of Poland (percentage)*

	1931	1946
Ethnic Poles	65	96
Jews	10	4
Ukrainians, Lithuanians, Belarusians, Germans, Tatars, and others	25	
Catholics	65	95

Sources: Michowicz 1988, Tomaszewski 1993, Casanova 1994.

processes. Yet this state of affairs was naturalized in the postwar period by both the socialist state and the Catholic Church. These institutions built or boosted their legitimacy by steeping themselves in the potent infusion of Poland's new ethnonational and denominational homogeneity, waving away even the aroma of diversity. Combined, these processes further tightened the association between Polishness and Catholicism (Zubrzycki 2006; Porter-Szűcs 2012).

Although the diversity that characterized Poland for most of its history is unlikely to return, progressive nationalists see the recognition of this legacy as a platform from which to build a more open society. They seek to push Poland toward an internationally normative model of nationhood, one that values and encourages pluralism and multiculturalism. Reaffirming Jewishness through memory work, social activism, and cultural practices symbolically reclaims the plural society eradicated during World War II, the memory of which was materially erased and ideologically suppressed by the socialist regime.[28] In this view, Poland's Jewish past holds the key to an imagined cosmopolitan future.

---

28 By "material erasure" I mean practices such as building over Jewish ruins and the conversion of synagogues into swimming pools, libraries, or cinemas, and of yeshivas into cultural centers. On the neighborhood built over the ruins of the Warsaw Ghetto, see Janicka (2011) and Chomątowska (2012). On the treatment of Jewish ruins more broadly in Poland and Germany, see Meng (2012, 2017). On Polish memory and amnesia with respect to Jews, see Irwin-Zarecka (1989), Kapralski (2001, 2015), Gitelman (2003), Steinlauf (1997), and Zubrzycki (2006, 2013b).

The historian Michael Meng has referred to this process as "redemptive cosmopolitanism," which he defines as the "commemorative display of multiethnicity that celebrates the cathartic, redemptive transformation of Germans and Poles into tolerant democratic citizens" (2012:10). The problem with redemptive cosmopolitanism, Meng argues, is that it replaces a critical examination of the liberal democratic nation-state's past and present failures (250). While I agree with Meng that a desire for cosmopolitanism is part of the motivation for Poland's Jewish turn, my research shows that many Polish activists also seek a critical engagement with the past and that at the core of their initiatives is a political critique of the present.

Resurrecting the Jew therefore has three primary objectives.

The first is empirical: to explain the origins, meaning, and significance of Poland's Jewish turn and of Polish philosemitism without reducing these to anti-antisemitism or a recent reaction to Poland's rightward turn. I show instead why and how they are related to the specific structures of Polish national identity and of nationalism.

The second objective is theoretical: to shed light on the impact of national scripts and their logics on symbolic boundary-making and re-making, and to clarify competing models of the relationship between nationalism, symbolic exclusion, and cultural appropriation, three key issues of our times.

The book's third objective is methodological: to propose a multifaceted approach to observing the making, unmaking, and redrawing of the symbolic boundaries of national identity via an analysis of discursive representations, material culture, and performative practices.

Symbolic Boundaries and the Logic of Ethnic Nationalism

"In order to focus on anything," Eviatar Zerubavel pointedly observed, "we must perceive some discontinuity between that which we attend and that which we ignore. . . . It is boundaries . . . that allow us—visually as well as mentally—to grasp any entity at all" (1991:118–19). Most of the literature on symbolic boundaries in the social sciences concerns the creation, maintenance, and transgression of group boundaries.[29] In studies of ethnicity

---

29 In sociology, Émile Durkheim's (1995 [1912]) work on the division of the world into the mutually constitutive and exclusive categories of the sacred and the profane is foundational for understanding symbolic boundaries and the role of the social in their making. Pierre Bourdieu (1984) has shown how social class and cultural capital interact to reproduce social boundaries and enforce gatekeeping. Michèle Lamont (1992) expanded Bourdieu's framework

and nationalism, the foundational work is that of Fredrik Barth (1969), who showed that ethnic identity is a feature of social organization and not a given of "culture," as the Herderian view would have it. By shifting attention away from a substantive notion of identity and toward its social organization, Barth demonstrated that ethnic groups were constituted via difference in the process of creating boundaries. From this key insight an important literature crossing disciplines and empirical objects was born. One subset has focused on showing that those symbolic boundaries have concrete consequences. Richard Alba (2005), for example, has shown that the *types* of boundaries between ethnic groups in immigration countries—"blurred" or "bright"—affected prospects of assimilation of second-generation individuals into the receiving society. Falling on either side of the color line in the United States and elsewhere is also known to have significant effects on educational and health outcomes, life expectancy, residential and professional opportunities, among many others (see Wimmer 2008a). The international standing of polities is also affected by the proportion of their citizens classified as "colored," hence political efforts to shift the criteria for "whiteness" to extend that category to more citizens (Loveman 2014).[30]

It was, however, the flip side of boundary making that animated Brubaker and his colleagues (2006) in their study of ethnicity in Cluj, a large Romanian city with a significant Hungarian minority. Instead of taking for granted that ethnonationality matters and assuming that Romanians and Hungarians constitute discrete and tightly bounded groups, Brubaker and his team studied when, why, and how that assumption did and did not hold. They found that ethnicity mattered less than local nationalist politicians claimed, and they concluded that ethnic boundaries are generally much more porous than even scholars had surmised. It is precisely because group identity and boundedness can be tenuous constructions that nationalists insist on hardening and policing boundaries—symbolic or institutional—between groups.

---

to include moral judgments people make in drawing symbolic boundaries between themselves and others. Other scholars, like E. Zerubavel (1991), focus on cognitive processes of boundary making and investigate how social context shapes the criteria by which symbolic boundaries are set. For insightful reviews of the literature, see Lamont and Molnár (2002), Lamont and Bail (2005), and Lamont, Pendergrass, and Pachucki (2015). On different dimensions and strategies of ethnic boundary making, see Wimmer (2008a, b).

30 Loveman and Muniz (2007) showed that after the First World War, Puerto Rico started to include individuals of "mixed" background (previously considered "colored") in the "white" category in its census, a process they call "boundary shifting." This reclassification resulted in an official "whitening" of the island.

Andreas Wimmer (2008b) analyzed an impressive corpus of case studies to identify four strategies used by social actors to negotiate ethnic boundaries: contraction, inversion, repositioning, and blurring. He showed that the choice of boundary-maintaining strategies depends on the characteristics of the social fields in which social actors operate: the institutional order, the distribution of power, and networks of alliances. Wimmer's "multilevel process theory" constitutes an important tool for understanding and explaining the making and unmaking of ethnic boundaries. Yet the theory, along with the empirical literature it is based on, understandably focuses on boundaries *between* ethnic groups—in immigration countries, majority/minority polities, and multiethnic societies. *Resurrecting the Jew* investigates instead the process of ethnonational symbolic boundary making and redrawing within a single ethnonational group.

As we have seen, Poland is one of the world's most homogeneous nation-states, with nearly 95 percent of its population ethnically Polish and 92 percent nominally Catholic. Almost 90 percent of Poles over the age of eighteen declare having religious faith. Forty-three percent participate in religious services at least once a week, and an additional 33 percent attend once or twice a month (Centrum Badania Opinii Społecznej 2021; Sadłoń 2021).[31] And yet ethnoreligious criteria are routinely used to draw distinctions *among* Poles. The Catholic Church and the Right discredit their opponents by accusing them of being "Jews," "Masons," "secularists" (the latter two being code words for Jews), "bad Catholics," and, increasingly, "terrorists-feminists" and the "LGBT lobby."[32] Given that Polishness

---

31 While the overall proportion of Poles attending church is very high (76 percent), it is in decline from what it was only a few years prior: in 2018, 87 percent of Poles participated in religious services, including 50 percent going to church at least once a week (Centrum Badania Opinii Społecznej 2018). The proportion of Poles participating in religious services today is also much lower than it was in the early 1990s, when 90 percent of Poles went to church (all frequency included, Centrum Badania Opinii Społecznej 2021) and 87 percent declared having religious faith. Concomitantly, the percentage of Poles *not* attending any religious services has nearly tripled since 1992, from 9 percent to 24 percent in 2021. The most drastic changes, however, can be observed among young adults (18-24 years of age). In 1992, 93 percent of Poles in this age group declared having religious faith; in 2021, 71 percent did. Between 1992 and 2021, the percentage of young adults declaring themselves *atheists* more than quadrupled (from 6.7 to 28.6) as did the percentage of young adults not participating in religious services (from 8 to 36) (Centrum Badania Opinii Społecznej 2021). For discussions of secularization processes in Poland, see Borowik (2017), Marody and Mandes (2017), Grabowska (2018), Zubrzycki (2020), and Sadłoń (2021).

32 The quotation marks indicate the symbolic and discursive nature of the categories. It is representations of Jews and Jewishness—not real, existing Jewish persons—that are used to sharpen Polishness, even when actual Jewish individuals are referred to or verbally and symbolically abused. Graff (2008) argues that gays are the "new Jews" and notes the ideological

is tied to Catholicism, this discursive strategy seeks to symbolically strip these groups and individuals of their Polishness.

This form of symbolic exclusion points to an interesting paradox. As we know from a rich literature on nationalism (e.g., Brubaker 1992; Schnapper 1994; Yack 1996; Nielsen 1999; Zubrzycki 2001), ideological forms of exclusion are typical of places where the nation is understood in civic terms, and where national identity, at least ideally, is therefore determined by an individual's adherence to the principles of the social contract rather than by ethnicity, race, or religious persuasion. The American case is paradigmatic of ideologically defined national identity: because being "American" implies supporting a specific set of values and practices, it is possible for citizens to be considered "un-American" by virtue of courting the "wrong" political or religious beliefs (including atheism).[33] This was the case during the 1950s' Red Scare and McCarthyism, when those suspected of supporting communism were accused of being un-American and, in consequence, suffered discrimination and prosecution, and in certain cases were forced into exile. The trope of un-Americanness resurfaced after September 11, 2001, to characterize critics of the Bush administration, and more recently to delegitimize the Affordable Care Act (so-called Obamacare) or those embracing "socialism" or declaring themselves atheists (Edgell, Gerteis, and Hartmann 2006; Edgell et al. 2016).

Nations imagined in the ethnic mode emphasize instead common descent, language, and cultural traits such as religion, passed on to individuals through the blood. Inclusion in the national community is primarily determined by ethnic or racial origins; identity cannot be chosen, acquired, nor escaped. Exclusion on the basis of politics or ideological leanings therefore ill befits places where the nation is primarily understood in ethnic terms, such as Poland. And yet the Catholic Right routinely excludes ethnic Poles from the imagined boundaries of the nation because of their ideological leanings, political identities, religious affiliation, or sexual orientation.

---

alliance between minority groups toward which the political Right and the Catholic Church are not especially benevolent. This argument has also been made by the feminist scholar and public intellectual Magdalena Środa (2014), who analyzes the witch hunt against feminists and the Catholic Church's blaming of "gender ideology" for all sorts of social ills, from broken families to pedophile priests. Moreover, it is common for far-Right editorialists and activists to directly refer to feminist scholars and activists as Jews. On the use of Jewishness and homosexuality as tropes for symbolic exclusion from the national community, see also Mosse (1985), Bunzl (2004), and Bratcher (2020).

33 The prefix *un*, unlike the more neutral *non*, implies active opposition to what is normatively considered "American."

How is it possible, given the dominant ethnic understanding of national identity, to exclude members of the prevalent ethnic group? How can the Catholic Right insist on the blood-based character of Polishness while at the same time symbolically excluding some ethnic Poles? How is the tension reconciled between these two modes of social closure—one based on blood and culture, the other on ideological orientations and political bonds?

Magical Antisemitism: Ethnicizing Ideological Otherness

In Poland, the tension between ethnic and civic modes of boundary-keeping is primarily solved by turning ideological divergence into ethnic divergence: individuals and groups who do not defend the prominent place of Catholicism and its symbols in the public sphere, but advocate instead for a civic and secular Poland, are discursively turned into "Jews" by the Right. That process makes ideologically based exclusion conform to the logic of ethnic nationalism.

This logic and the multiple cases of its application in the public sphere, in both verbal and nonverbal discourse, provide rich examples of a phenomenon analyzed long ago by Jean-Paul Sartre (1986 [1946]), who famously claimed that "if the Jew did not exist, the anti-Semite would invent him." For Enzo Traverso (1997), one can be Jewish, and become Jewish, merely by virtue of the Other's gaze. The former political dissident and Solidarity activist Adam Michnik, now editor-in-chief of Poland's most important daily *Gazeta Wyborcza*, refers to this reasoning as "magical antisemitism." He explains its workings as follows: "The logic of normal . . . antisemitism is the following: 'Adam Michnik is a Jew, therefore he is a hooligan, a thief, a traitor, a bandit etc.' Magical antisemitism however works this way: 'Adam Michnik is a thief, therefore he is most probably a Jew'" (1999:73).

Why single out Jews instead of Russians or Germans, also significant Others in the Polish social imagination? One key reason is that Jewishness is perceived as the polar opposite of the ethnoreligious category of the *Polak-katolik* (Krzemiński 1996, 2001). According to Kowalski and Tulli (2003:486–89), the invention of Jews in right-wing milieus is a response to their ideological creation of "imaginary Poles." Imaginary Poles embody the "true" qualities and values of Polishness—Catholicism, patriotism, traditionalism, and economic conservatism. But when actual Poles fail to live up to this model, right-leaning social actors can suffer from a cognitive dissonance that they resolve by spinning conspiracy theories of Jews infiltrating the nation. Furthermore, Jews are traditionally associated with capitalism, socialism, and cosmopolitanism. On the face of it, these three ideological forms might seem unlikely bedfellows, but all three are easily opposed to the traditional figures of the Polish Catholic peasant and nobleman-intellectual.

As Jewishness has become a symbol of a liberal, plural, and secular Poland, Poland is claimed by the Catholic Right to be ruled by "Jews"—symbolic Jews—who must be stopped. Poland is thus host to the perplexing phenomenon of antisemitism in a country with very few Jews.[34]

Figure 2 captures key components of that type and form of antisemitism. Posted on a far-Right website, the photo collage is entitled "A Very Virtual Poland," implying that the Poland represented here by (postcommunist Left) President Aleksander Kwaśniewski (1995–2005) is not the "real thing," nor what it should be. It depicts Kwaśniewski with his mouth covered by a photograph of Joseph Stalin, thus implying that the president is a communist mouthpiece. Prominently displayed at the top right corner of the image is the insignia of the Soviet NKVD, the organization that preceded the KGB and that was responsible for murdering some twenty thousand Polish officers in the forests of Katyń during the Second World War. The cloth Star of David that Jews were forced to wear in Nazi-occupied Europe, at the top left corner, suggests that Kwaśniewski is not only associated with violent communism but also a Jew—replicating the long-standing trope of Judeo-communism.[35] The juxtaposition of the Star of David with the yellow stars of the European Union flag, which Poland joined in 2004 under Kwaśniewski's leadership, visually alludes to a conspiracy theory often articulated in right-wing media, according to which the European Union is part of a communist/Zionist plot to take over Poland.[36]

A second example of magical antisemitism transforms various political elites representing a wide range of views, from Left to Right, into Orthodox

34 For survey-based analyses of antisemitism in contemporary Poland, see Krzemiński (1996, 2001, 2015) and Bilewicz, Winiewski, and Radzik (2012). On antisemitism and opposition to it, see Blobaum (2005) and Michnik (ed., 2010). On folkloric and historical representations of Jews in Poland, see Cała (1995), Michlic (2006), and Tokarska-Bakir (2008).

35 In Poland, Judeo-communism—*żydokomuna*—is a pervasive antisemitic narrative claiming that Jews collaborated with the Soviet Union to impose communism in Poland. The term underlines the fusion of the categories of Jews/Jewishness and communism. On the narrative of Judeo-Bolshevism in Eastern Europe, see Gerrits (2008) and Hanebrink (2018). On its Polish variant, see Michlic (2006) and Śpiewak (2012).

36 Such conspiracy theories were expressed numerous times by my interviewees in the early 2000s. One man in his sixties, for example, explained to me that the Jews knew that their situation in the Middle East was untenable in the long term and were therefore trying to come back to Poland, the "real Promised Land." As he saw it, the European Union was the structure through which they could accomplish that goal.

FIGURE 2. Antisemitic meme accusing President Aleksander Kwaśniewski of being a Jew and a communist, posted on the far-Right website "A Very Virtual Poland" (http://bardzo-wirtualna-polska.abceblog.com, accessed June 4, 2013).

FIGURE 3. Antisemitic meme turning Polish politicians into Orthodox Jews, posted on the far-Right website "A Very Virtual Poland" (http://bardzo-wirtualna-polska.abceblog.com/wp-content/uploads/sites/10/2013/08/zydzi-w-polsce.jpg, accessed June 4, 2013).

Jews (figure 3). The image implies that Poland is ruled by Jews. The prominent figure smoking a cigar and unceremoniously holding the Polish flag is Jerzy Urban, a former press secretary under communist rule who in the 1990s founded the vulgar, satirical, anticlerical weekly *Nie* (No).[37] Behind him, making the victory sign with his fingers, is Adam Michnik. On the left side of the frame, above the flag, is Donald Tusk, then leader of the Center-Right party Civic Platform (*Platforma Obywatelska*), prime minister of Poland from 2007 to 2014, and more recently president of the European Council (2014–19). Other notable political figures in the collage include Aleksander Kwaśniewski; the late Andrzej Lepper, leader of the populist party Self-Defense (*Samoobrona*) from 1992 to 2011; and Leszek Balcerowicz,

---

37 Urban is the only figure depicted without religious garb. This may be either because of his well-known animosity toward religion or because his Jewish origins are considered self-evident.

former minister of finance (1997–2000), responsible for Poland's so-called shock therapy during its transition to capitalism. Some of these figures have Jewish roots, but most do not. And that is the point: what matters is not whether they are Jewish by descent, but what Jewishness represents to the author of the cartoon.

These two arresting examples are emblematic of visual discourses common on far-Right social media but too extreme to be displayed on mainstream right-wing forums.[38] Magical antisemitism and discourses around *żydokomuna* are very much present in the public sphere, however, and commonplace in right-wing newspapers like *Nasz Dziennik* (Our Daily), *Gazeta Polska* (Polish Gazette), and the conservative Catholic weekly *Niedziela* (Sunday), as well as on the airwaves of Radio Maryja. In all these print and radio media, Poland's most popular daily, the progressive *Gazeta Wyborcza*, is nicknamed "Gazeta *Koszerna*," the kosher newspaper. In the same vein, the progressive, personalist Catholic weekly *Tygodnik Powszechny*, with which John Paul II was associated before his papacy and which has long worked toward building Polish- and Christian-Jewish dialogue, is nicknamed "*Żydownik* Powszechny" (Universal *Jewishy*) by people on the far Right.[39]

The process of casting opponents as Jews is so prevalent that some progressive Catholic bishops are sometimes accused of being Jewish. Even John Paul II, canonized in 2014, is not immune to this magical antisemitism (see figure 4). A graffito defacing a mural dedicated to the memory of the late Polish pope accuses him of being an "actor and an impostor," as well as a Jew, most likely because of his ecumenical preaching and rapprochement with Judaism and Jews, whom he commonly referred to as "our older brothers in faith." A Star of David is spray-painted over the pope's face, and the graffito includes a play on the vulgar "son of a bitch" insult, replacing the word "son" with "Jew" ("Jew of a bitch"—*z kurwy żyd*). The word Jew is sprayed over multiple times to achieve a bold effect. Though the graffito is not signed, the author left clues to its provenance. The symbol at the lower left is shorthand for the slogan "Poland Fighting" (*Polska walcząca*). It was used in the resistance against the Nazis during World War II and against communism in the postwar era, and is now used by the Right and far Right in their fight against the menace posed by so-called liberal issues.

38 While these images could be found on a popular far-Right website and are circulated on the web, it is impossible to identify their author or get in touch with the webmaster.

39 In a bold reversal, the weekly reclaimed the intended insult. For its sixty-fifth-anniversary issue in 2010, it printed *Żydownik Powszechny* on its masthead, commemorating its long-standing engagement with Polish-Jewish and Christian-Jewish relations.

FIGURE 4. Antisemitic graffito defacing a mural to the memory of Pope John Paul II, in Kraków, summer 2013. It accuses the pope of being an actor, a fraud, and a Jew because of his ecumenism and explicit rapprochement with Judaism. "Z kurwy żyd" is literally "Jew of a bitch," a play on the epithet "son of a bitch." (Photo by Marcin Karkosza / Polska Press, reprinted with permission of *Gazeta Krakowska*.)

Similar discourses find expression in everyday life. During my fieldwork at the Auschwitz-Birkenau Museum and the town of Oświęcim in the late 1990s and early 2000s, I was told on several occasions that the more liberal wings of the Catholic Church were led by Jews who had infiltrated the organization by "passing" as Poles/Catholics. A common theory is that many Jewish children who were hidden and saved by the Catholic Church during the Second World War later entered the priesthood for convenience and eventually rose in the church hierarchy. They are now ideally situated, the story goes, to destroy the institution from within. The fact that many Jewish children were in fact hidden in Catholic institutions, and that some of them later did become priests and nuns, lends plausibility and power to the conspiracy theory.[40]

In the examples cited here, Jewishness is understood as an ethnic or racial category rather than a religious one. The trope of passing—converting

40 See Paweł Pawlikowski's Oscar-winning film *Ida*, about a novice nun about to take her vows who is told by a family member that she is Jewish. See also the documentary *Torn*, by Ronit Kertsner, about Father Romuald-Jakub Weksler-Waszkinel, a Roman Catholic priest who found out at age thirty-five that he had been given by his Jewish birth mother to a Polish Catholic family in Święcany (near Vilnius) before the liquidation of the town's ghetto in 1943. Weksler-Waszkinel emigrated to Israel in 2008 (https://www.youtube.com/watch?v=DM4N2ecEaCo and https://sztetl.org.pl/en/biographies/4136-weksler-waszkinel-romuald-jakub).

and/or changing one's name to hide Jewish origins—is ever-present in the discourse of the far Right, as conversion cannot alter one's ethnicity or race. Revelations about the "real" names of public figures on traditional and social media platforms and the use of a modifier, such as "Polish-*speaking*" instead of the usual "Polish," are therefore common discursive strategies meant to unmask "impostors." Long before I started conducting research on antisemitism and philosemitism, someone's "real" identity would be "revealed" to me by others in confidence or casual conversations, not only with regard to public figures but also acquaintances and colleagues.

It is precisely this magical antisemitism that the street artist Peter Fuss critiqued in his project "Jesus Christ King of Poland." As part of the project, in January 2007 Fuss installed a large billboard in a residential neighborhood of Koszalin in northwestern Poland (figure 5). It displayed fifty-six stylized photographs of Polish public figures with the caption "Jews, Get Out of This Catholic Country!" By including several prominent figures from the Catholic Right—such as the president of Poland, Lech Kaczyński—Fuss underlined the convoluted logic and hysteria that perme-

FIGURE 5. A police car investigates street artist Peter Fuss's billboard "Jews, Get Out of This Catholic Country" in Koszalin in January 2007. The billboard included prominent members of the Catholic Right as well as the former prime minister Tadeusz Mazowiecki and the Nobel laureate Wisława Szymborska, both associated with the Catholic weekly *Tygodnik Powszechny*. (Photo by Peter Fuss, reprinted with permission of the artist.)

ates magical antisemitism. As part of the project, the artist observed and photographed reactions of passersby examining the billboard, as well as police cars slowing to investigate it. Those photographs became part of a multimedia exhibition in which Fuss blew up and framed transcripts of antisemitic discussions on popular web platforms and played recorded sound fragments from Radio Maryja.[41] The billboard was deemed racist and antisemitic by the Koszalin police, and the exhibition was shut down for propagating hate speech. Fuss documented this process, too, and posted it on his website.

Magical Philosemitism and the Tragedy of Civic Nationalism

If magical antisemitism involves the ethnicization of deviation from a strict ethno-Catholic model of Polishness, the same strategy is at the source of magical *philo*semitism. Whereas ethnoreligious nationalists contend that "Jews" are contaminating the nation with their civic ideals and building a pernicious cosmopolitan world, proponents of a progressive, liberal, and secular vision of the polity argue that "Jews" must be resurrected and Jewishness promoted for the same reason. Philosemitism in contemporary Poland is therefore not anti-antisemitism but is connected to the inner logic of ethnic nationalism in that country. Precisely because Jewishness carries specific significations and symbolic capital that other minorities (such as Ukrainians, Silesians, or Vietnamese) do not possess, it is primarily through Jews and Jewishness that a vision of a modern multicultural and secular Poland is articulated and liberal nationalism promoted.[42] In chapter 5 I explain in greater detail why that is the case.

In a context where national identity is primarily understood in ethnic terms, and where civic discourse of the nation can be perceived as a remnant of communist party-state rhetoric or as an import from the European

41 For photographs of the exhibition, screenshots, and radio segments used in the project, see http://peterfuss.com/jesus-christ-king-of-poland. The conservative weekly *Wprost* published a story on the project with the title "Police Searching for Author of Racist Billboard" (https://www.wprost.pl/kraj/100441/policja-szuka-autora-rasistowskiego-billboardu.html).

42 Broadly speaking, *Silesians* denotes the population inhabiting Silesia, a region that extends across the modern Polish, German, and Czech borders. Although few Silesians still speak the Silesian dialect (a mix of Polish and German), this regional identity is quite strong. In the 2011 census, the first to allow dual ethnonational identifications, 376,000 Polish residents declared "Silesian" as their only ethnic identity, 436,000 as their primary ethnicity, and 411,000 as their secondary one (https://stat.gov.pl/cps/rde/xbcr/gus/Przynaleznosc_narodowo -etniczna_w_2011_NSP.pdf).

Union and neoliberal Polish elites, progressive, "civic" nationalists must work doubly hard at rendering their vision of the nation legitimate and authentically Polish. Public intellectuals have therefore tried to promote this vision by reconstructing a narrative that emphasizes the civic heritage of the nation in Poland. They do so by looking back to sixteenth-century religious tolerance, to the First Republic's multiethnic and multiconfessional state, to the Democracy of Nobles' elective monarchy, to the Constitution of May 3, 1791, to the nineteenth-century Polish legions fighting "for your freedom and ours," to interwar liberal traditions, and to a certain extent to the 1970s Workers' Defense Committee (KOR) and Solidarity's peaceful resistance and civic activism in the 1980s.

Since the Right and far Right also use some of these historical themes, civic nationalists have few political stories and symbols at their disposal, and have therefore engaged in recreating Jewish culture as a visible counterweight to the ethnoreligious national community. Paradoxically, then, ethnicity remains the means through which they attempt to transcend ethnonationalism. That conundrum is at the basis of what I call the tragedy of Polish civic nationalism: to escape ethnic nationalism, civic nationalists must resort to deploying it. Part of that tragedy is that in order to achieve the goals of civic nationalism and multiculturalism, the Jew must remain irremediably Other. And whether real or symbolic, the category of the Jew remains malleable to those with power over it.

While Rogers Brubaker speaks of "ethnicity without groups" (2004) and Andreas Wimmer of "ethnicity without boundaries" (2008a) to highlight the fluidity of ethnic categories, in this book I analyze ethnic boundaries without ethnic groups, answering Lamont and Molnár's call "for greater attention to the cultural production of boundaries, of difference and hybridity, and of cultural membership and group classifications" (2002:169).

Methods, Data, and Guide to the Book

To explain the contemporary enthusiasm for all things Jewish and to explore the ways it is related to symbolic boundary (re)making, this study adopts a multiscalar approach, considering macro, meso, and micro dimensions of philosemitism. I analyze Jewish-centered initiatives sponsored by state institutions and nongovernmental organizations (NGOs), bottom-up civic projects, and everyday individual practices. On the basis of archival and ethnographic research conducted in multiple Polish cities and towns, I interpret the different meanings that Jewishness has for the diverse actors and organizations engaged in the Jewish turn: Jewish and non-Jewish, secular and religious.

In addition to its wide geographic reach, the study spans the last quarter century. It builds on previous fieldwork in Poland, during which I have observed and documented changing Polish-Jewish relations and the rising interest of non-Jewish Poles in Jewish culture. In the course of my research on the collective memory/nonmemory of the Holocaust in the 1990s and early 2000s, I conducted formal and ethnographic interviews with Poles (both Jewish and non-Jewish) interested in and dedicated to learning and teaching about Jews, Jewish culture, and Polish-Jewish relations. I participated in various commemorative events, such as the March of the Living at Auschwitz and the March of Memory in Kraków, and I have attended Kraków's annual Jewish Culture Festival on many occasions since 1990. These early encounters with the beginnings of the Jewish revival were significant because they served as a point of comparison when I returned to Poland in the summer of 2010 after a five-year hiatus.

I conducted thirty weeks of fieldwork over a period of ten years, from the summer of 2010 through the fall of 2019. Most of my fieldwork was in Kraków and Warsaw, where the Jewish turn is strongest, but I also conducted research in Lublin, Wrocław, Gdańsk, Łódź, Oświęcim, Chmielnik, and Szydłów. I was a frequent participant observer at the annual Kraków Jewish Culture Festival, which organizes workshops, courses, and tours focused on Poland's Jewish past and present. I was invited to numerous communal events in the Kraków and Warsaw Jewish communities, such as Shabbat dinners, anniversaries, weddings, bar mitzvahs, and religious holidays (Purim, Yom Kippur, Passover). I also attended the 2016 Polish Limmud, a three-day gathering of members of the Jewish community during which they learn from each other about Judaism, Jewish history and culture, and other issues relevant to their communal life in workshops, panels, and book readings. I participated in everyday work at Kraków's Jewish Community Centre (JCC), which opened in 2008, and I attended special events elsewhere for Catholics and Protestants who were eager to learn about Judaism and Jewish culture, such as a Christian enactment of a Passover seder. Lastly, I accompanied a group of Polish Jewish youth on a Birthright trip to Israel in July 2017, spending twelve days with them as they encountered that country, explored their Jewish heritage, and engaged in constant dialogue about their identities. I conducted follow-up interviews with a third of the participants in the months following the trip.

Besides participant observation, I conducted over one hundred open-ended interviews with key actors and representatives of institutions involved in initiatives and activities related to Jewishness: rabbis, cultural entrepreneurs, communal leaders, museologists, artists, and public intellectuals, as well as participants in communal and cultural events. Over half of these formal interviews were with non-Jewish volunteers at Jewish institutions, non-Jewish members of an Israeli dance group, Christian evangelicals observing Jewish holidays, and non-Jewish Poles who are in the process of converting to Judaism or who recently discovered they have Jewish ancestry. Many of the last are recovering a Jewish identity by registering for classes on topics from Hebrew to kosher cooking, and seeking to implement their learning in their daily lives.

Finally, I collected materials documenting the emergence and transformation of various Jewish-centered initiatives and state-sponsored institutions like festivals, museums, and university programs; memorials and significant artistic creations and projects; and the opening of commercial enterprises such as restaurants, cafés, and bookshops, with special attention to coverage of these in the press. I also analyzed primary texts such as political speeches, inscriptions on monuments, and newspaper editorials; iconographic documents (photographs, graffiti, ads, pamphlets); audio-visual materials (films and amateur videos, radio broadcasts, music and soundtracks); and artifacts (mementos and souvenirs). Although spatial constraints preclude my referring to all these materials in the book, they inform my overall analysis. A detailed discussion of methodology, specific sources, and different types of data used for individual chapters appears in appendix A.

These multiple perspectives provide me with a view of both the production of the Jewish cultural revival in Poland and its consumption and re-creation by participants. My interpretation of the varied meanings of Jewishness is firmly grounded in empirical data. By getting close to the actors actually engaging in Jewish-centered practices, paying careful attention to the local contexts in which those practices and projects arise, and seeing how they are interpreted and appropriated by ordinary people reacting to them, I can paint a nuanced picture of the phenomenal interest in all things Jewish in contemporary Poland.

Resurrecting the Jew is divided into two main parts. The first focuses on Poland's great mnemonic awakening after the publication of Jan Gross's *Neighbors*, and the emergence of nostalgic discourses on Jewish absence. Chapter 2 studies the material evocation of Jewish absence through an analysis of mnemonic initiatives by artists, NGOs, and official institutions to find and mark Jewish traces and ruins in urban landscapes. Chapter 3 digs into nostalgic discourses about Jews and what these reveal about

Poles. Chapter 4 analyzes the most important cultural institution articulating the history of Polish Jews, the Polin Museum of the History of Polish Jews.

Part Two shifts the focus to the active recovery of Jewishness and Judaism in the present. Chapter 5 analyzes the performance of Jewishness by non-Jews. It asks what cultural appropriation means in the Polish context before turning to the analysis of multicultural utopias embodied in the discovery, recovery, and performance of Jewish culture by non-Jewish Poles. Chapter 6 discusses the renewal of Jewish life proper, investigates how it intersects with the "Jewish turn," and asks what this all means for the community of Polish Jews. In the conclusion, I reflect on whether and to what extent the Jewish turn is a distinctively Polish phenomenon. I extend my findings to comparisons beyond Poland and articulate the theoretical contributions of the study to cultural sociology, the sociology of nationalism, and memory studies. By highlighting the role of cultural practices in the contest over national identity and its symbolic boundaries, *Resurrecting the Jew* disentangles the processes through which ethnonational, religious, and ideological identifications are bundled and mobilized.

The title of the book may be perplexing to some. The term *resurrection* is not one I have heard used in Poland to describe the Jewish revival. There, *rebirth* (*odrodzenie*) and *renaissance* (*renesans*) are used instead. I chose the metaphor of resurrection because it captures the story of the (unexpected, miraculous) passage from death to life, with a clear emphasis on life, which is central to the Polish narrative of Jewish history in Poland. I use that specific metaphor precisely to underline the Polish specificity of the phenomenon. I also use the metaphor in its present-participle form—*resurrecting* rather than *resurrection*—to emphasize the processual nature of the phenomenon and to stress that the revival of Jewish culture (and the renewal of Jewish life) in Poland involves human agency: it is a project enacted by specific people, most of whom are (nominally) Catholics but who are bringing Jewish culture back to life in order to transcend the religious definition of Polishness. The Jew in the title is not Jesus. It refers, rather, to an amorphous, ghostly Jew—a revenant—that Poles conjure to reinvent themselves.

PART ONE

The Great Mnemonic Awakening

CHAPTER 2

Traces and the Sensorium

THE MATERIALITY OF JEWISH ABSENCE

Before the Second World War, Poland had the largest Jewish population in Europe, and Warsaw was its epicenter. Fully one-third of the city's inhabitants—approximately four hundred thousand—were Jewish. After the Holocaust, Jewish life all but disappeared from the capital city, left in ruins, as it did from Poland at large. Only the city's Old Town and the large avenue leading to it were rebuilt in their earlier forms.[1] Other districts, like the former Jewish Quarter, disappeared as socialist construction rose over the rubble. Broad avenues absorbed smaller streets and alleys, and monuments to Polish martyrs began to pock the urban landscape. Material traces of past Jewish life and death were mostly erased (Janicka 2011; Chomątowska 2012; Klekot 2015; Meng 2017). Across Poland, Jewish homes that survived the war were taken over by new occupants, and Jewish communal buildings, including synagogues and yeshivas, were either destroyed or, more frequently, repurposed as libraries, cinemas, or cultural centers by the socialist state (Meng 2012; Wilczyk 2009). Cemeteries were abandoned and neglected; even tombstones were pilfered by local inhabitants for a variety of everyday purposes (Baksik 2013). Except for a few sites and exceptional memorials and monuments, the marks of Jewish life were nearly erased. And as Jewish survivors of the war aged and died and cityscapes were transformed, the very memory of Polish-Jewish history was slowly but surely buried.[2]

---

1 Despite the common claims that the reconstruction of Warsaw's Old Town was a faithful rendition of its prewar state, different parts of it were rebuilt according to its appearance at different historical periods (Martyn 2001; Elżanowski 2018; Klekot 2012). For a brief description of the rebuilding plan and process, see UNESCO's page http://whc.unesco.org/en/list/30.

2 With few Jewish survivors remaining in Poland after the war, it was difficult to organize the maintenance and repair of communal property, which was therefore often turned over to the socialist state. Since 2002, the Foundation for the Preservation of Jewish Heritage in Poland, established by the Union of Jewish Communities in Poland and the World Jewish Restitution Organization, has worked to recover, preserve, and commemorate "surviving sites

FIGURE 6. Commemorative path marking the location of the vanished Warsaw Ghetto wall. (Photo: Geneviève Zubrzycki, May 17, 2014.)

In the past two decades, memory activists have worked to resurrect Polish Jewish history and awaken Poles' memories of Jews. For them, the loss of Jewish memory is a wound in the nation's body. Jewish absence has come to represent the loss of a multicultural Poland—of what was, and what could have been. But if part of Polish society now experiences Jewish absence as something like "phantom-limb pain," an idea I explore in chapter 3, feeling the pain of amputation requires knowledge of the prior existence of the limb. For absence to be meaningful and experienced as loss, in other words, it must be discovered and brought to the surface of national history.

Absence has several potential dimensions that are important to distinguish. At the most elementary level, absence denotes something, or someone, that is basically "not there." As an example, consider a declaration like "There are no Jews in Poland." I call this an observation of *objective absence*. While this statement appears to accurately depict the

---

and monuments of Jewish cultural heritage in Poland" (interview with Monika Krawczyk, May 25, 2016, and http://fodz.pl/?d=3&l=en).

situation in post–World War II Poland, it obscures the fact of past Jewish presence, as well as the traumatic process by which presence became absence. This erasure is enabled by omission, silence and taboo, or what I call *discursive absence*. The objective and discursive absence of Jews has had a serious impact on Polish collective memory. With very few Jews left to tell their stories after the war, and in a climate that did not encourage discussing the Holocaust, most Poles remained enclosed within their own memories, repeating uncontested depictions and narratives (J. E. Young 1993:116; Irwin-Zarecka 1989). Within a couple of generations, past Jewish presence, and the causes and conditions of Jews' "disappearance" from the national landscape, receded into dim history. Jewish absence became an objective, but invisible, social fact.

The projects of memory activists have attempted to call attention to the *historical-temporal* dimension of Jewish absence. By calling attention to traces of former Jewish presence, they render visible contemporary Jewish absence. Through a variety of mnemonic practices, memory activists call attention to what and who is *no longer*: who is no longer *here*, and who *is* no longer tout court, an existential claim. This dimension of absence illuminates not only the empirical, observable state of objective absence but also the fact that this absence is of relatively recent origin.

Seen thus, absence is more than a neutral lack or objective fact. Its narrative has a genre, so to speak, and the genre is tragedy (White 1973). That narrative trajectory evokes reflection on the relation between the past and the present, even if the conditions that have brought about absence are not always fully acknowledged. Nevertheless, the recognition of Jewish absence in its historical-temporal dimension can activate a *phenomenological* aspect of absence: the experience of absence as a negative state, a void, a vacuum, a hole. Such experiences of loss often generate nostalgia, as we will see in the next chapter.

These dimensions of absence are not mutually exclusive, and they are implicated in complex historical, political, and sociopsychological processes of forgetting and remembering (Connerton 1989, 2009). This chapter analyzes a process of creative historical salvage through which socially conscious and politically engaged actors, NGOs, and official institutions give material form to historical-temporal absence. The signposting of vanished Jewish spaces, the marking of some ruins as Jewish, the resurrection of Jewish material culture, and the embodied commemoration of people and places are part of an attempt not only to acknowledge Jewish history but to make Poles cognizant of Jewish absence and perhaps even to feel it physically and emotionally.

Signposting the Missing

Warsaw and many other Polish towns today are so different from their pre-war incarnations that Jewish absence can be felt only by those who knew them before, or with the help of guides or physical cues indicating what was once there (Engelking and Leociak 2001; Zieliński and Majewski 2014). To help conjure this past, over the past two decades the city has been dotted by historical signs. This signposting project goes beyond the installation of bland memorial plaques to create instead memorials that engage the senses. The most prominent initiative is a walking path tracing the vanished walls of the former ghetto (see figure 6 on p. 34, and figure 7).[3] The symbolic path is marked by twenty-two concrete monuments, each embellished with a bronze map and a Plexiglas plaque that presents the history of the ghetto in Polish and English. Archival photographs of the specific site of a given monument are included as well (figure 8).[4] The project was conceived by Eleonora Bergman, an architectural historian and then director of the Jewish Historical Institute (ŻIH), together with the designer and architect Tomasz Lec. The pace of its realization was unusually fast: the City of Warsaw's monument conservator recommended adoption of the project in 2007, and it was approved on July 28, 2008. Only a few months later, on November 19, 2008, the path and the monuments were unveiled. The project was funded by multiple agencies, including the Ministry of Culture and National Heritage and the City of Warsaw, a collaboration that illustrates the close working relationship between Jewish, local, and national institutions at the time.[5]

With a new city grid superimposed on the old, until recently it was difficult for passersby to be aware of the sheer size of the ghetto and its exact location. The commemorative path not only marks the location and extent of the former ghetto but also provides a powerful reminder of the absent walls, whose trace crosses streets and parks and is sometimes interrupted by postwar buildings.

---

3 This initiative is akin to that of artist Gunter Demnig's stumbling stones (*Stolpersteine*) in Germany and other European cities: brass plates inscribed with the names and life dates of individual victims of Nazism. Warsaw's pavement and brass pathway visually and sensorially interrupts the walking surface to tell the story of the Warsaw Ghetto to the casual visitor. The ghetto wall, built in 1940, was 3 meters high (9.8 ft) and approximately 18 kilometers long, imprisoning at one point as many as 460,000 Jews within 3.4 km² (1.3 sqm).

4 Twenty-one of the monuments were dedicated between April and November 2008; the last one, in the courtyard of Sienna Street, was added in 2010. For a list of their locations, see https://pl.m.wikipedia.org/wiki/Pomniki_granic_getta_w_Warszawie (accessed April 18, 2016).

5 In 2007–8, both the city of Warsaw and the Polish Sejm were under the leadership of the Center-Right party Civic Platform (*Platforma Obywatelska*).

FIGURE 7. Commemorative path marking the location of the vanished Warsaw Ghetto wall. (Photo by Geneviève Zubrzycki, July 5, 2010.)

FIGURE 8. Monument marking a section of the vanished Warsaw Ghetto wall. (Photo by Geneviève Zubrzycki, July 4, 2010.)

The commemorative path brings the walker into three realities: that of the past, that of its erasure, and that of its reemergence through new spatial imaginaries in the present. Signposting the former ghetto wall highlights the Polish experience of Jewish absence on two levels: first, it reminds walkers of the extermination of Jews during the Holocaust; second, it reminds visitors of Jews' erasure from memory after the war.

In another project, street artist Adam X (Adam Jastrzębski) shows the location of the wooden footbridge over Chłodna Street that linked the small and the large ghettos (figure 9). (Chłodna Street was excluded from the ghetto because it was an important transport and communication route.) Titled *Here Was the Footbridge*, the piece highlights the different experiences of the war for Jews and non-Jews: packed crowds of Jews are depicted on the stairs and on the bridge crossing Chłodna Street, while a few gentiles appear to enjoy a stroll on the light, expansive "Aryan" street.

The mural was ceremonially unveiled on April 21, 2007, by Marek Edelman, the last surviving leader of the Warsaw Ghetto Uprising, to commemorate the uprising's sixty-fourth anniversary.[6] To the rare onlooker who can read Hebrew, the inscription in that language (top line) fascinates, because a small diacritical error on one of the letters in the word *bridge* transforms it into the word *void*. Thus "Here was the bridge" becomes "Here was the void." The mistake was most likely accidental—a correction has been added underneath the word—but the error that so acutely captures the meaning of the artwork was left in place and became a part of the work.[7]

Intended as an ephemeral piece, as street art often is, this creation eventually led to the establishment in 2012 of a formal, permanent monument to the footbridge, in the form of an art installation called *The Footbridge of Memory* (*Kładka pamięci*) (figure 10). The installation, created by Tomasz Lec, consists of two large steel pillars, linked by wires above the street, that mark the original sites of the staircases to the footbridge. At night the wires are illuminated, creating a visual bridge. The wires not only represent the platform of the original span but are also reminiscent of *eruvim*, the wires or cords strung around ultra-Orthodox Jewish communities. *Eruvim* conceptually extend the private domain, allowing residents to carry objects outside the home on Shabbat and Yom Kippur, when ritual rules proscribe engaging in work. On the pillars, at eye level, are historical inscriptions and bronze 3-D viewers allowing visitors to visually experience the everyday life of the former ghetto. The monument's imposing, electrically lit modernity, juxtaposed with grainy black-and-white archival photographs, is jarring. The site overwhelms the spectator with the weight of absence.[8]

6 http://puszka.waw.pl/tam_byla_kladka-projekt-pl-52.html (accessed October 23, 2014). Marek Edelman remained in Poland after the war, became a noted cardiologist, and was an active member of the Solidarity opposition. He died in 2009.

7 My thanks to Efrat Bloom for pointing this out to me.

8 This effect is perceived, of course, only to the extent that the passerby stops, looks at, and takes in the photos on the monument. The installation nevertheless imparts some awareness of past presence and current absence even with minimal engagement.

FIGURE 9. *Here Was the Footbridge*, by the street artist Adam X, on Chłodna Street, Warsaw. The title is given in Hebrew, Yiddish, and Polish. (Photo by Geneviève Zubrzycki, May 17, 2014.)

FIGURE 10. *The Footbridge of Memory* (*Kładka Pamięci*), by Tomasz Lec, at the corner of Chłodna and Żelazna Streets, Warsaw. (Photo by Franciszek Mazur / Agencja Gazeta.)

Other mnemonic projects likewise seek to invoke and amplify the world that was lost. The commemoration of Warsaw's Great Synagogue on Tłomackie Street is a case in point. Opened on Rosh Hashanah in 1878 for Reform Jews, the majestic building could seat 2,400 people, making it the largest synagogue in the world at the time. It was blown up by the Nazis at the end of the Warsaw Ghetto Uprising on May 16, 1943, and the site lay vacant until it was designated as the location for a modern skyscraper. Construction began in the 1970s but was not completed until 1991.[9] On May 16, 2013, the seventieth anniversary of the destruction of the synagogue, the Jewish Historical Institute in Warsaw "brought the synagogue back to remembrance," as it announced several weeks in advance. The commemoration was part memorial happening and part art installation. Called *The Great Absentee (Wielka nieobecna)*, the event included the unveiling of a 1:10 plywood model of the synagogue, erected in a plaza just adjacent to the Jewish Historical Institute and the former site of the Great Synagogue. The architect, Jan Strumiłło, also built walls around the structure on which he plastered photographs of prewar façades of the square where the synagogue stood, in order to give visitors "the feeling of strolling in the authentic square before the war" (figure 11).[10]

The scaled-down plywood synagogue could not truly enable visitors to experience the space as it once was. But its past existence could at least be intellectually grasped. Sited in the shadow of the Blue Skyscraper (as it is nicknamed) that now towers over the area, the synagogue's diminutive mock-up attuned visitors to the enormity of the transformation.

Five years later, on the occasion of the seventy-fifth anniversary of the beginning of the Warsaw Ghetto Uprising, on April 19, 2018, another commemoration took place. The Jewish Historical Institute and Open Republic (*Otwarta Rzeczpospolita*), an association fighting against antisemitism and xenophobia, organized a ceremonial virtual reconstruction of the Great Synagogue. Conceived by the Kraków-based artist Gabi von Seltmann, the performance consisted of the digital projection of an image of the Great Synagogue onto the Blue Skyscraper, accompanied by archival recordings

9 One of the reasons for the delay, Varsovians like to say, was that the rabbi of the Great Synagogue placed a curse on the site when the Nazis blew up the synagogue. Absence often comes with rumors, urban legends, and even ghost stories. Examples include Igor Ostachowicz's novel *The Night of the Living Jews* (2000), in which Jews-Zombies return to the Muranów district, and the ghost of Rivka haunting an old lady in Yael Bartana's *Nightmares* (chapter 5). For an incisive analysis of the use of ghost metaphors and phantom sites in popular culture and the post-Holocaust scholarly literature, see Sendyka (2016). Sendyka sees these stories as a sign that the traumatic events that took place at those sites have not been forgotten. See also the volume on the "spectral turn" edited by Dziuban (2020).

10 www.sztetl.org.pl/en/cms/news/3327,the-70th-anniversary-of-the-destruction-of-the-great-synagogue-on-tlomackie-st-/. More photographs of the replica and the square can be viewed on Strumiłło's webpage "The Great Absentee," www.janstrumillo.com/built/the-great-synagogue, and on the website of the design firm that executed the project: www.pracownia-tryktrak.pl/portfolio/wielka-nieobecna. A short film about the project is available at https://www.youtube.com/watch?v=JL_VoVvr0FQ&feature=youtu.be.

FIGURE 11. Art installation *The Great Absentee* (*Wielka nieobecna*), by Jan Strumiłło for the Jewish Historical Institute in Warsaw, April 2013. The unveiling of the plywood scale model of the Great Synagogue was part of the observances of the seventieth anniversary of the Warsaw Ghetto Uprising. The synagogue was burned down by the Nazis as the final act of crushing the uprising. The Blue Skyscraper is at the top-right corner, its glass reflecting adjacent buildings. (Photo by Jan Dybowski.)

of the synagogue's cantor and readings by the Polish-born Jewish American poet Irena Klepfisz (figure 12). Lasting approximately ten minutes, it was repeated over and over in a loop for two hours.[11] Hundreds of spectators watched with rapt attention. The performance was repeated in 2019 and 2020, and the events received coverage in national and international media.[12]

11 For a description of the event by the main organization sponsoring it, see http://www .otwarta.org/wielka-przywraca-pamiec (accessed June 13, 2018). See also the artist's description on her website, https://gabivonseltmann.com/portfolio/the-great-synagogue-restores-memory (accessed October 23, 2020). For a YouTube clip of the event, see https://www.youtube.com /watch?v=onlvd6hYz9U (accessed June 13, 2018).

12 See, for example, articles published in *Gazeta Wyborcza* and *Rzeczpospolita*: https:// warszawa.wyborcza.pl/warszawa/7,54420,26342452,wielka-synagoga-wirtualnie-odbudowana -przy-pl-bankowym-projekt.html and https://www.rp.pl/Warszawa/309269995-Wielka-Synagoga -odbudowana-cyfrowo.html. The magazine *Foreign Policy* commented on the event and the Polish art scene tackling antisemitism with the tagline "Poland Is Becoming a Global Capital of Chutzpah" (https://foreignpolicy.com/2020/02/07/poland-jewish-art-scene-anti-semitism).

FIGURE 12. During a memorial performance staged by artist Gabi von Seltmann on April 19, 2018, an archival photograph of the Great Synagogue is projected onto the Blue Skyscraper now occupying the space where the synagogue once stood. (Photo by Marta Kuśmierz. Copyright Gabi von Seltmann, https://gabivonseltmann.com/portfolio/the-great-synagogue-restores-memory/.)

In these different types of projects, signposting what is not there (objective absence) creates the knowledge necessary to perceive the historical-temporal dimension of absence: it allows the realization of what is *no longer*, and why it ceased to be. Evoking the absent synagogue tells the story of an entire world's destruction; signposting the vanished ghetto walls and footbridge tells the story not only of the Holocaust but also of the material and discursive erasure of the past after the war.

Ruins and Revelation

Another strategy of memory activists has been to transform sites of wreckage left after the Holocaust and render them visible as distinctively Jewish ruins. "Empty" objects like bricks and beams are animated; they begin to exert power and act as historical agents (Gell 1998).[13]

13 The winning design for the Polin Museum's *mezuzah*, for instance, was a brick from the rubble of the Warsaw Ghetto, dug out by father and son Andrzej and Maciej Bulanda (https://www.haaretz.com/jewish/.premium-warsaw-museum-selects-mezuzah-1.5224170).

FIGURE 13. Photographic installation on Próżna Street, Warsaw, the last remaining segment of the Warsaw Ghetto. The photographs of Polish Jews transform the ruined tenement house into a monument. (Photo by Geneviève Zubrzycki, September 25, 2012.)

Take, for example, Próżna Street, the only remaining block of Warsaw's Jewish Quarter, which had been left to fall into ruin (figure 13). The apartment buildings on the street were crumbling, to the degree that metal nets were suspended over the sidewalks to protect pedestrians from falling debris. In 2008, on the sixty-fifth anniversary of the Warsaw Ghetto Uprising, memory activists covered the boarded-up windows of the Próżna Street buildings with large portraits and candid photographs of Polish Jews. The images were collected through a campaign called "And I Still See Their Faces," initiated in 1994 by the Shalom Foundation and headed by the prominent Polish Jewish actress Gołda Tencer.[14] By the time the exhibition and installation were inaugurated fourteen years later, over nine thousand photographs of Polish Jews had been gathered.

The giant photographs on Próżna Street transformed the buildings from faceless, decrepit, even hostile spaces into "places": that is, into meaningful, if ephemeral, evocations of a Jewish home.[15] Próżna Street became the

14 For a description of the project, see "And I Still See Their Faces" on the Foundation Shalom website, http://shalom.org.pl/en/projects/i-ciagle-widze-ich-twarze/ (accessed April 26, 2016).

15 In social and cultural geography, *space* usually refers to a physical location, whereas *place* is a space imbued with meaning or a location created by human interactions and experiences. The distinction between a house and a home is a good example of space/place.

FIGURE 14. View of Próżna Street from Grzybowski Square. The renovated tenement house on the south side of the street was branded "Le Palais." (Photo by Anna Woźny, September 4, 2021.)

heart of "Jewish Warsaw," an important site of Polish attempts to remember and celebrate Jewish culture.[16] As with the *Great Absentee* and the *Footbridge of Memory*, the project's sensory impact derived from its striking material juxtapositions. Large sepia photographs show vivid people looking the viewer directly in the eye; the images cling to a dilapidated building with boarded-up windows and giant weeds burgeoning from its gutters, where construction fences bar anyone from coming too close. The assemblage served as a potent testament to the fates of long-forgotten Polish Jews and of a new movement pressing for their recuperation and revival. The depictions of faces and expressions also returned individual dignity to Jews whose lives and deaths were lost in the anonymity of the Holocaust's mass destruction and arithmetic reckonings like "the six million."[17]

Yet unlike the street-art piece *Here Was the Footbridge*, which led to a permanent commemorative installation on Chłodna Street, the Próżna

16 Próżna Street and Grzybowski Square is where Warsaw's Jewish festival, Singer's Days (named for Isaac Bashevis Singer), has been celebrated every August since 2004.

17 On making the "six million" figure an iconic number, see Stier (2016); on how Yad Vashem worked toward individualizing the six million Holocaust victims in its "recovery project" and the creation of a posthumous census, see Kidron (2016). On numerical commemoration, "a distinctive form of group remembrance in which the collective number of those who make up the group serves as the mnemonic key to the past," see Y. Zerubavel (2014).

Street project has so far not resulted in longer-term installations. The tenement houses on the south side of the street have been completely renovated in recent years, transformed from Jewish ruins into office and retail spaces and bourgeois *apartamenty*, callously marketed as Le Palais (figure 14). A plaque on the immaculate building at the south corner of Próżna and Grzybowski Square now explains that "this building—a witness to the history of Jewish Warsaw—was renovated and preserved for future generations thanks to the support from the Jewish Renaissance Foundation, Mr. Ronald S. Lauder and Warimpex. TRIUVA, as current owner, contributes to the revitalization process of Próżna St." The buildings on the north side have since been renovated, and the large portraits of Jews have been removed.

Another telling example of marking ruins as Jewish appears in a surviving section of the former ghetto wall, now enclosed in a courtyard (figure 15). Small plaques with a protective cover have been added as part of the Warsaw Ghetto wall memorial path.[18] While the wall itself is officially commemorated and now clearly marked as Jewish, the space where it stands is private. Experienced guides know how to find the site, but gaining entrance requires ringing random apartment doorbells until someone buzzes them in. Visiting the site feels slightly intrusive.

The situation of Kraków in Southern Poland differs sharply from that of Warsaw since the city was not destroyed during the war. Though its Jewish Quarter, Kazimierz, was left in a pitiful state until it underwent a slow process of gentrification in the 1990s (Murzyn 2006), its seven synagogues (two of them active), two Jewish cemeteries, and its Jewish street names remained.[19] The neighborhood now stages the largest festival of Jewish culture in Europe and boasts cafés, hotels, and music clubs where Jewish culture, from klezmer to cuisine, is performed and avidly consumed year-round.

Material, sensory, and spatial evidence of Jewishness in Kazimierz abounds, but there are also traces that remain invisible to the untrained

18 The United States Holocaust Memorial Museum (USHMM) affixed its own plaque to the wall in August 1989 to commemorate the site and acknowledge that "a casting and two original bricks of this wall erected by the Nazis to enclose the Warsaw Ghetto were taken to the United States Memorial Museum in Washington to give authentic power to its permanent exhibition." Konrad Matyjaszek (2016: 70–73) convincingly argues that it was the USHMM obtaining pieces of the wall that prompted "Polish state institutions to officially recognize, for the first time, the surviving ghetto wall sections as sites of commemoration" (71).

19 The gentrification of Kazimierz is related to the filming of *Schindler's List* in the early 1990s and the subsequent development of Holocaust tourism, as well as hipsters moving in because of low rent. See Kugelmass and Orla-Bukowska (2008), Murzyn (2006), and Lehrer (2013).

FIGURE 15. Segment of the Warsaw Ghetto wall, in the courtyard of apartment buildings accessible through 55 Sienna Street. Memorial plaques have been affixed to the wall, which is protected by tempered glass. A group of Israeli youth learn about the ghetto from their teacher as the group's security guard keeps watch. (Photo by Geneviève Zubrzycki, July 6, 2010.)

eye. The designers and memory activists Helena Czernek and Aleksander Prugar, founders of Mi Polin ("From Poland" in Hebrew), seek to provide precisely that training in discernment.[20] Cultural entrepreneurs in their mid-thirties, Czernek and Prugar create what they call "tangible Judaism"—modern Judaica design and commemorative objects—and

20 Interview with Helena Czernek and Aleksander Prugar, October 25, 2015. See also their website, Mi Polin, http://mipolin.pl.

host commemorative and pedagogical design workshops. At one such workshop, sponsored by Kraków's Jewish Community Centre during the Jewish Culture Festival in 2014, the designers distributed empty paper frames to participants, challenging them to roam through Kazimierz to find and mark Jewish traces with the frames to render them visible. One small group glued their paper frames on fragments of *matzevot* used in the wall separating Jakuba Street from the Old Jewish Cemetery.[21] Framing the tombstones brings attention not only to them but also to their fate, squeezed between fieldstones and bricks (figure 16).[22]

The exercise's intent was to "train the eye"—to change the way participants looked at their surroundings and to teach them to look for, to see, and then to render visible Jewish traces. By cultivating a different way of seeing, participants would be equipped to discover, uncover, and mark remnants of Jewish life all over Poland and to begin to learn and tell the story of a different Poland.

The participants were mostly young adults, some with children in tow, from different regions of Poland. Interested in discovering traces of Jewish presence in their own towns, they asked what they should look for, and where. Many saw discovering those Jewish traces as an important step in recovering a multicultural Poland. As we walked through Kazimierz, one young woman told me, "This [Jewish] culture was taken away from us. First by the Nazis, then by the communists who transformed old synagogues into storage facilities or neglected to care for cemeteries. Finding some of it again today is a bit like finding pieces of ourselves."

In another Mi Polin project, Czernek and Prugar look for holes and scars left by the removal of *mezuzot* from doorframes of former Jewish homes throughout Poland and cast new *mezuzot* from the traces left by the original ones. A *mezuzah* (plural *mezuzot*) is a piece of parchment inscribed with a Hebrew prayer from the Torah, contained in a decorative case. It is typically affixed to the doorframe of a Jewish home, and the family members and guests touch it before entering the home. Jews seeking to avoid persecution during the Second World War often removed and hid their *mezuzot*. The removals left indentations, etchings of absence, on the doorframes from which the *mezuzot* were torn (figure 17). Czernek and Prugar explain the project on their website:

---

21 *Matzevah* (s.), *matzevot* (pl.), Hebrew for "tombstones."

22 For a photographic essay on the postwar fate of *matzevot* in Poland, see Łukasz Baksik's photographic essay *Matzevot for Everyday Use* (2013). Jewish tombstones were routinely taken by local residents after the Second World War to be used for a variety of purposes, from retaining walls to pavement, or grinding stones.

FIGURE 16. Paper frames on fragments of Jewish tombstones used in the wall separating Jakuba Street from the Old Jewish Cemetery in Kazimierz, Kraków. (Photo by Geneviève Zubrzycki, July 5, 2014.)

FIGURE 17. Trace of removed *mezuzah*, Sokołowska Street, Siedlce. (Photo by Aleksander Prugar, reprinted with permission of A. Prugar and H. Czernek.)

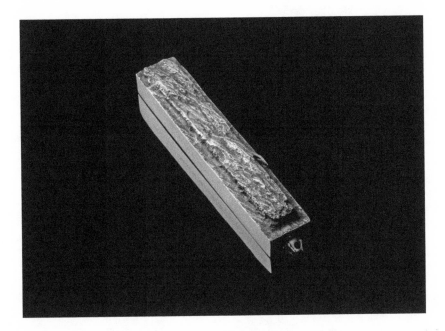

FIGURE 18. "Siedlce" *mezuzah*, cast in bronze by Mi Polin designers, from the traces left in the doorframe of a house on Sokołowska Street in Siedlce. (Photo by Aleksander Prugar, reprinted with permission of A. Prugar and H. Czernek.)

> After World War II almost all Jews vanished from Poland. Only void remained. The signs of former inhabitants' presence . . . are marks of the mezuzot on the doorframes of the houses, now inhabited by new residents. These marks, holes, are empty. "The mezuzot from this house" are new mezuzot, which are casts of these traces. Cast in metal, [they] commemorate Jewish life that was going on there years ago; [they] fill the emptiness. . . . The mezuzot tell stories about traces from difference places in Poland . . . . The mezuzot from the past get a new life and can be real mezuzot again. (original in English)

From void and emptiness, the artists create new objects that commemorate a past presence, but without erasing the gashes of loss and absence (figure 18). In the booklet that accompanies each new *mezuzah*, the artists write: "When you affix the mezuzah to your doorframe, you fill the emptiness and give it a second life. Touching the mezuzah activates a link between past and present."[23]

---

23 Thanks to Helena Czernek and Aleksander Prugar for providing me with copies of these unpublished materials.

Czernek and Prugar work with local activists and historians to learn about the buildings and neighborhoods, even attempting to track down the families of former inhabitants of dwellings where they find traces of removed *mezuzot*. Sold on the Mi Polin website and at the Polin Museum, each piece is unique and tells the story not only of a *mezuzah* that once upon a time graced the doorway of a house, but also the story of its removal and forgetting. As the trace of the vanished piece is cast in bronze, absence is made powerfully, durably present, in a material that will outlast the residents of a home or political regimes. And yet, casting absence into presence powerfully commemorates an original act of erasure. It is a presence that is also pain.

Filling empty space on blank building walls has been the strategy of multiple street artists who have painted over one hundred murals related to Polish Jews, Poland's Jewish past, or Judaism throughout the country in recent years (figure 19). Their creations tell different stories, and in 2021 the Polin Museum of the History of Polish Jews wanted to bring those to the four corners of Poland with an outdoor traveling exhibition reproduc-

FIGURE 19. Mural by Broken Fingaz, an Israeli collective of street artists. The mural was created during Kraków's Jewish Culture Festival in 2014, in memory of the Bosak family who lived in Kazimierz from the seventeenth century until 1941. The mural is inspired by the style of Maurycy (Ephraim Moses) Lilien, a Zionist art nouveau illustrator and printmaker who graduated from Kraków's Academy of Fine Arts. The large inscription at the top of the mural is a Yiddish translation of the artist collective's name. (Photo by Geneviève Zubrzycki, July 5, 2014.)

ing them on a smaller scale, "They Fill No Space: Reviving the Memory of Polish Jews in Public Space."[24]

The literal translation of the exhibition's Polish title (*Pełno ich nigdzie*) would be "Plenty of Them Nowhere," capturing the sense of void discussed here.[25]

Public Practices and Rituals

Activities commemorating the Warsaw Ghetto Uprising in the last several years offer an excellent illustration of the power of juxtaposing historical and personal narratives, symbols, and embodied practices. For years Marek Edelman, the sole surviving leader of the uprising, used to commemorate its beginning, on April 19, 1943, with a bouquet of yellow daffodils.[26] After his passing, in 2009, the tradition was taken up by several of his close friends and members of the Jewish community. In 2013, on the seventieth anniversary of the uprising, the designer Helena Czernek created for the Polin Museum a yellow paper daffodil to be worn as a pin. Some forty thousand were made and distributed by volunteers. The memento was effective because it linked the commemoration of the uprising with the memory of Edelman, a much-respected and beloved figure. It was also semiotically complex: once pinned onto clothing, the yellow paper flower opened up and looked much like a star.[27] Tens of thousands of Poles

24 For a film describing the exhibition, see https://polin.pl/en/wystawa-pelno-ich-nigdzie. The exhibition in individual cities was accompanied by educational and cultural events developed in collaboration with local partners: the Grodzka Gate NN Theatre Centre in Lublin, the Museum of the City of Kraków and the Jewish Community Centre in Kraków, and the Marek Edelman Dialogue Center in Łódź.

25 The Polish title of the exhibition is inspired by the last verse of "August 5, 1942," a poem by Jerzy Ficowski dedicated to the memory of Janusz Korczak. Korczak (Henryk Goldszmit) was a beloved Polish Jewish educator, children's book author, and pedagogue. He founded an orphanage in 1912 and directed it until August 1942, when he, the children, and some two hundred other educators were taken from the Warsaw Ghetto and sent to their death in Treblinka.

26 Press coverage of the tradition often mentions its origin: Edelman received a bouquet of yellow flowers every year from an anonymous sender, which he then brought to the Monument to the Ghetto Heroes.

27 Czernek told me she had not intended the daffodil to turn into a yellow star; the unfurling was a material flaw caused by poor glue and problematic execution by the volunteers who had assembled the paper flowers. It is, however, precisely that additional, accidental signification that made the small paper memento such an impactful one. This is an excellent example of the effect of "bundling" first identified by the anthropologist Webb Keane (2006). Keane argues that an object's very materiality—its weight and color, the materials of its composition, its relative malleability, permeability, mobility, and so on—endows it with a life of

FIGURE 20. Young couple strolling on Nowy Świat Avenue in Warsaw, proudly wearing the paper daffodil/yellow star on April 19, 2015. The closed version of the paper memento on the man's jacket more faithfully resembles the intended daffodil; the unfurling of the woman's paper flower has transformed it into a star. (Photo: Alicja Szulc / Polin Museum of the History of Polish Jews.)

affixed the flower/star to their lapels, others to their sleeves, replicating the branding of Jews with the yellow star during the Nazi occupation (figure 20). Commemorative marches and bike rides were organized, retracing the now-vanished traces of Jewish Warsaw. Some Poles wore the paper flowers for several weeks after the commemorative events.

The commemorative project was such a success that it has become an annual tradition: on April 19, 2016, over one thousand volunteers distributed sixty thousand paper daffodils in Warsaw alone. Eight hundred schools in small towns and villages across Poland made and distributed additional daffodils.[28] In 2019 over 2,500 volunteers distributed about two hundred thousand paper daffodils.[29] The daily newspaper *Gazeta Wyborcza* has since become the official patron of the event and includes six daffodils in its April 19 issue so that readers can share them with their loved ones.

its own and potentially allows it to acquire significations different from those its creators and social actors initially ascribe to it.

28 www.polin.pl/en/news/2016/04/22/4th-edition-of-the-daffodils-campaign (accessed July 13, 2016).

29 https://warszawa.wyborcza.pl/warszawa/7,54420,24682689,miasto-cale-w-zonkilach -warszawiacy-upamietniaja-bohaterow.html.

While the daffodil has come to symbolize the memory of the uprising, this paper representation of the flower also evokes the Holocaust. Wearing the daffodil/star has therefore become not only a commemorative act but also a posthumous act of solidarity and resistance to the distinction made by Nazis (and by many Poles) between Jews and non-Jews.

Even though events commemorating the Holocaust in Poland are not entirely new, their scope and frequency have dramatically grown since 1989, to the extent that they are now commonplace. In Kraków, for example, the annual March of Memory commemorates the liquidation of the Jewish ghetto. Participants walk from the Podgórze neighborhood, where local Jews were forcefully relocated in a ghetto, to the memorial on the site of the former Płaszów concentration camp.[30] For participants, this embodied practice attempts to reenact the forced exile of Jews. These rituals allow Polish Jewish history to be simultaneously internalized by individuals and externalized onto the material cityscape. The material and performative remaking of public space in turn motivates political discourses about citizenship and what constitutes Polishness. Although the march is conducted in silence, speeches are made at the departure and arrival points. In the multiple marches I have participated in since the early 2000s, the theme of citizenship has always been prominent, with the emphasis laid squarely on the fact that Jews were Polish citizens. The effect is to not only materially and performatively but also discursively reject a vision of ethnic Polishness narrowly predicated on its association with Catholicism.

The multifaceted initiatives undertaken by individual artists, NGOs, and local official institutions have, in the past two decades, created a climate where Jews, Jewish culture, and Judaism can finally occupy public space once again. Since the mid-2000s, a giant outdoor *hanukiah* is lit in Warsaw on the first night of Hanukah by Chabad rabbis, accompanied by city and state officials.[31] In 2021 Chabad Lubawicz Kraków followed suite, installing a large *hanukiah* in a small square of the Old Town. The chief rabbi of Poland, Michael Schudrich, also typically lights a *hanukiah* at the presidential palace. Those events are photographed and widely covered by news media. Such practices could be regarded as cynical electoral

30 Unveiled in 1964, the monument, designed by Witold Cęckiewicz, is dedicated to the "Victims of Fascism in Kraków." "Victims of Fascism" was the preferred expression of the socialist state, which presented the history of the Second World War as a conflict between socialism and fascist capitalism. That ideological framework de facto erased the specificity of the Jews' experience of the war and the fate of the millions murdered. The expression is no longer used in textbooks, museums, or on monuments dedicated after 1989.

31 A *hanukiah* is a nine-branched candelabrum used during Hanukah.

tactics by non-Jewish politicians, but the "Jewish vote" is of little significance given the small number of Jews in Poland. There can be little doubt,
however, that the Polish state's support of Jewish-related initiatives is addressed as much to international audiences as to national constituencies.
Jewishness is now seen as key to polishing Poland's image in international
venues, though the Law and Justice Party of late has displayed less interest
in this effort than its predecessors.

In Kraków the Jewish Community Centre (JCC) organizes every spring
since 2011 an event called 7@Nite. Inspired by the popular Night at the
Museum events, when museums open their doors free of charge until
early morning, Kazimierz's seven synagogues are open to Krakovians
eager to learn about the past and present religious landscape of Polish
Jews. Approximately eight thousand people flooded the narrow streets
of Kazimierz, surprising the organizers who had expected only about a
thousand.[32] Because of its popularity, 7@Nite was turned into an annual
event, which continues to attract similar numbers.[33] Each synagogue
hosts lectures or workshops and gives tours during which visitors/guests
can meet local Jewish residents, talk to rabbis, and become familiar with
spaces they otherwise rarely or never have occasion to enter.

In another example of Jewish traditions carried into public space, in
2012 Warsaw's JCC and the Polish chapter of the Joint Distribution Committee (JDC), an international humanitarian organization dedicated to
strengthening Jewish communities, invited architectural firms to design
contemporary interpretations of *sukkot* (sing. *sukkah*), temporary structures built on the occasion of the Jewish holiday of Sukkot.[34] Half a dozen
were built and exhibited on Grzybowski Square. As with the Kraków JCC's
7@Nite, the local population was invited to attend, meet members of the
Jewish community, and learn about the tradition. I asked random passersby what the installations represented. Many did not know or care, but
some were curious enough to enter the structures and read the informational panels about them. One man in his fifties correctly explained that
they were contemporary interpretations of *sukkot*, adding that he was

32 https://krakow.wyborcza.pl/krakow/1,44425,11684770,Rock__design_i_projekcje___7
_nite__Synagogi_Noca.html.

33 Visitor numbers have remained high, at about nine thousand, since 2016, with a peak
in 2017 when an estimated twelve thousand people visited Kazimierz's seven synagogues on
a single evening (personal communication, Sebastian Rudol, deputy director, Jewish Community Centre, Kraków, November 11, 2020).

34 The event was held to mark the opening of the Warsaw JCC. For a description and photographs, go to http://www.jccwarszawa.pl/news/81/n/23/?LangId=1. For a video of the event,
go to https://vimeo.com/55538006.

very happy that the tradition was being revived. "You know," he told me, his eyebrows raised, "Poland is more than the traditional Nativity scenes of Kraków."

Conclusion: Expanding the National Sensorium

Jewish markers, whether religious or secular, create visual and material diversity in the cityscape, monumentally, if modestly, diluting Catholicism's sensory dominance. Aneta, a longtime Kraków JCC volunteer who is expressly anticlerical and declares herself an atheist, expanded on this point during our conversation at a Shabbat dinner: "I think it's great to see all of that [Jewish activity]. I'm not religious, but I think it's good to see that there's something else than what we already know, and frankly speaking, we're sick of . . . processions, pilgrimages here and there, crosses everywhere."

Aneta's comment highlights the way the growing material presence of Jewish secular and religious markers, structures, and symbols de facto weakens the hegemony of Catholicism, much as the Catholic cross in the public sphere weakened the socialist state's claim of monolithic unity (Kubik 1994; Rogozińska 2002). But while the cross in Poland has come to signify a specific vision of the nation and the polity that has been increasingly contested in the past thirty years (Zubrzycki 2006, 2010, 2020), the menorah and the Star of David have acquired no such baggage for progressive Poles who support a secular vision of the nation. For progressives, markers of Jewish identity, be they religious or secular, point unswervingly forward; they serve to visibly create diversity and dilute Catholic dominance in castings of national identity. Resurrecting Jewish ruins, materially installing and animating Jewish absence to bring it to life and make it visible, disrupts claims of Catholic universality.

This is important. It is important because historical narratives and national myths are mostly learned and experienced through visual depictions and material forms like the built environment, landscapes, and embodied practices and performances, an assemblage I have elsewhere called the *national sensorium* (Zubrzycki 2011). Only through the sensorium does the abstract notion of the nation become concrete, perceptible, and real, such that subjects come to feel the nation, and feel *for* it. The national sensorium's multiple and diverse sites of material expression facilitate the convergence, exchange, and intersection of sensory perceptions, often weaving a dense tapestry of "national feelings." The creation and maintenance of a national sensorium is thus a crucial task undertaken equally by national and nationalist actors, as well as by those who seek to alter or subvert a given national identity.

Polish national identity, we have seen in the book's introduction, is articulated around myths of martyrdom and Poland's intrinsic Catholicity. The material creation of Jewish absence and the resurrection of Jewish culture in the public sphere challenge that vision of Poland. Mnemonic initiatives undertaken by individual artists, NGOs, and official, state-sanctioned institutions not only make Jewish absence and renewed presence visible in today's Poland. They also articulate a critique of, and corrective to, half a century's silence on the Shoah. Even more, they expand the Polish national sensorium and stretch the symbolic boundaries of Polishness.

It is not yet clear how to evaluate the "success" of attempts to reattach the Jewish limb to the Polish national body. One way to begin is to give close attention to the national sensorium. We can speak of a revived Jewish culture in Poland to the degree that Jewish histories are being discovered, named, and animated, and the proper attunement to their material traces is being cultivated—not only among memory activists and sensitive consumers but also as a matter of public pedagogy and city planning. By this measure, the so-called Jewish revival is well underway, though its effects in reforming Poland's national identity, or the manifold ways it is subjectively internalized, are far from clear.

CHAPTER 3

"The Way We Were"

In the fall of 2009, Rafał Betlejewski, an activist and performer then in his early forties, painted the words "I miss you, Jew" (*Tęsknię za Tobą, Żydzie*) under the Powiśle Bridge in Warsaw. The graffito was the first individual gesture in what became a multipronged collective memorial project, one that aimed to recover the "true" Poland that was lost with the euphemistic "disappearance" of Jews from the national landscape. As Betlejewski writes on the project's website: "I miss you, Jew. I miss you in Poland, in all these little villages and big cities. You left a vacuum there, both in space and my heart. I just wanted you to know that." He signed the declaration "Pole" (*Polak*) (see figure 21 on p. 60).[1] A banner at the bottom of the webpage asserts that the word *loss* (*utrata*) should be a synonym for Holocaust (*zagłada*) in Polish.[2] The Holocaust is a loss for Poland, for the Polish nation, the site claims; hence the signing of the graffito with a national instead of a personal signature.

In the previous chapter, I discussed initiatives that materially highlight Jewish absence in such a way that it becomes possible to experience that absence as a void. In this chapter, I examine the experience of loss through a study of Betlejewski's project and his description of it, as well as through an analysis of statements by participants in the "I Miss You, Jew" project. The website provided a venue where Poles could post remembrances—their own, their parents', or their grandparents'—of specific Jewish individuals or vanished communities, of places and encounters. I collected and analyzed 349 testimonies posted on the "I Miss You, Jew" website.[3]

1 Betlejewski intended the website to be accessible to an international audience, hence his use of English on a few prominent pages. All translations from Polish in this chapter are my own.

2 The term *extermination* (*zagłada*) is commonly used to describe the genocide of Jews during the Second World War. *Holokaust* is now also common, but *Szoa* less so and primarily used in academic contexts.

3 The testimonies appeared on the website http://www.tesknie.com, which is no longer operational. I downloaded and archived every entry up to December 15, 2012, when the testimonial part of the project was for all purposes over. Testimonies I cite in the chapter are

FIGURE 21. Rafał Betlejewski posing in an iconic Polish landscape, next to an empty chair representing the missing and missed Jew. The image was posted on the main page of the "I Miss You, Jew" memorial website. (Photo and design by Rafał Betlejewski, with permission of author.)

The analysis of these testimonies offers a glimpse of how Poles who are invested in the new mnemonic awakening speak of Jews—how they explain Jewish absence from Poland, how they experience that absence, what it means to them, and what that says about them and their vision of Poland. Their discourse shows how the experience of loss may be cast in the genre of nostalgia, even for a time that many of these participants cannot recall because they were not yet born. As I show below, many testimonies of longing for a Jewish-Polish past skew into familiar lanes of stereotype and caricature. There is no shortage of self-serving evasion and elision in relation to the violence of the twentieth-century past, even for those professing heartfelt admiration for all things Jewish. Yet even these deeply problematic recollections and testimonies disrupt the *Polak-katolik* vision and the political Right's mostly pernicious use of it to close the fist. However romanticized the Jewish past they recall and suffer the "loss" of, these imaginative renderings nevertheless open space for new ways of thinking about history in relation to the Polish future, and they derail the Catholic Right juggernaut, if only for a while and in part. Moreover, some of these discourses engage in genuine historical reckoning with Polish antisemitism. The reports heave with sorrow, guilt, and shame about what the authors knew, didn't know, or should have known. They also hold out hope, and for that, especially, they are worth our attention.

---

identified by their original page identification number on the website (for example, "Testimony 674" instead of the inactive url www.tesknie.com/index.phd?id=674). Descriptions of the website and of the specific methods employed to analyze the testimonies appear in appendix A.

Nostalgia for Those Never Known

Knowing "what once was" is a necessary (though not sufficient) condition for experiencing absence as loss, as phenomenological absence. Memory activists, cultural entrepreneurs, and educational organizations work to uncover Jewish stories—those of individuals, families, and places—so that participants or students can register, and feel, Jewish absence.

Rafał Betlejewski explained in interviews that the project "I Miss You, Jew" originated with the shock caused by the publication of Jan Gross's *Neighbors*. Jedwabne, explained Betlejewski, is "the central point of 'I miss you . . . .' [With Jedwabne], I understood with horror . . . that my nonmemory of the Jews was active, fostered forgetting." He described how Jedwabne threw him into a double narrative shock: first, with the realization of how little he knew about those who had lived and were then murdered in Poland, sometimes by Poles; and second, with the conclusion that this lack of knowledge had not been inadvertent but had rather been "shaped by the Polish school, the romantic-messianic tradition, and the Polish Church" (Testimony 674). The very institutions credited with keeping Polish identity alive through the ages were the cause of his ignorance of national history; they were responsible for stunting and deforming an "authentic" Polish identity. The purpose of the project, then, was to cure himself (and others) of "antisemitic reflexes, from [their] forgetting about Jews," by actively "remembering."

Missing the Missing Jew

The confession that became the title of the project is significant. The original Polish verb used in the project's name, *tęsknić*, and its related noun, *tęsknota*, were translated by Betlejewski as "missing." But as Eva Hoffman (1989) noted in the first paragraphs of her celebrated *Lost in Translation*, "tęsknota [is] a word that adds to nostalgia the tonalities of sadness and longing." The verb *tęsknić* can be used in personal form, with a direct subject ("*Ja tęsknię za*" / "*I miss x*," or "*I long for y*"), or in a subjectless, impersonal one (*tęskno mi za*) that has no proper equivalent in English ("x is missed by me"). The difference between the two forms is subtle; the impersonal is indirect, diffuse, and perhaps expresses a more existential condition. Betlejewski chooses the first-person singular (*tęsknię*). Though the project involved groups and communities, and the national community was very much at the center of the project, the statement is intended as personal, an address of one individual ("I") to another ("you, Jew") instead of to a faceless, collective mass ("Jews"). As such, it has the effect of rendering intimate and proximate what is unknown and now gone, and of personalizing the commemorative act.

Although Betlejewski's work includes no reference to Martin Buber's celebrated short text *I and Thou*, and any direct influence is unlikely, the text resonates with the words of the opening page of Buber: "The one primary word is the combination I-Thou. The other primary word is the combination I-It. . . . Primary words do not signify things, but they intimate relations. Primary words do not describe something that might exist independently of them, but being spoken they bring about existence" (1937: 3). *I-You*, in Betlejewski's scene, tries to establish an inseparable union. The phrase does not seek to describe but rather to instate, to "bring about existence." In J. L. Austin's nomenclature, it is a performative (1975).

Between the author and the Jew stands the message: I miss you, I care, I feel a loss, a painful void left by your absence. Of course, in a practical sense, the message is not really addressed to any particular Jew but rather to those who read the graffito—Poles, for the most part. And the message is less than straightforward in other respects as well, not least because the Polish word *Żyd* (Jew) is complex and nefarious. Hidden in the three letters are layers of negative connotations, long-standing flotsam of fear, hatred, and disgust. *Żyd*, or its diminutive form *Żydek* (plural *Żydki*), is usually an insult or a hurtful accusation ("*Ty, Żydzie!*"—"You, Jew!").[4] Far too many use it unhesitatingly as a slur, but others shy away from using the word in public, repeating it only sotto voce to hint at, or reveal, a secret: "Is he *Jewish?*" "A *Jew*, mind you."

Given those specific connotations of the word, Betlejewski's graffiti were ambiguous and provocative on several levels. First, the form clashed with the content. The graffiti were reminiscent of antisemitic graffiti scrawled anonymously on walls at night. Second, the use of the word Jew, considered a slur, overshadows the rest of the text and renders the

---

4 Despite its pejorative connotations, the noun *Żyd* remains the official descriptive term for *Jew* in Polish. This is not the case in Russian, where *Zhid* is considered antisemitic and *Yevrai* (Hebrew) is used instead. The diminutive Polish forms *Żydek* and *Żydki* imply contempt and condescension, in a manner analogous to the English "Jew-boy." *Żydocha/Żydochy* (masculine singular and plural) and *Żydówa/Żydówy* (feminine singular and plural) are augmentative forms that evoke disgust and hatred toward a threatening other. Another offensive formulation is *Żydy*, which improperly uses the plural form reserved for feminine nouns or animals. (I'm grateful to Dariusz Pasieka and Ewa Pasek for their help in unpacking the grammatical underpinnings of these antisemitic formulations.) In addition to these nouns, several related verbs have antisemitic roots, such as *żydzić* (to stint), *ożydzić/pożydzić* (to bamboozle, to cheat), and *wyżydzić* (to bargain aggressively).

message ambiguous. Can a Jew, a common object of derision, contempt, and hatred, truly be missed? Why would that be so? What is the graffito saying? What does it mean? Read only quickly, or misread, the graffito may easily be interpreted as an antisemitic gesture.

In fact, Betlejewski was quickly arrested for hate speech, which suggests the power of the expletive "Jew" in Polish, and, at least hypothetically, demonstrates increased sensitivity to antisemitism.[5] But his experience at the police station, which he recounted in a television interview, is telling. He noted that the police officers who held him reviled him for being a petty criminal, a "graffiti vandal," rather than for being a presumed antisemite. When he explained the project and said that he actually longed for Jews, he was told, "You stupid philosemite! If you love Jews so much, why don't you get the fuck out of here and move to Israel!"[6]

Betlejewski's experience with the police prompted him to expand the project and bring it to the center of the public arena. One of his goals was to reclaim the word Jew from antisemites who had hijacked it.[7] Betlejewski repeated the word out loud in performances on television and invited others to do the same, shouting collectively, "I miss you, Jew!" The goal of these public "happenings" was to restore the word's dignity, purging it of its negative connotations. For many Jews and non-Jews alike, however, both the graffiti and the performances were too much. The word Jew was covered with white paint on some of Betlejewski's graffiti to erase it. The University of Warsaw balked at the project, requesting that the word Jew be omitted from a happening planned on its grounds. Betlejewski refused. The project's objective, he argued, was precisely to reclaim the word from antisemites. In fact, the shouting of the slogan, "I miss you, Jew!" became the crux of the event, drowning out the visual dimension of Betlejewski's work. The university's objections to the happening generated a meaningful discussion in the public sphere about the word Jew and the need to free it from its negative associations.[8]

---

5 This incident recalls Peter Fuss's problems with authorities for his provocative billboard and controversial exhibit, discussed in the introduction.

6 Personal interview with Rafał Betlejewski, audio recording, Warsaw, March 24, 2011.

7 Unlike *négritude* in the francophone world, which was primarily a literary movement initiated by Black intellectuals in the 1930s, or the "Black is beautiful" cultural movement in the United States, here it is non-Jews who want to destigmatize the term by taking it back from those who stigmatize it. Some might see in this use of the term by non-Jewish Poles a form of symbolic violence (Janicka and Żukowski 2021); yet symbolic violence, as defined by sociologist Pierre Bourdieu (1991), is a different process, whereby stigmatized groups themselves internalize the dominant group's values and prejudices against them.

8 See Karpieszuk, "Na UW krzyczeli: Żydzi-tęsknimy!," *Gazeta Wyborcza*, March 29, 2010 (https://warszawa.wyborcza.pl/warszawa/1,95190,7710658,Na_UW_krzyczeli__Zydzi___tesknimy_.html); Kowalska, "Odczarujmy słowo 'Żyd'," *Gazeta Wyborcza*, March 23, 2010 (https://

FIGURE 22. "I Miss You, Jew" graffiti-mural in Łódź, painted with participation of locals in June 2016. A late addition to the project, it is one of the very few murals that still remain. (Photo by Geneviève Zubrzycki, April 6, 2018.)

It's Not (About) You

In the wake of the controversy, public interest in the project spread throughout Poland. Betlejewski, joined by local residents and youth groups, painted "I miss you, Jew" graffiti and murals across the country (figure 22).

In addition, groups of ordinary citizens turned memory activists engaged in the project by posing in spaces formerly occupied by Jewish individuals, families, or communities in order to call attention to Jewish lives: in Poznań's former synagogue, which was repurposed into a swimming pool by the Nazis in 1940 (figure 23); by a store; in a train station; in the forest.

They posed next to an empty chair, signifying the missing—and missed— Jew. The chair, covered by a sheepskin and a kippah, highlights absence (figures 23, 24). The absence, moreover, is not a simple, objective absence. Rather, it is, according to Betlejewski, a "vacuum." The absent Jew is at once

warszawa.wyborcza.pl/warszawa/1,95190,7690303,Odczarujmy_slowo__Zyd_.html); and the radio reports on TokFM, "'Tęsknię za Tobą, Żydzie!' nie na UW? 'Boją się zabierać głos'," (https://www.tokfm.pl/Tokfm/1,103085,7687793,_Tesk-nie_za_Toba__Zydzie___nie_na_UW___Boja_sie _zabierac.html).

FIGURE 23. "I Miss You, Jew" event in the New Synagogue in Poznań, February 2010. Built in 1907, the synagogue was repurposed as a swimming pool for Wehrmacht soldiers by the Nazis in 1940. It was returned to the Union of Jewish communities in Poland (*Związek Gmin Wyznaniowych Żydowskich w Rzeczypospolitej Polskiej*) in 2002. The swimming pool closed in 2011, and the building was temporarily converted into a gallery space. A proposal to establish a Center for Judaism and Dialogue there was abandoned. (Photo by Rafał Betlejewski, reprinted with permission.)

the central subject of the photograph and the missing element that makes the picture incomplete. The absence of Jews from the Polish landscape, the photographs imply, throws Polishness into a state of incompleteness.

Consider, for example, the powerfully evocative photograph of the young woman posing as a Polish *góralka* (highlander) next to the Jew's empty chair (figure 24). Dressed in her folk costume against an archetypically Polish background, she is not and cannot be herself without the Jew. Artist Anna Kolek, who collaborated with Betlejewski on the project, created the scene by juxtaposing several symbols that "compress Polishness," she explained to me (December 18, 2020). Kolek chose to set the photograph in Istebna, a village in the Silesian Beskids Mountains, and asked her friend to pose as a highlander because for her, "highlanders [*górale*] are the group most characteristic of Polishness: . . . They are very attached to tradition, and that tradition is very strongly based on Catholicism." The wooden church, the tall cross, and the forest, all emblematic of Poland, provide the perfect background to the odd couple. Her focus, as an artist, was not on creating an authentic portrayal but to distill Polishness

FIGURE 24. Young woman posing as a Polish highlander (*góralka*), next to an empty chair and kippah symbolizing the missing Jew, circa 2010. The wooden church of the Exaltation of the Holy Cross (*kościół pw. Podwyższenia Krzyża Świętego*), in the Silesian Beskids Mountains, frames the visual discourse. (Photo by Anna Kolek, ca. 2010, reprinted with permission.)

and Jewishness so that they could be juxtaposed—the *góralka*, representing Polish culture, healthy and standing tall; and the empty chair with the kippah representing the annihilation of Jewish culture in Poland.[9]

The mnemonic project "I Miss You, Jew" is thus built around the attempt to recover a memory of the past that has been erased and to instill a feeling of loss in participants and viewers. The project brims with nostalgia for a time when Poland was different. As Betlejewski told the editorialist Piotr Pacewicz in a television interview, "For me, as a Pole, [the project] is the exploration of the unconscious at the source of weaknesses, phobias, complexes but also of wonderful dreams of the past" (Testimony

9 Kolek's curiosity was initially sparked upon learning that her maternal grandfather was Jewish. As she discovered the history and culture of Polish Jews, she became "fascinated," she told me. She volunteered at the Jewish Culture Festival in Kraków and participated in several other Jewish cultural initiatives. Her master's thesis was about blood libel in Poland. Her personal journey is in many ways typical of the experience of "new" Jews, as I discuss in chapter 6, although in her case it did not lead her to adopt a new (Jewish) identity.

674).[10] Jewish absence (objective and historical-temporal) feeds the nightmares of the Right and their negative stereotypes of Jews as well as the dreams of the Left. The absent Jewish body is an empty container, filled with Polish aversions, fears, desires, and aspirations.

Perhaps the empty chair can be interpreted as conveying a welcome. The sheepskin warms the seat for one who will soon arrive and rest; the kippah is ready for the awaited guest to don. In this reading, the chair communicates not only loss but also hopeful expectation. The object, like the artist's original statement, "I miss you, Jew," is a performative that aims to "bring about existence," in Buber's phrase. Perhaps.

In photographs taken early in the project, the empty wooden chair was not covered, and it disappeared against the background. Betlejewski added the sheepskin for visual effect, to focus the viewer's gaze on the chair and the absent Jew (interview with Rafał Betlejewski, Warsaw, March 24, 2011). His aesthetically driven decision had a significant effect on how the Jew, as a symbol, is constructed and perceived in the images. The missing Jew in those photographs is not the Bundist, the Zionist, the assimilated intellectual, or the feminist activist, but the Orthodox shtetl Jew. Thus the Jew becomes a flat, one-dimensional figure—perhaps even a fetish, since it is invoked to enable Poles to become a "truer, better version of themselves," closer to the romanticized multiethnic and multidenominational Second Republic that existed before the Second World War, fulfilling contemporary Poles' "wonderful dreams of the past" (Testimony 674). These are pervasive tropes of the Jewish turn, as I will show.

"In Search of Lost Time": The Romance of the Past

The companion website to "I Miss You, Jew" documented collective graffiti actions, as well as provided a space where private individuals could share remembrances, thoughts, and feelings about Jews. A total of 301 individuals posted 349 testimonies. Slightly more women than men posted memories or testimonies.[11] While it is impossible to determine participants' level of education unless they referred to it in their testimonies, the language

10 That nostalgia can be observed in Yael Bartana's trilogy *And Europe Will Be Stunned* (2011) and especially in the first film of that project, *Nightmares* (2007), which I analyze in chapter 5.

11 Forty-nine percent of testimonies were authored by women and 36 percent by men. Two percent were coauthored by women and men. Because Polish is a gendered language, I was able to identify the author's gender for most of the anonymous posts. This proved impossible for 13 percent of testimonies.

Type of memory

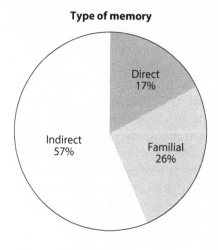

GRAPH 1. Type of Memory.

used in most entries (vocabulary, spelling, grammar, and syntax) suggests that the overwhelming majority were educated individuals, and the content also suggests that most had significant cultural capital. Many recounted how they discovered Poland's Jewish past through reading or conducting their own investigations into local history. Participants obviously needed access to a computer and the internet to post a testimony online. Most importantly, they needed to be aware of Betlejewski's project, which would have required that they follow news coverage of it or be involved in cultural activities where it might be discussed. In short, the participants are not representative of Poland's population as a whole.[12] At the same time, they are not the cosmopolitan elite that critics might suspect them of being: only 14 percent of authors/participants were from metropolitan areas (e.g., Warsaw, Kraków, Gdańsk), while 36 percent were from smaller towns and villages with populations of less than two hundred thousand.[13]

Participants posted three general types of testimonies (graph 1). Fewer than one in five (17 percent) related a direct remembrance, that is, a memory of people they knew or of events and places that they themselves experienced. One in four (26 percent) testimonies drew on familial recollections, most often accounts passed on to the author by parents and grandparents. Slightly over half (57 percent) were "indirect" remembrances: testimonies of events, people, or places learned about through history books, literature, or encounters with material traces of Jewish life. Testimonies about antisemitism and those sharing general impressions about Jews and their absence in contemporary Poland are included in this category.

---

12 In the 2011 census, nearly 20 percent of Poles had only a primary school education; 26 percent had attended middle school or had basic vocational training; 29 percent had secondary education and 17 percent postsecondary education (Narodowy Spis Powszechny, 2011, https://stat.gov.pl/spisy-powszechne/nsp-2011/nsp-2011-wyniki/ludnosc-stan-i-struktura-demograficzno-spoleczna-nsp-2011,16,1.html).

13 Twenty-three percent were from cities with a population greater than two hundred thousand. I was unable to determine author's place of origin in the remaining 27 percent.

Some authors signed their posts with their full names, some with nicknames, and still others with only descriptors. Some testimonies were as short as one line, others several paragraphs long. While the style and content of the testimonies varied greatly, many share broad themes that grant the collection a certain coherence: nearly half of the testimonies conveyed feelings of loss and addressed the issue of Jews' "disappearance," and a quarter of testimonies expressed nostalgia for multicultural Poland. About a third used Jewish stereotypes in their testimonies, and only one in six articulated a critique of antisemitism. Testimonies often addressed more than one theme; those I present and analyze here are especially emblematic exemplars.

Discoveries, Feeling of Loss, and Longings

The feeling most commonly expressed in testimonies is that of loss, in keeping with the overall spirit of the project. One woman, who uses the screenname mlenia, explains with striking lucidity the impact of realizing that contemporary Jewish absence was not merely objective ("There are no Jews here") but also historical-temporal ("Jews are *no longer* in Poland"). Only after realizing that Jews were no longer in Poland, which she describes as an amputation from the Polish body, did she begin to experience longing:

> At first I didn't know [Jews] used to be here at all. . . . Later I began reading more, and I slowly realized that . . . in one instant, a piece of OUR society was amputated (even though some claim that they [Jews] were not part of us). Ever since, I continue to read and I long, even though I do not know a concrete person for whom I could long.
> —mlenia (Testimony 551, emphasis in the original)

As this testimony highlights, the experience of Jewish absence—phenomenological absence—occurs through, and is predicated upon, formal knowledge about the past. It is possible only through an awareness of Jewish absence in its historical-temporal dimension.

While mlenia did not use the term Jews, opting for a more impersonal (and perhaps neutral) "they" throughout, a testimony from a participant named Kuba, addressing abstract Jews directly, expresses similar feelings. These include, first, the discovery of the absence of Jews; second, the realization that something that was not, was in fact *no longer*; and third, an emotional response:

I miss you, Jews. I miss the awareness that until recently you were together with us. You created the culture, the atmosphere of the town. Today there are only ruins left from your temple, a few stones, and a great void, which I feel while walking through town. Until recently I did not miss you at all; I was not aware of what really happened. Nobody talked about you, the old people did not reminisce about you . . . . I feel robbed of you, dear Jews. . . .
—Kuba (Testimony 276)

Another man explains that until he learned the story of a wartime Jewish colleague of his grandmother, he thought about the Jews,

like everyone else, textbook-like [*podręcznikowo*]—they used to be here; they no longer are [*byli, już ich nie ma*]. Germans murdered them. I didn't wonder about the lack of traces of their presence, the lack of the few who managed to survive. They used to be here, now they are not [*Byli, nie ma*]. Something terrible happened, but it was distant, far away, and not ours.
—Tommy (Testimony 1382)

Discovering the Jewish past is often challenging and requires personal investment, as a writer named Radosław described:

I learned late, in high school, [that] before the war Białystok was one of the most important Jewish cities in Europe. That knowledge was not provided in a systematic lecture. In primary school (in the days of the People's Republic of Poland), there wasn't much space in textbooks dedicated to Jews, nor to Polish Jewish or local history. My study of that past resembled piecing together a puzzle. First, I learned from my parents' and grandparents' stories, later from my own research in libraries, and then thanks to independent "discoveries in the field."
—Radosław Poczykowski (Testimony 398)

That knowledge about Jewish Białystok pushed the author to wonder what might have been:

What would Białystok look like now, with Jews as its largest "minority"? Who would I myself be? Would I know the name of the rabbi teaching in my school? Would I know Yiddish? Would I have the courage to defend Chackiel and his Esterka from hooligans? Unfortunately, I will never know.[14]

In another testimony, Joanna notes that before the war there were many Jews living in her small town near Warsaw, and yet today people do not remember them: "Only old buildings, dark courtyards, and crumbling cornices do. Jews, in the memory of locals, were transformed into an impersonal generality, an abstraction" (Testimony 251). Hence her desire to tell the story of one Jew she learned about by chance, in a book.

Other participants in the memory project reflected on the very idea of longing for something or someone one does not know:

> Longing is a very good word, but it does not completely convey what I feel. A lot of emotions and memories fill the word "longing." Yet I do not have memories in my longing. There haven't been Jews in my town for so many years. . . . I've never heard singing from our synagogue, and I never will. When I think about them, the irreversibility of history paralyzes me. It is like the partial amputation of collective consciousness.
> —Grzegorz Meisel (Testimony 534)

Another participant explained that absence pushes her to long and look for Jewish presence:

> I miss Jews always and everywhere. Traveling through Poland, in every place I visit I look for traces of Jewish presence. . . . Alas, my longing cannot be expressed toward a concrete Jew. I was born much too late, and in my family the memory of Jewish neighbors and acquaintances did not survive.
> —krulenka (Testimony 662)

Sometimes it is a chance encounter that summons the feeling of loss:

> The day before yesterday I saw a Hasid walking down the street. Older, in a fur hat and black winter overcoat. Walking briskly. It reminded me of the poet [Zbigniew] Herbert, for whom Poland without Jews on the street is not Poland. I felt just then that my post-Jagiellonian [i.e., postmulticultural] Fatherland had come back to me. I'm for "landscape

---

14 Chackiel and Esterka are stock characters in Polish idiom, analogous to the English Jack and Jill.

patriotism"; the landscape of my Country without black hats on the street is . . . full of holes. Like the coat of the poor Jewish tailor before the war. Like a heart riddled with bullets. Like the teeth of a [socialist] fighter under foreign rule. . . . I miss all Polish Jews, whom Lady History took away from me, ripping out a piece of my heart.[15] (capitalization as in original)
—Wielisław M. (Testimony 702)

The absence of Jews is described, in the collection of testimonies, as a lack (*brak*), a hole (*dziura*), a piercing emptiness (*przejmująca pustka*), a great void (*wielka pustka*), a loss (*utrata*), and am amputation (*amputacja*). What was lost? A look, a landscape, a language, a teacher, a neighborhood, a history. But all of these itineraries and lists of things and persons longed for, despite never having been known or experienced, share a project and a premise: Jews made Poland multicultural, piquant, and alive. Now it is but a monochrome shadow of its former, authentic self.

Longing for Multicultural Poland

Some participants specifically express a feeling of loss for Polish Jewish authors and the world they created, and through which contemporary Poles "know" Poland's Jewish past. As one woman laments, "I miss the unknown Jews who lived in Warsaw's Nalewki [neighborhood]; I miss the known ones who created our literature, I miss the entire Jewish culture" (Testimony 476). That "entire Jewish culture" is the one presented in the literary universes of Bruno Schulz and Isaac Bashevis Singer, evoked in many testimonies.[16] One man explains that since Jewish culture has vanished from Poland, he listens instead "to wonderful Jewish music and reads the books of Singer and Schulz" (Testimony 705). Some try to recreate that world in their own testimonies, with heavy doses of caricature:

---

15 "Jagiellonian Poland" today refers to the multicultural Polish-Lithuanian Commonwealth (1569–1795). It derives its name from the Jagiellonian dynasty that enacted the union of Poland and Lithuania in 1569. It is often opposed to "Piast Poland," which refers to the early Polish state and its alleged monoethnic character.

16 Isaac Bashevis Singer, the Yiddish writer, was born in Poland in 1902, emigrated to the United States in 1935, and died in Florida in 1991. Bruno Schulz was born in Drohobych (now in Ukraine) in 1892 and wrote in Polish. He was executed by the Gestapo in 1942, on his way from the "Aryan" side of Drohobych to its ghetto.

I miss the tenants and traders, their nervous gesticulations and their forked beards, their eyes twinkling like coal . . . ; I miss the Golem crossing godforsaken alleys . . . the Jews from Tarnów from my grandmother's stories; I miss Bruno Schulz . . . Bruno Schulz . . . Bruno Schulz . . . (Testimony 702)

These testimonies evoke a romanticized, objectified culture, frozen in time and literature: "I miss the world of Singer, which will never return. Our cities and towns will now always remain half dead and deprived of their Jewish soul" (Testimony 1385). Another writer explains that she "satisfies her longing for years now with the Kraków Jewish Culture Festival, where people from the entire world meet each other, aficionados of a nonexisting and yet still living culture" (Testimony 476).

What many participants miss is the multiculturalism that this lived culture made possible. A contributor to the website named Zara lamented that the absence of Jewish neighbors in her city altered its identity:

I miss the Jews of Poznań, whom I do not know. I miss multicultural Poznań, remembered from old stories. When I walk around the city and look for those few traces left by former inhabitants, I see this piercing emptiness, the absence of Jewish neighbors. I can only imagine who they were, whether they were happy here, or at least while their home was here. This lack, never filled, has been with me for a long time. Now I can express it. (Testimony 446)

Barbara, twenty-seven years old, also comments that "it is a great shame that Poznań, given its prewar Jewish community, today is boringly monocultural," adding that "it's good that there are a few foreigners thanks to Erasmus [EU study and training fellowships], because otherwise foreigners don't come here" (Testimony 601). This regret about living in a "boringly monocultural" society, of not experiencing multiculturalism, is common. Daga, a young woman, writes incisively that

Poles "long" above all for what is undiscovered, what they never could know (especially the younger generations, of which I am a part), what is for them a secret and what unfortunately will most likely never return. It is sad and as striking as the slogan on the page, "For Poles a synonym of the word Holocaust should be Loss," because our life could have been more interesting and culturally rich were we to share it every day with Jews. (Testimony 242)

Karol, a twenty-year-old resident of Łódź, explained that "by losing Jews, Łódź . . . lost a piece of its unusual climate, its history." He went on to say that he "miss[ed] the words uttered in Yiddish on the streets, Jewish songs, Hasidim on the streets, men with sidelocks [*pejsy*] and kippahs on their heads, beautiful Jewish women" (Testimony 751). Nostalgia for the olden days, for "the beautiful, colorful, fragrant but modest" interwar towns is rampant in the "recollections" found on the website (Testimony 322). Like Grzegorz, who felt "paralyzed by the irreversibility of history" (Testimony 534), Karol regrets that the lost world

> will never come back; my generation and the next likely will never know what it means to live in a multicultural environment—Polish Jew next to a Catholic Pole, atheist, Protestant; a Jew next to a polonized [*spolszczonego*] German, a Russian next to a native, "ancestral" Pole. (Testimony 751)

The result is an "impoverished" world (Testimony 270), made "boring" because "homogeneous." As Michał expresses it:

> It's difficult to say that I long [for Jews]. . . . I'm twenty-seven years old. But I do feel regret that a part of our country, of our coloring, disappeared. We became a boring society. I regret that I don't have Jewish friends with whom I could celebrate the days important for their culture and for mine; I would like to be able to argue about worldviews. (Testimony 463)

Yet another participant, born after the war, likewise regrets losing "the specific climate, the atmosphere of the shtetl, the poor sinuous streets, the markets, the Jewish holidays, Yiddish, or Jewish humor—unique in its genre." The author of this nostalgic enumeration, a woman who signed her full name, concludes that "our generations are impoverished by the loss of that world; we didn't have the opportunity to live together with neighbors of another faith, traditions, customs; get to know each other" (Testimony 270).

For participants in the "I Miss You, Jew" project, the lost diversity, the enchanting multiculturalism that will never return, is significant not only because Poland has become a "boring," "monocultural," "homogeneous" society but because the nation is no longer itself:

> There no longer are such places [like Krynki] in Poland. There are no places of such coexistence, places built over the years by people of di-

verse cultures that still co-constitute them. . . . I did not live in prewar Poland; I didn't have the opportunity to live in multicultural places, even if only Polish-Jewish. And I would have liked to. Loss is the right word. *We lost a big part of ourselves.* I miss it. (emphasis added)
—Polka (Testimony 683)[17]

Like Betlejewski in some of his own testimonies, the author of this last post used the nickname Polka—the feminine form of *Pole*. As she writes, without Jews, Krynki and hundreds of other small Polish towns like it are deformed, no longer "themselves." The transformation is felt as an injury because it entails not only a loss of diversity but also of authenticity. Another participant writes that

somewhere inside me I always had a feeling of loss and emptiness, created after the Second World War and this "boring" Polish national homogenization. Of course, after some years Poland changed, and instead of Jews we have . . . Vietnamese. (Testimony 1799)

This author makes it clear that for him, Vietnamese immigrants are a poor substitute for Jews. They do not count toward that multiculturalism that is so longed for.

All That Nostalgia Conceals

Fewer than one in five participants shared remembrances of personal acquaintances.[18] References to World War II and its immediate aftermath came from individuals telling stories they had heard from their parents or grandparents. When participants reminisced about Jews they had personally known, it was mostly in reference to the aftermath of the 1968 political crisis. In March 1968 students protested throughout Poland against the regime and its attack on free speech, demanding "socialism with a human face." The Polish United Workers' Party responded by spinning conspiracy theories that leaders of the student movement, some of whom had Jewish

---

17 Krynki is a small town in northeastern Poland, on the Belarussian border, about forty-five kilometers from Białystok. Before the war about 80 percent of the town's population was Jewish.

18 This is not too surprising, since participants who would have reminisced about Polish Jews they knew during or shortly after the war would have been over seventy years old in 2009–10, and less likely than younger generations to participate in a web-based platform.

roots, were attempting to destroy the country on behalf of Israel. These anti-Jewish accusations came on the heels of official condemnation of Polish Jews who had supported Israel during the Six-Day War a few months earlier. By evoking common antisemitic suspicions of Jewish anti-Polish plots, the party-state raised the specter of *żydokomuna* and managed to quell public support for the protests. It then proceeded to purge academic institutions, state organs, and other public offices of Jews, who were accused of revisionism and Zionist sympathies. As a result, between 1968 and 1970 approximately fifteen thousand Polish Jews were stripped of their Polish citizenship. Many emigrated to Israel, Europe, and North America (Stola 2000, 2005, 2010; Plocker 2022). These were traumatic times for Polish Jews, and yet memories of the writers' own sense of loss mostly eclipse any sustained reflection on what the displaced Jews themselves experienced. Karol W., for example, wrote:

> I miss Henryk, a pal from primary and middle school; and his sister and mother, who used to give us kids cake. With time passing, I don't even remember the names of these women anymore. [Our] ideal youth in Wrocław—courtyard, school, cheap wine—ended abruptly in 1968, when Henryk announced that they were all getting out of Poland. Apparently, he became a great engineer in Denmark.
> —Karol W. (Testimony 259)

Another participant, Mała, lost contact with Sara, a close friend until they graduated from university in 1969. She addresses Sara directly:

> I miss you, Sara! There was "chemistry" between us, and not just because we were majoring in chemistry. You shared with me even the smallest sandwich, the last cigarette, the lunch tickets and everything you didn't have that much of. We graduated in 1969. We parted ways. After that I learned that you left for Israel. . . . We were beautiful, young, and happy. Do you remember? Get in touch! (Testimony 171)

In both these examples of testimonies addressed to specific persons, the missing and missed Jew stands for an idyllic period in the participant's life, and it is not clear whether the nostalgia and longing expressed are for the person or the vanished time.

Another participant speaks of a specific individual whom she knew as a child. Her elegant mother's seamstress, Ms. Anda, left Tarnów for Israel with her beautiful daughters, whose "unusual southern appeal" so impressed the narrator that she had hoped, as a child, to grow up to resemble them. Recalling the time when she learned of the family's departure, she comments:

> To this day I remember the sadness and regret that overcame me. There would no longer be colorful garments for my dolls, beautiful daughters, or promenades through the cemetery to Ms. Anda's small wooden house at the other end of the world. Today I look at photographs where my mother and I look great in Ms. Anda's dresses, coats, and suits. And now we reminisce about her because she and her daughters are undoubtedly gone from our world.
> —Grażyna Corr (Testimony 270)

The self-centered nature of the description of Ms. Anda's disappearance is perhaps not surprising, given that it is rendered from the perspective of a five-year-old child. The writer's adult musings, however, still focus on herself rather than on Ms. Anda and her daughters. She writes only of the material effects of the Jewish seamstress's work on her body and her mother's. Absent from the testimony is any reflection about Ms. Anda herself: of how she and her daughters might have felt about leaving Poland; the reasons for their departure—whether they left by choice or under compulsion; or what might have become of them after they left for Israel (probably ca. 1968).

A younger participant tells another story related to 1968, involving recollections of a man his grandmother knew. It is longer than some other testimonies, and worth citing in almost its entirety:

> I come from Warsaw and I'm 35 years old. I know Jews only from stories, primarily from my grandmother's stories. . . . I don't know what his name was, but I heard quite a bit about him. I know that in the 1950s he worked in the Ministry of the Interior and had an apartment on Kwiatowa Street in Warsaw. My grandmother cleaned his place when she was still a young married woman with four children. . . . At that time the Jew in question recommended her at the ministry, and she received a cleaning position there thanks to him. The '50s passed, the '60s began and were about to be over when the ground suddenly opened under the Jew's feet. I don't know the details, my grandmother never recounted details about what happened, but I know that through some circuitous moves by my grandmother's boss, the apartment was transferred to my grandmother and her family after he had to leave Poland.

Thanks to the Jew, her family moved from a village outside War-saw to an apartment building in this charming corner of the Mokotów neighborhood. My grandmother always talked about him as "the Jew-boy" [Żydek], but more from affection and care than from any negative subtext. For her the word Jew didn't have a negative connotation. She knew a bunch [of Jews] and had similarly favorable opinions about them. And she transmitted that attitude to me, her grandson . . . in strange, fragmented stories . . . that I could later put together into a whole. I will never know this whole, the whole truth about the Jews that my grandmother knew. But what I do know I will share with pleasure so that we do not forget.

—Krzysztof Wiśniewski (Testimony 249)

This testimony offers clues to the story of a Jewish man who survived the war, who was likely a member of the Communist Party,[19] and was appar-ently forced to leave Poland in 1968. It is not clear how much of that history the author is aware of, since the protagonist in his story is his grandmother. The central point of his testimony is how his grandmother's destiny and that of her family was transformed "thanks to the Jew." The grandmother is twice the beneficiary of the Jewish man's actions, first when he secures a job for her and second when he arranges the transfer of his vacated apartment. But according to the narrative, it is through historical events and "circuitous" circumstances—when "the ground suddenly opened under the Jew's feet"—that the grandmother obtains the apartment. This change transforms the family's life. Most startling is the mention of the grand-mother's name for her benefactor—"Jew-boy"—an expression the author implicitly acknowledges as antisemitic with his explanation that his grand-mother meant it affectionately. The author concludes that she has trans-mitted her "favorable attitude" toward Jews to him and that he will gladly pass on what he knows about Jews to others, "so that we do not forget." Yet his testimony includes almost no details about the Jewish man in question: where he was from, how he survived the war, what kind of work he did, whether he had a family, where he might have gone after leaving Poland, or whether he ever got in touch with his former cleaner, now living in his previous home. We learn what the author's family gained from the man's departure, but not what the Jewish benefactor lost.

---

19 Although housing was often provided for workers in socialist Poland, party members and officers, like this Ministry of the Interior employee, were often allotted nicer accommo-dations, in better locations, and ahead of other workers.

The testimonies that touch on the events of 1968 quickly back away from the actual Jewish trauma. Few participants are able to confront the trivial nature of their own desire for a recovery of the lost past in comparison to the violence suffered by Jews pushed into exile.

Even when the testimonies refer to the Holocaust, authors are often incapable of deeper reflection. Here, a young man relates an incident experienced by his great-grandparents that has become part of family lore:

> I miss you, Jew! I live in western Wielkopolska. Today I'm twenty-one years old, and I deeply regret that I was not given the opportunity to know the entire history of my town. In the very center of Wolsztyn stood a beautiful synagogue, just by the square. Today there is no trace of it. I want to retell the history that my great-grandfather told my grandmother, and which she then told me. During the war my family had a big farm. The entire day was spent working in the field, especially during the summertime. That field was next to a forest. One day, some Jew who was hiding in the forest came to ask my great-grandfather . . . for food. They agreed. I remember how my grandma described the fear. . . . They left food in the forest, between trees, and that Jew, I don't know his name or age, took the food and hid himself underground. This didn't last too long, probably a few months. One day the food was left untouched. Same thing the following morning. I don't know what happened to that Jew but I hope that he survived! Jew, I miss you! I would very much like someday to talk with him, ask how he managed, help him find his roots. I very much regret that there are no Jews left in Wolsztyn. It is a huge loss. I'm also sorry that in 2009 someone burned the synagogue. We still don't know who did it. I only hope that someday I'll see a smiling Jew who will be walking the streets of my town and be part of it, like it used to be.
> —Aleksander (Testimony 1416)

Aleksander's recollection is an earnest narrative, filled with stereotypical details but also with yawning gaps. The story is one of benevolence, of his great-grandparents helping a Jew in hiding. Aleksander assumes that the Jewish man survived the Holocaust and transfers onto him his own nostalgia, assuming the fugitive might be interested in coming back and reconnecting with "his roots." Most disconcerting is the conclusion of Aleksander's testimony, referring to the destruction of the "beautiful synagogue" of Wolsztyn. Missing is any critical reflection on what the relationship could be between the past event he recalls, his own nostalgia, and the antisemitism that endures. After lamenting the burning of the synagogue, Aleksander snaps back to his musings on the quasi-mythical past and his naive hope to see one day "a smiling Jew who will be walking the streets of [his] town and be part of it, like it used to be." The abruptness of the pivot is chilling.

While Aleksander fails to reflect on antisemitism, another participant, Tommy, puts his finger on what remains unsaid:

> Once my grandma casually reminisced about a young Jew who taught at the same village school as she did before the war. During the occupation, not much in his life changed. Germans only came to the village to requisition livestock and agricultural products. The teacher still lived in his house, taught at the school, and did not even wear the Star of David.
>
> "Until one day the boys from the forest came and took him," said Grandma.
>
> "What does that mean, 'They took him'?" I asked naively.
>
> "Well, the usual, they took him."
>
> "And what?" I still didn't get what my grandmother was trying to say without using horrible words.
>
> "And nothing. He didn't come back."
>
> That sentence—"And nothing. He did not come back"—was left hanging between us; the air was heavy, hot, and it started to hurt [*zaczęło dusić, parzyć, uwierać*]. And then I understood.
>
> "Grandma, what kind of boys from the forest?"
>
> "Boys from the forest. Who knows. No one would ask, after all."

From the grandmother's perspective, this story needed no explanation, since it relied on familiar tropes and codes. It was "usual" for "boys from the forest"—Poles—to come and take away Jews. Her grandson, however, needed an explanation. Tommy explains how he felt when he finally understood:

> I don't know what made the biggest impression on me. Probably that my grandmother, an enlightened, educated woman with leftist and liberal opinions used the expression "They took him." So impassively, as if she was talking about an evident, everyday, normal thing. . . . This was long before [Jan] Gross. But it etched [*przeryło*] my understanding of Polish-Jewish relations during the occupation. . . . Maybe I misunderstood, though? Maybe the teacher survived the war and settled down somewhere else? Does anyone know what happened to the young Jewish teacher of Rzeczniów?
> —Tommy (Testimony 1382)

Tommy didn't misunderstand. It's impossible to determine from the grandmother's statement how she felt at the time about the Jewish teacher's "disappearance." Her grandson, however, describes her detached retelling of his murder as having brought home to him the nature of Polish-Jewish relations: both the violence toward Jews and the indifference of those witnessing it. Yet Tommy still hopes that he misunderstood the story and that the Jewish teacher from Rzeczniów survived.

Other testimonies tell of contemporary antisemitism. A teenage girl shares her outrage at "banal," everyday antisemitism:

> I'm overwhelmed with an inexpressible rage, and that is the worst feeling; a feeling of helplessness when I hear my older brother, whom I consider a truly intelligent person, calling me a Jew and talking about my Jewish characteristics [semickie cechy] when I don't want to lend him two złotys. I can only stop talking to a friend who calls ONR people "fascists" but herself laughs out loud at all the "soap" jokes, screams "Jude raus!" [sic], heils as a greeting (such a funny joke), and calls people she doesn't like "faggot" [pedał].
> —Julia Majewska (Testimony 1392)[20]

If Julia's "intelligent" brother and cool friend don't see the antisemitism in their speech, how can it be annihilated?

Others express shame at all the violence committed against Jews by Poles over the ages:

> I'm tormented by the thought of the vandalized Jewish shops, of Jewish mothers' and children's fear during pogroms, of the ghetto benches, of the firing of Janusz Korczak from the radio,[21] of the Stars of David on gallows, painted on the walls of our houses, of the use of the word Żyd as an insult, of the greed of those grabbing Jewish property and occupying Jewish houses and shops, of the people on the merry-go-round when the [Warsaw] ghetto was burning, of the abandoned Jewish cemeteries, of the presidential candidates advertising antisemitism. . . .

20 ONR stands for *Obóz Narodowo-Radicalny*, or the Radical-National Camp, a fascist organization founded in the 1930s and still active today. With other radical-Right groups, they coordinate the infamous "Marches of Independence" on November 11, celebrated in Poland as Independence Day.

21 Ghetto benches (*getto ławkowe*) were a form of discriminatory segregation in Polish universities in the 1930s, wherein Jewish students were required to sit in specific sections of classrooms. Janusz Korczak had a popular radio show about children in the early 1930s. He was fired in 1936 when antisemitic arguments were made in the press that the "Jewish doctor" had a bad influence on Polish children. See also chapter 2, n. 25.

I tremble when I think that so many among us were indifferent when Jews were murdered during the war; that there were some among us who themselves did the murdering; who stoned Jews in Kielce; that so many Jews had to leave Poland in 1968. That there was this terrible barn in Jedwabne.

From these historical events the author passes to the present:

I'm ashamed when I hear jokes about the Holocaust, when I see anti-semitic books . . . , when I hear . . . things are bad because Jews are in power, when I see photos of antisemitic protests. I am ashamed of the silencing of history and its untruthful telling. I'm ashamed that we're ashamed.
—Alina Pietrzak (Testimony 1401)

Another participant noted the violence committed against Jews "at home" in times of "peace":

I miss those who upon their return to their fatherland were received with cruelty, this time from their compatriots. I miss those who had to leave Poland in 1946, the '50s, in 1968, to survive, to find some kind of safety. Paradoxically, they went to Germany! To Berlin! Because they felt safer there. A year after the end of the war! To the USA, to Canada, to South America and finally to the dreamed-about Israel.
—Marcin Wygocki (Testimony 322)

Jewish Stereotypes and Antisemitic Tropes

Stereotypes about Jews are present in almost one-third of testimonies of Poles expressing longing. One woman, for instance, writes that she is fascinated by Jewish people, that she "admires their skills and their intelligence." Without their contributions, she writes, "the Polish nation wouldn't be what it is, and Poles would be 'worse'" (Testimony 33). Another contributor misses Jewish "wisdom and tradition. [Their] pride, loyalty, humility, faith, and diligence. [Their] music, dance, literature, and humor. [Their] otherness" (Testimony 621). A man from Białystok, who has "never met a single Jew [there]," despite the fact that "before the war almost half of the population was Jewish," was "impressed by the intelligence and the manners" of the Jews he met in Warsaw and especially in the United

States, and also by "this sort of absolute secrecy inscribed in their history, religion, tradition" (Testimony 705). Another participant asserts that

> we must admit that Jews had good business sense [*głowę do interesów*]. [Our family was] thus grateful for their help and for having a heart during difficult situations, forgetting [our] childish resentment; we liked them for their wisdom and even cleverness [*lubiliśmy ich za mądrość a nawet spryt*].
> —BJ (Testimony 299)

These apparently complimentary remarks, describing Jews as wise and clever moneylenders whom the writer's family turned to "in difficult situations," have their basis in long-standing antisemitic tropes. The writer acknowledges a certain resentment for having to depend on Jews' help. The stereotypical traits that are often admired and apparently missed are often the same ones, then, that antisemites fear—like intelligence, pride, and secrecy—or mock, like styles of dance and humor.

Sometimes writers express longing for the beauty of Jewish women in a sense that is already familiar from scenes of the perception of exotic others in situations of unequal power, a form of orientalism (Said 1979) that is also extended to Jews and Jewish culture more generally (and generically):

> I miss you. . . . I long for your beautiful names, your beautiful language, your beautiful music. I remember the moment in the Włodaw synagogue, where while listening to your music I touched your things, [things] of people who are now gone and . . . I longed. I longed for you, Jews. You are a wonderful nation.
> —Marek Roman (Testimony 120)

Conclusion: The Limits of Nostalgia

"I Miss You, Jew" was inspired by Jan Gross's book *Neighbors*. After reading that book, Betlejewski "understood with horror . . . that [his] nonmemory of the Jews was active, fostered forgetting" (Testimony 674). "I Miss You, Jew" was meant to break that active forgetting; to remember Jews. But did it succeed?

In the megabytes of testimonies, what perhaps stands out most clearly is the lack of acknowledgment of the Holocaust and other turning points that brought Poland from "then" to "now." Authors use a variety of metaphors for those responsible for the murder of Polish Jews or their subsequent expulsion from Poland—"the war," "boys from the forest," "1968," "Lady History"—and refer to the consequences in oblique language, saying that a Jewish acquaintance "left," "disappeared," "didn't come back," or was "gone." The passive voice persists; the euphemisms pervade; the dodging metonyms abound. The perpetrators and acts are never directly named. This language is emblematic of Poles' problematic attitude toward the Holocaust. According to Andrzej Leder, the philosopher, psychoanalyst, and Lacanian cultural critic, Poles are "interpassive subjects": they were not the main agents of the Holocaust, yet they benefited, directly or indirectly, from it (2014).[22]

This might explain why some Poles turn to denial and others toward nostalgia. One thing is certain: according to participants in the "I Miss You, Jew" project, the "disappearance" of Jews left Poles in an "impoverished," "boring," "half dead," "monocultural" country. Jews are missed for the kind of Poland their presence created—"colorful and fragrant." Even the few testimonies addressing Jewish individuals known personally by the authors express less concern about the missing and missed Jews—Ms. Anda, Henryk, Sara—than about the feelings of those who miss them—Grażyna, Karol, and Mała.

Svetlana Boym defines nostalgia as "a longing for a home that no longer exists or has never existed" (2002: xiii), altering the original signification of the word, which combines the Greek roots *nostos* (to return home) and *algia* (pain). It is that mythical "home," that multicultural Jagiellonian Poland, that many Poles are pining for when they express missing, or longing for, Jews. If nostalgia is "a sentiment of loss and displacement," Boym argues, it is also "a romance with one's own fantasy" (2002: xiii). Just as nostalgic love can survive only in an impossible relationship, Poles' nostalgia for Jews can exist only because there are very few Jews in Poland. It is possible because Poles can imagine Jews more or less as they please. The Jewish body is a blank canvas, skillfully adorned—symbolized by Betlejewski's empty chair with its sheepskin and kippah—and painted with progressive Poles' "wonderful dreams of the past."

---

22 Leder's book *Prześniona rewolucja: Ćwiczenia z logiki historycznej* has been widely discussed and debated in academic circles and in public forums in Poland, and it received two prestigious awards. Its title can be translated as "The Slept-Through Revolution: Exercises in Historical Logic." It argues that the extermination of Jews and the emigration of Holocaust survivors in the late 1940s and early 1950s, coupled with the communist regime's socioeconomic reforms, changed Polish social structure, leading to the emergence of an ethnically Polish middle class. That social revolution was carried by external forces, and its traumatic causes and origins remain repressed in Polish collective consciousness.

Betlejewski attempted to go "a bit deeper" (personal interview, March 24, 2011) by organizing a follow-up commemorative performance on the sixty-ninth anniversary of the Jedwabne pogrom. The crux of the event was the burning of a barn. He explained his motivation as follows:

It is time to face the most important problem in Poles' relationship to the Holocaust—the absence of common feelings of suffering. Years of postwar demagoguery and propaganda not only removed traces of Jewish presence from our collective memory, but also anesthetized us . . . to Jewish suffering. We became subjects of our own social anesthesia. We do not feel, we have no compassion, we don't relate to Jewish suffering, and the Jewish narrative appears to us as a huge dispossession. But here is a symbol that brings us closer to that drama in a direct way, without mediators, without third parties, without Germans. Just us and the Jews. Through this drastic act I'd like to try to reconstitute a community of suffering. I'd like to wake up from our "pharmacological coma." Just as I need to write on those walls, now I need that barn. (Testimony 674)

Betlejewski therefore had a barn built for the occasion on farmland in central Poland. He invited Poles to send "thoughts" and "confessions" beforehand, which he printed on white sheets of paper and brought into the barn to burn, as a form of collective expiation. He also invited the local population and readers and participants in the "I Miss You, Jew" project to gather for an outdoor banquet and witness the burning. The entire event was documented with photos and film clips on the "I Miss You, Jew" website, with details about the making of the barn, the bureaucratic red tape involved in the preparations, the controversies that arose (the local authority first granted but then refused to give a permit for the burning; two young students "occupied" the barn to prevent the burning), the conflagration itself, and the crowd of witnesses.

While "I Miss You, Jew" received positive coverage and support from various public figures, institutions, and Jewish communities, "Burning Barn" was much more controversial. Many argued that some things should not be shown, that a performance re-creating this brutal event was pornographic. Betlejewski was accused of seeking the limelight, of reveling in his provocateur role, of taking the Jedwabne pogrom too lightly. Many of my Jewish interviewees were outraged that the tragic and violent death of innocent victims had been trivialized by the performance of a camera-ready artist in a self-promoting stunt. Members of the Jewish community wrote on a web-based forum that the "Jedwabne barn is the symbol of the death of over 1,000 people. But ["Burning Barn"] takes away the symbol from the victims."[23]

Despite protests, threats, and the cost of the project (including the construction of the barn, the banquet for dozens of onlookers, and the filming), Betlejewski proceeded with the burning and posted a film of the event on his website.[24] As he told me when we met, he instantly became a pariah, losing all credibility with the Jewish community, which until then had been quite supportive of the first project.[25]

Unlike "I Miss You, Jew," which generated discussions in the public sphere about collective memory, amnesia, and antisemitism, "Burning Barn" was so controversial that it did not provide a space for a productive discussion on violence and collective responsibility. The performance upset both Jews and non-Jewish Poles. Perhaps it was the "spectacle" involved in "Burning Barn" that many found reprehensible, including the kitsch showmanship of Betlejewski casting himself in the role of the Polish peasant. It is also possible that the objections to the project were based less on its form than on its content and intentions. Unlike "I Miss You, Jew," which indulges in a rather sanitized and sentimental portrayal of the past, "Burning Barn" confronted Polish violence against the Jews whom Poles now profess to miss. It is certainly easier to commemorate the lives of the departed than to revisit their violent murder. Perhaps the trauma of Jedwabne remains too fresh for Poles to be willing to confront the burden of complicity. For Polish Jews, the graphic reenactment of mass murder was indecent and too much to bear. In any case, by going ahead with the performance despite Jewish requests to cancel it, Betlejewski privileged the expiation of the perpetrators' sins over respecting Jewish trauma.

23 Piotr Pacewicz, Paweł Jędrzejewski, and Zuzanna Marczyńska, *z Forum Żydów Polskich* (http://wyborcza.pl/2029020,76842,8146511.html?sms_code=). See also Paweł Dobrosielski's (2017b) incisive analysis of the barn as a symbol of the Holocaust and its place in Polish-Jewish relations.

24 The film has since been removed from both the website and YouTube. It was, however, available on Facebook (https://www.facebook.com/watch/?v=795454570661421) as of March 8, 2022.

25 Personal interview, March 24, 2011.

CHAPTER 4

Museum Encounters

History museums, like memorials and commemorative events, play an important role in the creation and maintenance of collective memory and national identity.[1] In posttotalitarian societies, they take on the additional social functions of demythologization and *ree*ducation. Because museums also *objectify* memory and identity, they often first have to *undo*, to deconstruct some of their previous museological narratives, before they can rebuild. This is a complex process, not least because it typically faces resistance from segments of the public for whom certain historical revisions are difficult to accept. Then, too, the modifications risk opening the way to new, equally knotty forms of national myth-making.

The period of postsocialism and European Union membership has been prolific for history museums in Poland and throughout Eastern Europe. Old museums are being redesigned, their narratives revised. New institutions are opened every year (Sarkisova and Apor 2013; Iordachi and Apor 2021). In examining various aspects of socialism, from its political configuration to its material culture, new museums have also brought the history of the Second World War and the Holocaust under scrutiny. Until 1989 the Holocaust had been mostly effaced or diluted from the Polish narrative of the war, folded into a broader history of fascist aggression and Soviet liberation (J. E. Young 1993; Zubrzycki 2006). Since the fall of state socialism, Jewish-history museums in particular have enjoyed a renaissance in the region (Gershenson and Kirshenblatt-Gimblett 2015; Manchin 2015; Deme 2015).

In Poland alone, over half a dozen museums of Jewish history have been inaugurated in the past two decades. These include Kraków's Galicia

---

1 I have in mind, in the European context, commemorative practices such as marches, the laying of wreaths or lighting of candles at monuments, visiting the tombs of national heroes at cemeteries on All Souls' Day, or going on a pilgrimage on the occasion of a national holiday.

FIGURE 25. Poles queue to enter an empty Polin Museum of the History of Polish Jews in April 2013, eighteen months before its core exhibition was inaugurated. (Photo by Jakub Nowotyński/ Polin Museum of the History of Polish Jews.)

Jewish Museum, established in 2004 "to commemorate the victims of the Holocaust, present the diversity of Jewish culture and the complexity of Jewish history, as well as to participate in the revival of Jewish life in Poland";[2] Oskar Schindler's Enamel Factory Museum, which opened in 2010 and focuses on the Nazi occupation of Kraków; Kraków's Eagle Pharmacy Museum, which was unveiled in 2013 in the former ghetto and tells the story of Kraków's Jews during the Second World War, commemorates victims of the Holocaust, and celebrates Tadeusz Pankiewicz, a pharmacist who was awarded the Israeli designation of Righteous Among the Nations for assisting local Jews; and Warsaw's Polin Museum of the History of Polish Jews, which opened its building in April 2013 and its permanent exhibition in October 2014. The content of numerous preexisting exhibitions has also been revised or expanded to (better) address the history of Polish Jews, and smaller museums and educational centers scattered across Poland have opened their doors to local populations and Polish

2 https://galiciajewishmuseum.org/en/press-kit.

tourists.[3] These include the Świętokrzyski Shtetl Museum in Chmielnik, which opened in 2014 in the former synagogue of a small town whose population was 80 percent Jewish before the war and is 100 percent Polish now.[4]

Because they are legitimized by official authorities, museums are privileged sites for the transmission of historical narratives and the construction of collective memory. They often have access to significant resources, allowing them not only to affirm and promote a given historical discourse but also to transmit that knowledge with dynamic and technologically sophisticated pedagogical tools. The new museums seek to impart knowledge less by offering rooms full of artifacts and displays of information than by telling stories, engaging the senses, and kindling emotions. As Michał Niezabitowski, director of Kraków's Schindler's Enamel Factory Museum, explained:

> Museums are (seemingly!) no longer needed. . . . The visitor nowadays does not want to be a spectator; he wants to be a participant. . . . [So] we thought the exhibition had to be more than an exhibition! More than theater! More than a movie! . . . We invite [visitors] to take part in the exhibition. [Come and] look, touch, hear—and most importantly—feel and experience.[5]

Schindler's Enamel Factory Museum therefore plays with visitors' vision and orientation (as they traverse a narrow, dark passage), hearing (through music and archival radio broadcasts), and sense of touch (as they walk on uneven surfaces).

The new "narrative museums" are phenomenological factories, generating scenarios in which the visitor directly encounters and engages with the recreated history in a multisensory way.[6] This creates a certain

---

3 The Polin Museum set up a traveling education exhibition, *Museum on Wheels*, which visits smaller towns (pop. up to fifty thousand) and tours selected cultural festivals. Since the opening of the museum's core exhibition in 2014, the *Museum on Wheels* visited over eighty-nine towns throughout Poland (https://polin.pl/en/education-culture-jewish-cultural-heritage-project /museum-on-wheels).

4 I discuss Chmielnik, its festival, and the Świętokrzyski Shtetl Museum in chapter 5.

5 Michał Niezabitowski and Bartosz Piłat, "Tramwaj historii," *Gazeta Wyborcza*, June 24, 2010.

6 Narrative museums are museums whose main exhibits are stories. Whereas traditional museums are typically based on a collection—physical artifacts and/or historic buildings—in narrative museums artifacts are important only insofar as they support the story being told. Some narrative museums therefore have no collection and few or no artifacts. The Holocaust Museum in Washington, DC, was one of the first narrative museums. Its first curator, Jeshajahu Weinberg, articulated the original statement on this type of museum (1994). For analyses of

emotional investment in the story being told, the materials visitors see, and the facts they learn.

The Polin Museum of the History of Polish Jews likewise invites the visitor to experience different Jewish worlds through stories and sensory experience. Together with the Auschwitz-Birkenau Museum and Memorial, and the Museum of the Warsaw Uprising, it is among the most visited museums in Poland. It has also become an important agent of Polish cultural diplomacy abroad and national pedagogy at home, and for that reason the museum and some of its staff have been targets of the Law and Justice government. My goal here is not to explore the political controversies surrounding the museum but to analyze its core exhibition, assess how the narratives it presents are assimilated by visitors, and discuss its place in the broader mnemonic field.

My analysis is primarily based on participant observation at the museum—at the opening ceremony and activities on October 28–30, 2014, and on visits from November 2014 to September 2015. During the latter period, two research assistants and I conducted a total of 110 visits to the museum. We joined guided tours, followed individuals and small groups visiting on their own, and carried out postvisit interviews with individual visitors and small groups. (For more details on the research, see appendix A.) This ethnographic observation allowed us to capture how visitors "read" the exhibition, both in accordance with and beyond the intentions of its curators; to see how they react, where they linger, where they reach for phones or cameras to take photographs; to listen to the conversations they engage in during the visit; and, finally, to learn what they themselves think they learned from the exhibition, and whether or not they perceive themselves as changed by it. To keep abreast of changes or addendums to the museum narratives or displays, I have revisited the core exhibition every year since that initial ethnographic research.

Cultural Diplomacy

While Schindler's Enamel Factory Museum focuses on a specific time and place—wartime Kraków—the permanent exhibition of the Polin Museum

---

narrative museums in Poland, see Wolska-Pabian and Kowal (2019). For a presentation of the Polin museum and a discussion of curatorial choices, see the book chapter authored by its chief curator, Barbara Kirshenblatt-Gimblett (2015), as well as an interview with her conducted by Ewa Klekot (Kirshenblatt-Gimblett and Klekot 2016).

takes a *longue durée* approach, leading the visitor on a journey of "1,000 years of the history of Polish Jews."[7] The initial idea for the museum came from Dr. Grażyna Pawlak, then vice-director for development at the Association of the Jewish Historical Institute, who had attended the opening ceremony of the United States Holocaust Memorial Museum (USHMM) in Washington on April 22, 1993. The vision was to create in Poland a modern narrative museum that would focus on the story of Jewish life before the Shoah.[8] Two decades in the making, the museum was the result of a public-private partnership unique in Poland: the City of Warsaw donated the land and contributed to construction costs, the Polish Ministry of Culture and National Heritage paid for the building, and the Association of the Jewish Historical Institute of Poland, supported by philanthropic organizations and individual donors from Poland and abroad, financed its permanent exhibition and cultural programming. Over one hundred scholars from Poland, Israel, and North America worked on the overall concept and individual galleries.

The end result is stunning. The building's design, by the Finnish architect Rainer Mahlamäki, is at once understated and brilliantly cutting-edge. It stands in the center of Muranów, the former Jewish neighborhood and wartime ghetto. The museum's entrance faces Nathan Rapoport's 1948 iconic Monument to the Ghetto Heroes, built on top of the rubble left after the Nazis crushed the 1943 uprising (figure 26).[9] The building's simple lines do not oppress the empty space it occupies or detract from the monument and postwar buildings it faces. It blends organically with its environment. The exterior glass panels reduce the sense of the building's size and weight while permitting the interior to be flooded with light (figure 27).

7 This is the title of the core exhibition on the Polish-language webpage (https://www .polin.pl/pl/wystawa-stala, accessed October 28, 2020). The English-language page gives no title for the exhibition.

8 Jeshajahu Weinberg, originator of the "narrative museum" and of the concept of the USHMM and of the Diaspora Museum in Tel Aviv, served as chair of the Polin Museum's design team from 1996 until his death in 2000 (https://artsandculture.google.com/exhibit/how-to -make-a-museum/wR7xiggx?hl=en-GB.) For a detailed history of the museum, see Małgorzata Niezabitowska (2015).

9 Dignitaries on official visits to Warsaw typically bring wreaths to the monument. Some historic moments of the postwar era were captured there, such as the German chancellor Willy Brandt kneeling at the foot of the monument, a gesture and image that came to signify Germany's recognition of collective guilt. The moment with its image became so iconic that in 2000 it was commemorated in its own monument in Willy Brandt Square, just behind what is now the Polin Museum.

FIGURE 26. Polin Museum of the History of Polish Jews, its entrance facing Nathan Rapoport's 1948 Monument to the Ghetto Heroes and the Tree of Memory, dedicated in 1988 to the "shared memory of Polish Jews murdered between 1939–1945 by the Hitlerite invader, and to the Poles who died helping Jews." (Photo by Wojciech Kryński / Polin Museum of the History of Polish Jews.)

FIGURE 27. View of the Muranów neighborhood from the museum's lobby. (Photo by Geneviève Zubrzycki, March 28, 2013.)

The museum's reception hall is an open space enclosed by curvy, sand-colored walls and ceiling.[10] Mahlamäki intended the open space to symbolize the biblical parting of the Red Sea, but former museum director Dariusz Stola (2014–19) prefers a historical interpretation: for him the hall is reminiscent of a canyon in a Middle Eastern desert, underlining the geographic origins of a civilization that Jewish immigrants brought to Poland in the Middle Ages. "The museum tells the rest of their story."[11] Another popular interpretation I have heard from guides is that the narrow hall symbolizes the rupture in the Polish memory of Jews, a tear that the museum seeks to mend via its exhibitions, lectures, workshops, and events.

Windows at both ends of the hall frame the visitor's view: of modernist apartment buildings, the edge of the Monument to the Ghetto Heroes, and the Tree of Memory on one end (figure 26), and of a park and more apartment buildings on the other (figure 27).

Even before its core exhibition was installed, the Polin Museum was the object of intense curiosity: thousands of Varsovians lined up on a cool April day in 2013 to visit the empty building, which opened its doors on the occasion of the seventieth anniversary of the Warsaw Ghetto Uprising, and thousands more a month later during Warsaw's Night at the Museum (see figure 25 on p. 88).

The much-awaited core exhibition was finally inaugurated on October 28, 2014, in the presence of dignitaries and VIPs from around the world as well as members of the Jewish community in Poland and the Polish Jewish diaspora. Some 1,500 guests attended the ceremony, seated outside the museum facing the Monument to the Ghetto Heroes.[12] President Bronisław Komorowski of Poland and President Reuven Rivlin of Israel spoke at the event. Komorowski's speech was tailored to Polish audiences:

I am happy to be opening the exhibition of a museum that has a beautiful name—*Polin*. Polin means "Here you will rest," because that is how Jews referred to Poland, long ago, in Hebrew.[13] And not without reason! For centuries the multinational, multireligious, and tolerant republic was a safe haven and a generally friendly place for Jews. It was a beautiful exception in Europe at that time. The downfall of the

10 On the architecture of the building, which won several prestigious awards, see Polin's page https://polin.pl/en/about-museum/building.

11 Personal communication, July 20, 2021.

12 https://www.polin.pl/pl/aktualnosci/2014/10/28/witajcie-w-polin-otworzylismy-wystawe-stala-wideorelacja.

13 In English, *Polin* is sometimes translated as "Here you will *dwell*."

Polish state with its partitioning in the eighteenth century put an end to that Polin as well. . . .

The museum itself attests to the changes since Poland regained its freedom twenty-five years ago. Without Polish freedom, the museum would not have been possible in its present form. One of our key duties after recovering our freedom was to rectify the history that had been corrupted, manipulated, and distorted in so many ways under the nondemocratic communist system. That task concerned the entire history of modern Poland, including the history of Polish Jews and Polish-Jewish relations.

It is only by telling the story of greatness and pettiness, heroism and cowardice, sacrifice and crime, life and death, that we can perhaps get close again to the idea of Polin.[14]

President Komorowski's speech was remarkable for the extent of its focus on Poland rather than Polish Jews. While he acknowledged the existence of "pettiness, cowardice, crime, and death," the Poland depicted in his speech is that of a country mostly benevolent toward Jews until it was partitioned and invaded by its neighbors and its history distorted by communists. That interpretation of history is a powerful one, and it exerts differing effects on domestic and foreign audiences.

The ceremony concluded with a brief but forceful address by Marian Turski, an Auschwitz survivor and chair of the museum's council, who reminded everyone that Polish Jews were still in Poland: "We are here," he proclaimed in Yiddish and Polish, an important message addressed to Poles and to the world, and affirming the narrative of one thousand years and counting. He then walked toward the museum with thirteen-year-old Joanna Widła, a graduate of the (Jewish) Lauder-Morasha School in Warsaw, to symbolically open the museum.

The atmosphere at the ceremony was solemn but festive. The two-day program included lectures, a gala, an outdoor concert, film screenings, and workshops.[15] It served as the occasion for many reunions and as an opportunity for Polish Jews who had left Poland to reacquaint themselves with a much-changed country. The festivities were not without intrigue. Gossip circulated: Who got the best seats at the ceremony?

---

14 https://www.polin.pl/pl/aktualnosci/2014/10/28/witajcie-w-polin-otworzylismy-wystawe-stala-wideorelacja.

15 See the full program on the museum's website, https://polin.pl/en/grand-opening-of-the-core-exhibition.

Who was snubbed? Who sat with whom, who got to talk with VIPs? Others speculated on who had managed to talk to or snap a picture with the filmmaker Roman Polanski, recently arrived in Warsaw for the occasion.[16]

The opening ceremony made clear that the museum was meant to write a new page in Polish-Jewish relations. Under the honorary patronage of President Komorowski, the multiday event became a formidable instrument of cultural diplomacy, an unprecedented public relations feat. Six hundred reporters from around the world were invited to cover the events.[17] They obliged, and coverage in the foreign press was overwhelmingly favorable: the *Jerusalem Post* claimed that "few things in this world are absolutely perfect, and there are some minor criticisms which can be leveled at the museum, but all in all it is a superb project;" *Le Monde* characterized the museum as "the successful outcome of a delicate and controversial project;" Anne Applebaum announced in *Slate* that the museum was "a testament to people everywhere who have fought to exist," while Timothy Garton Ash, in his review for the *Guardian*, called it a "small miracle."[18]

In Poland, too, the response was generally positive, and the museum and its core exhibition became instantly popular with both the critics and the public.[19] Between 2013 and 2019 the museum hosted nearly four

16 Polanski's attendance itself was turned into evidence of Polish hospitality and benevolence toward Polish Jews as rumors circulated that Polish authorities protected him, as a Polish citizen, from being extradited to the United States to serve his sentence after his 1977 guilty plea for unlawful sexual intercourse with a minor (https://wyborcza.pl/1,75398,16905362,Palac_Prezydencki_negocjowal_w_sprawie_Polanskiego_.html).

17 https://www.polin.pl/pl/aktualnosci/2014/10/28/witajcie-w-polin-otworzylismy-wystawe-stala-wideorelacja.

18 http://www.jpost.com/Diaspora/Another-reason-to-go-Poland-the-Polin-Museum-381187; https://www.lemonde.fr/arts/article/2014/10/31/un-musee-juif-dans-l-ancien-ghetto-de-varsovie_4515853_1655012.html; https://slate.com/news-and-politics/2014/10/museum-of-the-history-of-polish-jews-this-new-museum-empathizes-with-all-those-who-have-fought-to-exist.html; https://www.theguardian.com/commentisfree/2014/nov/01/polish-jewish-relations-warsaw-museum-history-polish-jews.

19 Reviews were published in all major Polish newspapers, most emphasizing key elements of the museum's master narrative: Poles' and Jews' common history and peaceful coexistence, and Poland's openness and past multiculturalism. Important critiques were formulated by several academics and public figures, including scholars who had worked on the exhibition. See Leopold Sobel's interview with Helena Datner cited in Tokarska-Bakir (2016: 55) and those of Zofia Waślicka and Artur Żmijewski with Jacek Leociak (2015: 88) and with Dariusz Stola (2015). In-depth critiques were presented by academics at a workshop hosted by Irena Grudzińska-Gross at Princeton University in April 2015: see Janicka (2016), Matyjaszek (2016), Forecki and Zawadzka (2016), and Tokarska-Bakir (2016). A balanced assessment of critiques can be found in Kijek (2017).

TABLE 2. *Number of Visitors to the Polin Museum, 2013–19*

YEAR	VISITORS TO THE MUSEUM	VISITORS TO THE CORE EXHIBIT
2013	190,210	n/a
2014	348,140	72,130*
2015	576,347	316,426
2016	583,528	336,974
2017	731,420	381,437
2018	683,187	358,157
2019	604,020	310,156
Total	3,716,852	1,785,979

Source: Unpublished data, Polin Museum of the History of Polish Jews.

Note: The total number of visitors to the museum comprises all individuals entering the building, including those attending events and visiting the café or the gift shop. The number of visitors to the core exhibition is based on tickets sold for individual visits and guided tours, as well as the number of visitors on free days, when tickets are not sold but visitors are counted upon entrance to the museum. In all cases the data represents "visits" rather than unique visitors, as one individual could visit the exhibition a couple of times or attend other events at the museum.

*Numbers based on visits after October 28, 2014, when the core exhibition was inaugurated.

million visitors, and it has become one of the few obligatory stops for foreign dignitaries on official visits (see table 2).

Even before its core exhibition opened, people flocked to the museum for temporary exhibitions, concerts, films, lectures, workshops, and activities for children. In 2013 more than 190,000 people visited the museum; in 2014 it had more than 348,000 visitors. Attendance exceeded all expectations, especially given that the core exhibition was open only for the last two months of 2014. More than half of all visitors (55 percent) are Polish.[20]

20 Based on unpublished data provided by the Polin Museum of the History of Polish Jews. I'm grateful to Katarzyna Lewandowska for providing those numbers. For comparative purposes, during the years 2016–19 the Auschwitz-Birkenau Memorial and Museum hosted an average of 2,150,000 visitors annually, of whom approximately 20 percent were Poles. The Museum of the Warsaw Uprising hosted, on average, nearly 700,000 visitors per year during that period, the majority of whom were Polish. See http://auschwitz.org/muzeum/aktualnosci/2-32-miliona-odwiedzajacych-miejsce-pamieci-auschwitz-w-2019-r-,2105.html and https://www.1944.pl/artykul/jak-wygladal-rok-2016-w-muzeum-powstania-warsz,4606.html.

"Here You Will Rest": Narratives and National Pedagogy

As President Komorowski noted in his speech, the museum's very name, *Polin*, captures one of its key messages: that Poland was a hospitable place for Jews. It adopted the Hebrew name for Poland, itself related to the myth of origin of Jews settling in Poland. The museum's core exhibition was conceived as a deliberate rejection of the tendency to reduce the long and complex history of Polish Jews to their destruction in the Holocaust. The 43,000-square-foot exhibition tells instead the story of Jewish presence on Polish lands for a millennium, from the Middle Ages to the present. Its eight galleries, organized chronologically and thematically, immerse visitors in everyday life at specific points in history, circumscribed by the political events that shaped them. The thousand-year history is narrated through a series of multimedia, multisensory displays.

The curators also dispensed with the formal, authoritative metadiscourse of an omniscient narrator. Instead, as the English-language introduction to the core exhibition explains:

> The Core Exhibition is a narrative: visitors will be drawn into a story told by artefacts, paintings, interactive installations, reconstructions and models, video projections, sounds and words. Our focus is on life, therefore at each stage of the journey we strive to remain close to life by letting people speak—Jewish merchants, scholars or artists from a given era, rabbis, housewives, politicians, chroniclers and revolutionaries. We give the floor to those who perished and to those who survived.[21]

That rhetorical strategy was chosen to avoid a teleological reading of history, as if all of Jewish history in Poland was inevitably moving toward the Holocaust. The exhibition seeks to transport the visitor to times when Jews did not yet live in the shadow of the Holocaust or have the same historical hindsight as modern visitors (Kirshenblatt-Gimblett 2015). The museum presents itself, in its catalog, ad campaigns, and public relations, as a "Museum of Life" (Kirshenblatt-Gimblett and Polonsky 2014). The Holocaust nevertheless shapes the museum's narrative, if only because it is articulated in opposition to one that portrays Poland as the land of ashes.

Visitors, moreover, cannot escape knowledge of the Holocaust. After all, the museum stands on one of its most iconic sites. This knowledge

21 https://www.polin.pl/en/exhibitions/core-exhibition (accessed October 28, 2020).

can create a certain disjuncture or dissonance between visitors' expectations and their museum experience. In multiple conversations with Polish visitors in exit interviews, however, most said that the core exhibition "works" in the sense that it succeeds in evoking a thousand years of Jewish life, though this history is not always assimilated as the curators intended. A retired journalist in her eighties described the most valuable lesson of her visit:

> I knew that the history of Jews was tied to that of Poland for centuries, but it was only kind of recorded in some fragments of memory, you know; it wasn't present. And here, . . . Poles' and Jews' common life on Polish lands was shown in such a rich and vivid way. Because these events, the Holocaust, have dominated how we remember Polish Jews and their history. These events were tragic, macabre, cruel, terrible—there are no words to describe those events. But it is to those events that we returned, that were commemorated in monuments, plaques, discussions. But that is only some part of history. [So] it was very valuable to me that the [museum] showed that for so many centuries we lived together.

Her daughter, a mid-level manager in her forties, interjected that what she "liked best about the exhibition was the 'de-Holocaustization' of the topic":

> Because here [*u Nas*], Jews are most often associated with the Holocaust. . . . But they [Jews] were present on our lands not just in concentration camps, right? Yet, that's the association we have. . . . And that's interesting; this nation was present for many, many years of our history—whether we like it or not, as people think in Poland—as if those Jews were present [only] during the interwar years.

This assessment is factually correct; Jews did live in this part of Europe for many centuries. Yet the observations made by this middle-aged professional expose fault lines too deep, it seems, for the exhibition to fix, and which it may even exacerbate. Throughout her explanation, the woman not only uses expressions that reinforce a distinction between "us" and "them," but she also uses formulations that betray her view of "those Jews" as "guests" on Polish soil. The phrase *U nas* means "at home, here" but literally refers to "us" (much like the French *chez nous*). She then distinguishes the Jewish nation from that of Poles and "our" history. Ultimately, the woman emphasizes Polish hospitality over Jewish history. Her comments also betray a lack of any sense of Jewish agency. Jews were simply "present" within "our history." This was a common locution repeated by museum guests in interviews, in which the existence and fate of Jews are expressed in passive constructions: "Jews were persecuted," and so on. The Polish hosts, in this perspective, retain the leading role.

The Paradox of Hospitality

The exhibition points to Polish hospitality from the start, as the story begins with the arrival of Jews and their settlement on Polish land. In postvisit interviews, visitors emphasized the Jewish legend surrounding the settlement of Jews in Poland—with God telling Jews traveling through dense forests that "here [they] will rest," and King Kazimierz granting rights to Jews—as a key takeaway point. This may be because independent visitors tend to spend a disproportionate amount of time in the first two galleries of the exhibition (titled "First Encounters" and "Paradisus Iudaeorum").[22] Perhaps the beginnings capture their imagination because they know key characters of the story (e.g., King Kazimierz and his lover, the beautiful Esterka) but not the historical details and facts of the period.[23] Perhaps they spend more time in those galleries simply because at the beginning of the exhibition they are more motivated to read everything and interact with every prop. Or perhaps they prefer to spend time steeped in images of the distant past than to view (or avert their eyes from) the violence of the recent Polish Jewish past. In any case, by the time visitors reach the Holocaust gallery, they have noticeably less energy. Those with small children often leave because of fatigue or because of the graphic nature of the exhibition. Thus the impression many visitors retain is of the mostly peaceful coexistence of Poles and Jews over centuries, and the vision that President Komorowski conjured in his speech of Poland

22 "Paradisus Iudaeorum" [Jewish Paradise] is a Latin expression that most likely origi- nates in a sixteenth-century political critique of the Polish-Lithuanian Commonwealth. It then became part of a popular proverb describing Poland as a "heaven for the nobility, purgatory for townspeople, hell for peasants, and a paradise for Jews." Tokarska-Bakir (2016) finds the use of the expression by the Polin Museum, without quotation marks and explanation of its origins, counterproductive because it normalizes and legitimizes a view of Poland that should instead be problematized.

23 According to a popular legend, King Kazimierz the Great (r. 1333-70) had a beautiful and intelligent Jewish lover, Esterka, for whose sake he extended privileges to the Jews in the kingdom.

as "a safe haven and a generally friendly place for Jews, . . . a beautiful exception in Europe at that time."

In our observations, Polish visitors demonstrated a keen interest in Jewish "otherness." They peppered guides with queries about religious beliefs, practices, and customs. Interactive props concerning rules for keeping kosher are popular, and this topic generates many questions and comments during guided visits, as do life-cycle rituals like weddings and funerals. Frequently these discussions lead visitors to compare these practices with Christian rituals. Guided tours often become an occasion for visitors to ask about rumors they have heard about Jewish practices: whether Jews are buried sitting up, for example, or why Jews ate "so much garlic." Visitors often pointed out curiosities to each other.

On one occasion, a guide pointed to the rise in the number of Jewish communities during the mid-eighteenth century, estimating that approximately eight hundred thousand Jews lived in the Polish-Lithuanian Commonwealth at that time. The guide asked the group what they thought the causes of that population increase might be. One woman conjectured that the growth was due to the number of Jews escaping persecution elsewhere and settling in the tolerant First Republic. Another suggested that keeping kosher is more hygienic, which increased life expectancy and population. Yet another mentioned that Jews could divorce easily and quickly, and therefore Jewish men remarried younger women and had more children. In the end, the guide explained that while some of these hypotheses might have played a role, the Jewish population increased primarily because Jews started to live in cities and were therefore more mobile and more likely to be able to escape life-threatening events.

I recount this anecdote to underline how visitors attributed the rise in the Jewish population either to Polish benevolence (Poland as refuge) or to some assumptions about Jewish dietary and matrimonial practices. No one hypothesized that the number of Jews increased because of conversions to Judaism, for example. Likewise, no one offered explanations that could also have been the cause of an increase in the *Polish* population, such as advances in medicine or hygiene that lowered infant mortality and increased life expectancy, or economic growth. Nor was it proposed that the demographic growth could have resulted from decreased violence against Jews. Thus, even in the context of guided discussions among a population of museum visitors evidently interested in Jewish history, hypotheses tended to drift toward exotic or stereotypical arcana rather than to the most obvious reasons, and to conform to the narrative of Polish hospitality, "Paradisus Iudaeorum."

Senses and Sensibilities

Polin's exhibition relies on digital magic and strong visual, aural, and tactile cues to engage the visitors. As Anda Ziembińska-Witek noted in a public roundtable at the museum (April 23, 2015), the Polin Museum is "a spectacle of knowledge," and because of its interactive platforms, it is a "game" into which visitors are drawn.

The re-created synagogue impresses visitors the most. Located in the third gallery ("The Jewish Town"), it is where the visitors most frequently stop, linger, express delighted surprise, and snap photos and selfies (figure 28). The space is constituted by replicas of the bimah and ceiling of the seventeenth-century wooden synagogue in Gwoździec (now in Ukraine), damaged by fire in the First World War and destroyed in the Second World War. It was constructed on the basis of archival photographs, using only traditional methods and tools, and hand-painted with natural pigments by volunteer artists and students from Poland and the United States.[24] For most Polish visitors, the reconstruction is their first glimpse of a synagogue interior, and they comment on what they perceive as different, unique, or, more rarely, similar to sacred structures already familiar to them. Many visitors lament that they never had the opportunity to visit a "real" synagogue, or they tell stories of what happened to the synagogue in their own town. This display, a midpoint in the core exhibition, plays a pivotal role in imparting lost Jewish heritage. "Even though it's not an authentic monument, [even if] it's re-created, it creates a wonderful mood," observed one visitor. During a different visit, a woman in her seventies explained to her daughter that she was very interested in that synagogue because "you know, I'm from Radziwiłłów, [so] we might not have pure blood."[25] These scenes become significant sites where visitors pause and often share stories.

The shtetl marketplace, with its stand displaying fish, goose, and garlic, staples of Jewish cuisine, is another space in the exhibition that stimulates visitors' conversations. The large table at the re-created tavern (*karczma*) is rarely empty; tired visitors sit down and rest, listening attentively to the

24 On the project of construction of the replica, see the fascinating documentary film *Raise the Roof* (2015) by Yari and Cary Wolinsky.

25 Before the Second World War, about half of the population of Radziwiłłów (now in Ukraine) was Jewish. Three things are interesting in the woman's statement: the first is the notion of "pure" blood to refer to the family's origins; the second the invocation of her possibly mixed ancestry as an explanation for her interest in the synagogue; and the third her inclusion of the daughter in this speculation ("so *we* might not have pure blood"). This brief comment exemplifies the strength of the ethnic understanding of national identity in Poland.

FIGURE 28. Replica of the seventeenth-century wooden synagogue from Gwoździec, Polin Museum of the History of Polish Jews. (Photo by Geneviève Zubrzycki, October 28, 2014.)

stories about tavern life and innkeepers, who are major figures in Polish folklore and literature. It was also a fortuitous location for our research team to catch up on note-taking and record passing guests' impressions, and to observe tour groups with guides padding through. Guides typically explain that Jews collected rent from peasants on behalf of lords and served them alcohol at the inn, which led to the stereotype of the Jew as a perverting influence. Jankiel, the Jewish character in Adam Mickiewicz's national epic *Pan Tadeusz*, was sometimes evoked as a counterexample, that of the patriotic innkeeper.[26] The character of Jankiel reminded many visitors of fragments of the epic they had once learned by heart at school: "Many men played the dulcimer; / With Jankiel present, though, no one would dare" (2018: 414).[27]

---

26 Jankiel was a "good Jew": he spoke Polish flawlessly, knew dozens of Polish patriotic songs, and was involved in the national fight for independence.

27 Translation from Bill Johnston. The original is "Było cymbalistów wielu, ale żaden z nich nie śmiał zagrać przy Jankielu." This is a nice example of synesthesia, the "transposition of sensory images or sensory attributes from one modality to another" that "express . . . a relationship between features of experience that properly belong to different senses" (Marks

Farther along, in the gallery devoted to the interwar period, is the "Jewish street," a replica of a narrow, cobblestoned street with storefronts, a newspaper office, a cinema, a dance hall, and a café. Visitors can step into the newspaper office and learn about interwar politics, enter the dance hall and try a few dance steps, listen to popular songs from the period, and watch movies in Yiddish at the cinema. When asked to choose which of these exhibitions they most wanted their guide to speak about at greater length, groups nearly always opted for the cultural ones.[28]

In one postvisit conversation with a family who had visited the exhibition without a guide, the mother and her adult daughter explained why they found these re-created street spaces especially engrossing:

DAUGHTER: The street was great! . . .
MOTHER: It was exquisite. . . . You were transported to that world. . . .
DAUGHTER: And real cobblestone! At the beginning I even wanted to touch it.

At that point the father interjected, "But who walked on those stones? Who drove over them? That's the question."

It is the sensory nature of these spaces that attracts visitors and draws the vanished world close. They can sit at the inn's table; "touch everything," as another visitor remarked; "grab" a newspaper and read the news for a given day, or dance to a jaunty air from a given year. That physical connection is important. It increases the shock of what is literally just around the corner: the Holocaust gallery. And this is what the father hinted at with his poignant questions.

By the time the visitor enters the cramped and dark Holocaust gallery—a spatial arrangement meant to summon feelings of confusion and anxiety, as a faint evocation of the emotions generated by confinement in the overcrowded ghettos—she has, in theory, gained a sense of the variety of worlds that were annihilated during the Second World War and the challenges of rebuilding Jewish lives in postwar Poland. The claustrophobic proximity to history is crucial in the Holocaust gallery. One wall displays, in alphabetical order, the names of towns where ghettos were created.

2014: 8,1). In this case, standing in the tavern and hearing of Jewish innkeepers brought back to memory verses learned in school.

28 The café represented on the Jewish street is the famous Mała Ziemiańska Café, where Warsaw's artists, actors, and writers gathered. Visitors can hear the Polish Jewish authors Julian Tuwim and Antoni Słonimski in a playful simulated discussion. On café life in Central Europe, see Shachar Pinkser's *A Rich Brew: How Cafés Created Modern Jewish Culture* (2018).

Though some visitors rush through that gallery for reasons hypothesized previously, most of those we observed sought out their own towns, places where they had family, and locales they knew and had visited. Many were shocked to learn that ghettos existed in those places during the war and expressed dismay that they were ignorant of the full histories of even their intimately known worlds.

For some Polish Jewish visitors, the Jewish street and the Holocaust gallery are far more than reconstructions or pedagogical adventures, however innovative. The sites depicted and the historical events described are part of their personal experience and family history. For some survivors and their families, these spaces can reignite trauma, but they also serve to validate their personal, familial, or communal experiences.[29] On one afternoon, an elegant elderly couple speaking English to each other examined the interwar gallery with rare attention to detail. When they moved on to the Holocaust gallery and reached the section marked with the names of the streets from which Jews were taken to the *Umschlagplatz* during the Warsaw Ghetto's liquidation, the elderly gentleman read aloud, his voice breaking: "Twarda, Żelazna, Ciemna, Grzybowska."[30] "All these streets," he continued in Polish, weeping. "I know them . . . our streets." His companion took his hand, repeating softly "I know" in English, and then, switching to Polish, "I know, I know."

If some sections of the exhibition can be traumatic, some Jewish visitors from abroad nevertheless describe visiting the museum as redemptive. The space rekindles past relationships to people and places, and may even hold out the prospect of some reconciliation with Poland. During the opening festivities, invited guests were able to visit the exhibition between special events with relative privacy. I encountered an older couple and overheard the husband tell his wife, in Polish: "Look at this. . . . Who would have ever thought we'd see this in our lifetime. . . . That our world would be on display, and that we'd be back after so many years, as guests of honor! Look! There's that traditional wedding you always wanted and never had. Let's ask this lady to snap a picture of us." It was clearly a deeply moving experience for this couple, born shortly before or during the war,

---

29 For that reason, the exhibition offers a shortcut allowing visitors to bypass the Holocaust gallery. The museum also indicates on its website that the Holocaust gallery is not recommended for children under twelve.

30 This is a German term denoting a collection point where Jews were assembled to be deported to the death camps. The largest such site was in Warsaw, next to the ghetto. During Operation Reinhard in 1942, over 250,000 Jews passed through Warsaw's *Umschlagplatz* on their way to Treblinka where they were murdered.

raised in Poland, and still speaking Polish together even after a long time away from the land of their youth.

For members of the 1968 generation who were expelled from Poland as young adults, the postwar gallery is especially intriguing. This cohort pauses to watch a speech by First Secretary Władysław Gomułka and archival footage of the student protests of March 1968 and its aftermath on small television screens. Some visitors scan the screens avidly, looking for fleeting images of themselves, their friends, and their family. On one afternoon, a group of three women and two men, who appeared to be in their late sixties, were scrutinizing photographs when one of the men identified several acquaintances: "Oh, there's this guy who was a [student] leader from Łódź, and another one from Wrocław!" One of the women insisted on taking a picture of him as he gazed at the photos: "Come," she insisted, "You'll have it"—a photo trace of past negatives of yet other pasts, a memento of the encounter with his past at the museum. A bit farther along, another man from the group found a list of belongings deportees carried with them, which they had to declare to the authorities, and exclaimed, "Oh, our documents!" The woman who had taken the photograph apparently had not gone through the same experience, because she asked him, bewildered, "And you had to list *everything*?" "Yes," he replied, "Yes, underwear, socks. . . ."

Toward the end of the section of the postwar gallery, the group commented on images of the boat moored in Copenhagen Harbor that served as accommodation for Polish Jewish exiles. The other woman in the group mentioned that she had in her possession "a whole video filmed on that boat," and that perhaps she "should send it to the museum?" The second man, her companion, became distracted and abruptly burst out, "There are our friends!" The woman responded in resigned tones, "Argh, give me a break. These are terrible memories of those days. Let's go." The group walked on to the next room, on the 1980s democratic opposition movement, which sowed the first seeds of the current revival of Jewish communities.

It is to that revival after 1989 that the last gallery is devoted, with contemporary videos featuring members of the Jewish community who explain what being Jewish in Poland today means to them. Most of the visitors we observed—with or without guides—walked through that final section of the exhibition without much more than a quick perusal. By then the story (and the visit) seemed to be essentially over. Guides typically offered some generic concluding statement about the number of Jews currently living in Poland, the Jewish revival, and advertised some museum cultural activities.

Conclusion: Narrative Corrections, Pitfalls, and Civic Horizons

By adopting a *longue durée* approach, the museum strives to make two important correctives to the narratives visitors enter with. The first is addressed to foreign audiences. The core exhibition emphasizes that Poland is not just the graveyard of European Jewry but also the place where it flourished in rich and diverse ecologies. It is the place that saw the birth of important religious and secular movements and significant political projects. As a "Museum of Life," the institution becomes an important tool of national rebranding and cultural diplomacy for the government, regardless of who is in power.

The second corrective is directed to Polish audiences. It undermines the dominant mythology of Poland's intrinsic religious and ethnonational homogeneity. By emphasizing that Poland was the place where Jews dwelled for a thousand years, the museum highlights that the current demographic makeup of Poland is the exception rather than the rule in Polish history.

To be sure, this is a significant intervention. Yet in its transmission to Poles, and the frameworks through which it is interpreted, it risks turning into a romantic view of Poland's multicultural past. For two thematic strands are intertwined in the museum's master narrative: that of Polish hospitality, and that of a millennium of Jewish presence on Polish lands, made possible by that hospitality. That "mostly peaceful coexistence," as President Komorowski described it at the museum's opening ceremony, was disrupted only when Poland was subjugated to foreign powers. The structure of that narrative reinforces the common belief that Poland was a generous "host" and Jews the beneficiary "guests"—despite their having lived "on Polish lands" for centuries.[31]

Poland/Polin, in that telling, is recast as a promised land, a gift from God, as recounted in the legend that starts the exhibition. According to Joanna Tokarska-Bakir, the museum thus participates in a process of rebranding Poland to foreign audiences, at the cost of a potentially deleterious impact on *Polish* knowledge—since, she argues, that rebranding is a "self-colonizing operation that will lead to less self-reflection on Poland's past on the part of its citizens." She continues: "Unlike some of the German museums, Polin does not require the audience to reflect upon difficult issues. Instead of being thought-provoking, the Museum tells a

---

31 An extension of that narrative is often expressed in the antisemitic trope of the "ungrateful Jews."

self-complacent tale of a colorful past life and the pitiful and somewhat incomprehensible 'disappearance' of Jews from Poland" (2016: 55).

Another critique comes from Konrad Matyjaszek, who asserts that both the museum's architectural form and the exhibition's content erase the very materiality and history of the actual site on which the building stands (2016: 70). The descent down a large, bright stairway to the basement where the exhibition is located, for example, makes no reference to the layers of rubble buried behind the walls. In the museum's sand-colored, womb-like interior, the visitor does not "confront the ruin of modernity but rather bypasses it" (89). That architectural and curatorial choice, he argues, provides more stable ground on which to build a nostalgic dream of Poland's multicultural past, a process he calls "the Polinization of Jewish history" (74).

These incisive critiques raise important questions of another order: Why *should* violence and death be the prism through which Jewish history is presented, and why should the museum serve as a space in which Poles confront their history? And why do others prefer to turn away from that violence and emphasize Polish hospitality and peaceful coexistence instead? The answer to these questions resides in what is considered the national interest. James Edward Young, in his comparative study of Holocaust memory (1993), has shown that the history of the Second World War was narrated and commemorated everywhere in accordance with specific national myths and state imperatives. In a different context, Diana Pinto (1996) argued that Jewish spaces in 1990s Europe provided the occasion for different nations to work through their national histories. In the United States, one might consider the four hundredth anniversary of the beginning of American slavery as such an occasion, and the 1619 Project as a space where the US and its values, institutions, and policies have been debated.[32] The Polin Museum, then, serves as a battleground for Poles with different visions of what Poland was and should be. This is

---

32 The 1619 Project was initiated by the *New York Times Magazine* in August 2019 with the objective of "reframing the country's history by placing the consequences of slavery at the very center of our national narrative" (https://www.nytimes.com/interactive/2019/08/14 /magazine/1619-america-slavery.html). The project garnered strong interest and support from the public, but also generated some debate within academia as well as vehement opposition from political conservatives. Some African American leaders refuted the 1619 Project and proposed instead 1776 Unites, "a movement to liberate tens of millions of Americans . . . by helping them become agents of their own uplift and transformation, by embracing the true founding values of our country" (https://1776unites.com/). For a summary of the historians' debate, see https://www.theatlantic.com/ideas/archive/2019/12 /historians-clash-1619-project/604093.

why the harshest criticisms of the museum's exhibition were articulated in Poland, and why the Law and Justice government fought very hard to remove the museum director, Dariusz Stola (who was not complying with their politics of history).

The Polin Museum faces enormous political pressure in addition to being presented with a challenging pedagogical mission—telling a set of rich and complex histories to domestic and foreign audiences of various ages and with wildly varying levels of knowledge of both Polish and Polish Jewish history. The museum is keenly aware of its dual mission of serving both domestic and foreign audiences, and the need to pitch the core exhibition differently to each. The Polish-language introduction to the core exhibition on the museum's website addresses the Polish visitor directly:

> We invite you on a journey through a thousand years of history of Polish Jews. Along the way, you'll find stories about kings, discoveries, thinkers and industrialists. You'll [learn about] Jewish holidays, customs, religion and culture. About love, friendship, sacrifice and fighting. About the lives of those known from chronicles and newspapers and of those who were known on the streets of Jewish districts.

The tone is light. The exhibition is presented as an adventure; a saga of encounter and intrigue, promising to reveal to Poles what for most remains a mystery—Jews' customs, religion, and culture—even after a thousand years of coexistence. Farther down the page, in a larger font, the potential Polish visitor is again addressed in the second person:

> You will get answers to the [following] questions: When and under what circumstances did the first Jews appear in Poland? How did our country become the center of the Jewish diaspora and the home of the largest Jewish community in the world? How did it cease to be that home, and how is Jewish life being revived?

On the English version of the page, addressed to foreign audiences, this latter paragraph becomes the opening text. The next paragraph hints at the darker turn to come:

> We present 1000 years of Polish-Jewish coexistence, speaking of cooperation, rivalry and conflicts, autonomy, integration and assimilation.

While seeking to confront thorny issues, we also bring attention to bright chapters in our common history.[33]

Both versions accurately describe the exhibition. The difference is in what the museum assumes the Polish and foreign audiences hope to find in it. What will convince them to visit, and even return? The "average" Polish visitor we observed was, as the curators anticipated, most interested in the origins of Jewish settlements on Polish lands; in Polish Jews' religious beliefs and customs; in famous industrialists and literary characters; in poets and writers. The main goal with regard to Polish visitors is to impart knowledge about Polish Jews and Poland's Jewish past. The museum fulfills that objective. The museum also addresses so-called difficult topics in Polish-Jewish relations, although those topics neither drive the core exhibition's main narrative arc nor constitute its primary pedagogical goal.

The challenge for any museum is that it does not control how its message is received. The specific challenge for the Polin Museum is that it exists in physical, cultural, and political contexts that affect the reception of its exhibition. In the immediate vicinity of the museum are located the Monument to the Ghetto Heroes; the Tree of Memory, dedicated in 1988 to the "shared memory of Polish Jews murdered between 1939–1945 by the Hitlerite invader, and to the Poles who died helping Jews"; and the Irena Sendler Alley, dotted with monuments to the Polish Righteous. Behind the museum is the Willy Brandt Square, with its monument recalling the German chancellor's acknowledgment of German guilt for the Holocaust. Taken together, these sites convey a narrative of centuries of Jewish life on Polish lands, its destruction by the Nazis, and the rescue of Jews by Poles. Hence the nickname given to it by the cultural critic Elżbieta Janicka (2015)—"the Square of Polish Innocence"—and the vigorous opposition of many Poles (Jewish and non-Jewish) to the project of yet another Monument to the Polish Righteous in the vicinity of the museum.[34]

---

33 https://www.polin.pl/en/exhibitions/core-exhibition.

34 In 2013, the Polish-born Jewish American philanthropist Zygmunt Rolat established the Memory and the Future Foundation (*Fundacja Pamięć i Przyszłość*) to promote the memory of survivors and those who saved them during the Second World War. The foundation board was composed of representatives of Jewish organizations in Poland, the United States, France, and Israel, and intended to fund a monument commemorating Poles who saved Jews, to be erected in the vicinity of the Polin Museum (https://www.facebook.com/fundacjapip). The planned location of the monument generated strong opposition from members of the Polish Jewish community in Poland and abroad, as well as from Jewish organizations in Poland. The authors of a widely circulated petition wrote that the former ghetto is "a place sanctified by blood and the martyrdom of hundreds of thousands of Jews who died there of hunger and

When we expand the geographic context of the museum to Warsaw and its other memorials and museums, or to Poland as a whole, the picture becomes even more complex. Despite efforts to signpost important sites of the Holocaust in Warsaw and elsewhere in Poland, as I discussed in chapter 2, new monuments and museums promoting Polish martyrdom have mushroomed over the past two decades in an effort to reinforce the Polish martyrological narrative. The Museum of the 1944 Warsaw Uprising, opened in 2004, is a case in point. Created by Lech Kaczyński, then mayor of Warsaw and the future president of Poland, the museum was the first project carried out by the Law and Justice Party under the mandate of its new historical policy. For years the topic of the Warsaw Uprising was taboo because it was ideologically inconvenient under state socialism: the uprising, which lasted sixty-three days, was led by the anticommunist Home Army. The Soviet army was stationed just across the Vistula River but did not intervene. Approximately sixteen thousand members of the Polish resistance were killed, and up to 150,000 Polish civilians died during the uprising (Snyder 2010: 308).[35]

In the face of Soviet passivity, and because the members of the Home Army were considered enemies of the new regime, official commemoration of the uprising was strictly controlled during the socialist period (Sawicki 2005). This does not mean that the memory of the events disappeared: it retreated underground, preserved in personal stories of surviving participants and their families, and disseminated through samizdat productions and graffiti of the uprising's symbol (PW for *Polska walcząca*, "Poland fighting").

The 1944 Warsaw Uprising Museum was therefore explicitly built to counter the imposed silence under socialism, to rehabilitate the uprising, and to officially commemorate it, a process initiated with the unveiling of a monument on the forty-fifth anniversary of the uprising on August 1, 1989.

---

disease, and from where they were transported to their death in the gas chambers of Treblinka. It is also where, in April and May 1943, Jews died in their last, terrifyingly lonely fight against the Germans. The site symbolically remembers the martyrdom of three million Polish Jews." A monument to Poles who saved Jews at that specific site, they wrote, "would inevitably be read as a polemical addition to the museum, as a 'Polish supplement' to the 'Jewish' story which would de facto act as a negation of the museum's main idea" (https://www.otwarta .org/list-otwarty-w-sprawie-lokalizacji-pomnika-sprawiedliwych-polakow-srodowiska -centrum-badan-nad-zaglada-zydow).

35 During the urban combat, approximately 25 percent of Warsaw's buildings were destroyed. Following the surrender of Polish forces, German troops systematically leveled another 35 percent of the city, block by block. Together with damage suffered in the 1939 invasion of Poland and the Warsaw Ghetto Uprising in 1943, this meant that over 85 percent of the city was destroyed during the war.

The museum, which opened its doors on the sixtieth anniversary of the outbreak of fighting in Warsaw, includes a memorial and a chapel. As a memorial and ritual venue, it honors those who fought, and it also serves as a site of state pedagogy that aims to socialize a new generation of Poles to the narrative of sacrifice for the nation.[36] Since its opening the museum has been visited by almost 3.5 million, including over 150,000 schoolchildren and students participating in museum workshops on the uprising.

Today, then, schoolchildren visiting the capital might visit the 1944 Uprising Museum on one day and the Polin Museum on the next. On the way, they would pass the myriad markers to Polish martyrs and some tributes to the Righteous Poles who saved Jews.[37] On a field trip to Kraków, they might visit the Auschwitz-Birkenau Museum in the morning and an exhibition on life in Kraków's Ghetto, housed in the Righteous Tadeusz Pankiewicz's Eagle Pharmacy Museum, in the afternoon. The following day, on their way home, their bus might pause at the Ulma Family Museum of Poles Saving Jews in World War II, opened in 2016 in the village of Markowa near Rzeszów in southeastern Poland. That museum tells the story of a couple and their six children who were executed by Nazis for hiding Jews in their home. Józef and Wiktoria Ulma were recognized as Righteous Among the Nations by Yad Vashem in 2005. The beatification of the entire family is under consideration at the Vatican. President Andrzej Duda was present at the ceremonial inauguration of the museum, which was broadcast live in Polish consulates across the globe in a massive public relations push (Wóycicka 2019).

My point here is not that Poles who saved Jews are not important or that their actions should not be celebrated. Rather, it is to underline that as a result of this proliferation of sites of memory, the museological field

---

36 Like the Polin Museum and the Schindler's Enamel Factory Museum, this is a narrative museum. Its collection was created by appealing to the local population to donate mementos. Thirty thousand artifacts were donated, of which nearly one thousand are presented on the exhibition area of 3,000 m². For an incisive analysis of the museum and the mnemonic activity around the uprising in the 2000s, see Napiórkowski (2016); for a study of the complex politics of memory of the Second World War in Poland, see Wawrzyniak (2015).

37 Consider, for example, the commemorative plaque honoring Jan Żabiński, the Warsaw zookeeper, and his wife, Antonina, who hid Jews in the zoo during the occupation. Or the three plaques affixed to different buildings where Irena Sendler lived or worked in Warsaw, in addition to the alley named in her honor close to the Polin Museum. Many streets and schools throughout Poland also now bear Sendler's name. In 2009, a commemorative coin was minted bearing images of Irena Sendler and two other Polish Righteous, Catholic nun Matylda Getter and Zofia Kossak. All three worked with Żegota, an underground organization helping Jews during the war, and the year 2018 was officially dedicated to Sendler's memory by the Polish parliament. A commemorative postage stamp was issued for the occasion.

in which Polin operates potentially skews the ways its core exhibition might be received by Polish visitors. Different memorial enterprises and entrepreneurs compete with each other for the control of collective memory and Polish identity. When the mnemonic field and the objectives of the state coalesce, causing their themes to converge around the tropes of Polish generosity, heroism, and martyrdom, they form tenacious strands of narrative that are difficult to counter.

The Polin Museum addresses this challenge by expanding its mission well beyond the walls of its core exhibition with extensive public offerings, educational programs, and publications on antisemitism, xenophobia, and discrimination. The everyday practices of ordinary citizens also play a significant role, as we will see in the next chapter.

PART TWO

Recovering Jewishness for a Better Polish Future

CHAPTER 5

"With One Color, We Cannot See"

MULTICULTURAL DREAMS AND REGISTERS OF ENGAGEMENT

Fantasies of the past determined by needs of the present
have a direct impact on realities of the future.

—Svetlana Boym, *The Future of Nostalgia*

With one religion, we cannot listen
With one color, we cannot see
With one culture, we cannot feel
Without you, we cannot even remember
Without you, we remain locked away in the past
With you, a future will open before us.

—Sławomir Sierakowski in Yael Bartana's *Nightmares*

In her short film *Nightmares* (2007), the Israeli visual artist Yael Bartana showcased Sławomir Sierakowski, a Polish public intellectual and founding member of the leftist collective *Krytyka Polityczna*, imploring Jews to "come back to Poland, [their] country."[1] Sierakowski, dressed as a 1950s politician, is standing in the middle of an empty Warsaw stadium overrun by weeds, declaiming a forceful speech:[2]

---

1 *Krytyka Polityczna* was established in 2002 and consists of an online daily, a quarterly magazine, a publishing house, and cultural centers in Warsaw, Gdańsk, and Cieszyn (https://krytyka-polityczna.pl/o-nas/eng/). The idea for *Nightmares* came about after Bartana's first visit to Poland, when she discovered a Białystok very different from the one she knew from family stories. After experiencing the shock of finding no Jewish traces, she sought to understand what that absence might mean to Poles. She enlisted Sierakowski and Kinga Dunin, whom she met at *Krytyka Polityczna*, to express the new Polish Left's feelings about Polish-Jewish relations (interviews with Sławomir Sierakowski, Warsaw, September 26, 2012, and Yael Bartana, Berlin, January 17, 2013).

2 The Stadium of the Tenth Anniversary (*Stadion Dziesięciolecia*) was built in 1955 to commemorate the end of the Second World War. It was largely constructed with rubble from the

Jews! Compatriots! People! . . .

You think the old lady who still sleeps under Rivka's quilt doesn't want to see you? That she has forgotten about you? You're wrong. She dreams about you every night . . . and trembles with fear. Since the night you were gone and her mother reached for your quilt, she's had nightmares. Only *you* can chase them away. Let the three million Jews that have been missing from Poland return, stand by her bed, and finally chase away the demons. Come back to Poland, to your and our country!

Rivka's quilt is a metonym for Jewish property stolen by non-Jewish Poles after their neighbors were forcibly relocated to ghettos or murdered.[3] Sierakowski alludes to the nightmares arising from guilt over the use of this stolen property. He asks Jews to return, to "stand by the old woman's bed, lay [their] hands on that old quilt, now thin as a sheet, and tell her: 'We give it to you. What use would we make of it now? There's not even down left in it, only pain. Heal our wounds, and you'll heal yours.'" Those invisible wounds left by the unacknowledged guilt can be healed only by Jews forgiving Poles.

Sierakowski continues with a soft mea culpa and a lament over Poland's national homogeneity:

When you disappeared, we were secretly happy. We kept saying "At last we are home by ourselves. Polish Poles in Poland, no one to bother us." And because we were still unhappy, once in a while we managed to find some Jew to kick out of our country. Even when it was clear that there weren't any of you here, there still were some people who managed to kick you out. And what? Today, it is with boredom that we watch our faces, all similar to each other . . . and today we know that

---

Warsaw Uprising of 1944. After 1989 it became Europe's largest open-air market, where one could buy anything from Soviet army uniforms, cameras, and watches to fake French perfume, pirated American videocassettes, caviar, exotic spices, and cheap household items. It was certainly the most cosmopolitan space per square foot in Poland at the time. It was demolished in 2008 to make way for a new stadium for the 2012 Euro Cup.

3 There exists an adjective in Polish to describe property formerly owned by Jews: *mienie pożydowskie*, literally property "after Jews," sometimes translated as "post-Jewish" or "formerly Jewish." A similar term refers to property formerly owned by Germans who were forcibly relocated after Poland gained Silesia and Pomerania in the postwar settlement—*mienie poniemieckie*. On the plundering of Jewish property during the war and its aftermath, see Gross and Grudzińska-Gross (2011), Grabowski and Libionka (2014), Dobrosielski (2017a), Matyjaszek (2019). See also the films *Aftermath* (by Władysław Pasikowski, 2012) and *Ida* (by Paweł Pawlikowski, 2013). In both films the theft of Jewish property is an open secret that leads to tragic outcomes.

we can't live on our own, that we need the Other, and there isn't an Other that is closer to us than you. Come live here! Changed, but the same! Let's live together!

Acknowledging traditional as well as magical antisemitism is the first and essential step in exorcising old demons. Yet the ultimate goal of this appeal is the utopian recreation of multiculturalism. Only through the "return" of Jews to Poland might Poles be saved from the dour monotony of the ethnically homogeneous society in which they live. In an allusion to the cinematography of Leni Riefenstahl, Bartana's camera pans the similar faces of blond scouts while Sierakowski speaks the words "It is with boredom that we watch our faces, all similar to each other." In the scene immediately preceding this one, the scouts are shown stenciling the call "3,000,000 Jews can change the life of 40,000,000 Poles" on the stadium green.

Bartana went on to imagine what might happen if Jews did indeed "return" to Poland. In *Wall and Tower* (2009), she tells the story of the fictional Kibbutz Muranów, founded by young Israelis building a new life on the site of the former Warsaw Ghetto.[4] In *Assassination* (2011), the third film of the trilogy *And Europe Will Be Stunned*, Sierakowski's character, now the leader of a multicultural Poland, is murdered. The movement solidifies around the martyr's death.[5] Together, Bartana's films present a critical commentary on the nostalgia-infused, multicultural Poland the new Left desires, while at the same time knowingly participating in that political fantasy.[6]

4 While the Polish viewer contemplates what that Jewish presence might mean for Poland, an Israeli might contemplate what the departure of three million Jewish Israelis might mean for Israel and for the "Palestinian question" (interview with Yael Bartana, Berlin, January 17, 2013).

5 The story of this third film is evocative of the assassination, in 1922, of Poland's first democratically elected president, Gabriel Narutowicz, following rumors and conspiracy theories that he was a Jew (see Brykczynski 2016).

6 Sierakowski wrote the monologue with sociologist Kinga Dunin and told me in a conversation that they "truly, genuinely meant" what his character expressed. And that is the tension the film so poignantly captures (Warsaw, September 26, 2012). *And Europe Will Be Stunned* was expanded through the creation of a "real" (i.e., noncinematographic) movement, known as the Jewish Renaissance Movement in Poland. Further blurring the line between art and politics, and between fiction and reality, the movement/art project was replete with a manifesto, publications (Cichocki and Eilat 2011), congresses, delegates, and supporters advocating for the return of Jews to Poland and human rights more broadly. *And Europe Will Be Stunned* was selected by the Ministry of Culture, led by the Civic Platform Party, to represent Poland at the 2011 Venice Biennale, making Bartana the first non-Pole to represent Poland at this prestigious event. For an analysis of these different aspects of the project and a discussion of other

The key point here is that the creation of a multicultural Poland is imagined not with the small but visible community of Vietnamese who now constitute the largest ethnic minority in Warsaw; nor through Silesians, Poland's largest ethnonational minority; nor Ukrainians, the country's largest immigrant group; nor through the welcoming of Syrian or Afghani refugees. A multicultural Poland is imagined through *Jews*—"real, living ones" whom Sierakowski invites to return to Poland, or long-gone ones, like Rivka, whose ghosts Poles attempt to exorcise. A multicultural Poland is created by and made possible solely in and through Jews, the "Other" Sierakowski identifies as closest to Poles.

Svetlana Boym defines "restorative" nostalgia as a longing for a lost home and the desire to recover or rebuild it. That is why it is most often evoked in religious or nationalist revivals. The nostalgia is both prospective and prescriptive. At the very least, it is aspirational. Polish nostalgia for Jews is about what many Poles believe Poland should be. Whereas in previous chapters I focused on backward-looking mnemonic discourses and material practices that highlight Jewish absence, in this chapter I turn to various cultural initiatives, projects, and practices of individuals and organizations focused on "resurrecting" Jewish culture to save Poland from its bland homogeneity. I show that the cultural-appropriation paradigm is inadequate to capture the variety of processes at play in Poland's Jewish turn and propose instead a typology of "registers of engagement" with Jewish culture.

Producing, Performing, and Consuming Jewish Culture

Kraków's Jewish Culture Festival

For over three decades, Kraków's Jewish Culture Festival has been devoted to the revival of Jewish culture in Poland.[7] It has contributed to the renewal of the city's Jewish Quarter, Kazimierz (Murzyn 2004). Founded in 1988 as a modest, two-day, local affair consisting primarily of films and lectures with limited public appeal, it has grown enormously in both size and stature and now has an international reputation.[8] Under the patron-

---

artistic, performative, and participatory memory works in contemporary Poland, see Lehrer and Waligórska (2013).

7 For a discussion of the festival's role in Poland, see Gruber (2002); for a detailed history, see Dodziuk (2010).

8 In 2012, for example, the festival was invited by the Polish embassy in Belgium to represent Polish cultural achievements there. An exhibition about the festival was organized in

age of the president of the Republic of Poland since 2001, the festival now lasts ten days and is attended by some thirty thousand people from Poland and abroad. Between fifteen thousand and twenty thousand people attend its closing-night open-air concert, titled "Shalom on Szeroka Street," which is also televised nationwide.[9]

The festival is sometimes portrayed in the West as a kitsch Disneyland, and Kazimierz as a Potemkin village (figure 29).[10] Such criticisms overlook the fact that the festival not only allows non-Jewish Poles to learn about different facets of Jewish culture but also offers a safe space in which Poles who are rediscovering their Jewishness can acquaint themselves with some of its cultural forms. It also provides the occasion for Jews from across Poland to gather for symposiums, book releases, reunions, and celebrations. The festival is a significant space where Jewishness is performed and celebrated at multiple levels. My encounters and conversations with Polish and non-Polish, Jewish and non-Jewish festival participants, Jewish community members and activists, tour guides, and volunteers illuminated some of the varied meanings that these practices have for ordinary visitors.

Having participated in the festival in the 1990s and early 2000s, when the program was much leaner and primarily focused on music, film, and theater, I was struck by how dramatically it had expanded by 2010, when I embarked on this book project. The number of events on its program had almost tripled, and twice as many workshops and four times more lectures and symposiums were offered than ten years earlier (graph 2).

To be sure, the fact that the festival was celebrating its twentieth anniversary in 2010 in part accounts for the record number of events that year. But, as depicted in graph 3, the number of events that year reflects the general growth trajectory of the festival. From 2010 to 2019 the festival offered on average 150 events on its main program, nearly three times more than in the 1990s. In the years 2011–19 an additional one hundred events, on average, were offered by partner organizations.

---

the embassy's foyer, but the main event was a public conversation with Janusz Makuch, the festival's cofounder and director, with a concert by the Kraków klezmer band Bester Quartet.

9 From published and unpublished reports, Jewish Culture Festival in Kraków. I'm grateful to Janusz Makuch and Robert Gądek for providing me with data on events and attendance.

10 See, for example, the *New York Review of Books* blog of Shelley Salamansky, "Disney Diasporas" (http://www.nybooks.com/blogs/nyrblog/2011/dec/23/diaspora-disneys); or the *New York Times* travel report on Jewish communities around the world, in which the author praises Kraków's revival of Jewish culture while remarking that the old Jewish Quarter "is a bit of a Disney World experience" (http://www.nytimes.com/2014/09/21/travel/exploring-the-worlds-jewish -communities.html?_r=0).

FIGURE 29. Customers have drinks outside *Dawno temu na Kazimierzu* (Once upon a Time in Kazimierz), a restaurant, bar, and klezmer club in Kraków's Kazimierz neighborhood. Its front reproduces interwar signs advertising a grocery store, a carpentry shop, and a tailor's atelier, producing an impression akin to a Potemkin village or Disneyland's Main Street. Its interior is decorated in the style of a late nineteenth-century bourgeois home. On its website, the club explains that "Kazimierz was originally a town in its own right. Over the years, it was gradually absorbed into the city of Krakow becoming [a] district [where] two communities, Polish and Jewish, once lived side by side. Those two communities differed in just about everything: language, customs, creed and culture. And yet like all good neighbours, they mingled together, worked alongside one another, day in and day out. This is what kept them so close to each other. All barriers between them appeared to just disappear and melt away" (http://en.szeroka1.com). (Photo by Geneviève Zubrzycki, July 6, 2014.)

As graph 2 shows, the festival grew rapidly following Poland's entry into the EU in 2004. By 2006, it was twice as large as four years earlier. From 2000 to 2009, the number of lectures, symposiums, workshops, and tours increased, shifting the festival's emphasis from the arts to pedagogy.[11] By the second decade of the twenty-first century, 70 percent of the events on the festival's main program were educational in nature.

11 Popular tours include "Kraków's Famous Rabbis," "Jewish Women's Kraków," "Jewish Cemeteries," "the Jewish Ghetto," and "Jewish Synagogues." Many are conducted by historians and Jewish studies scholars.

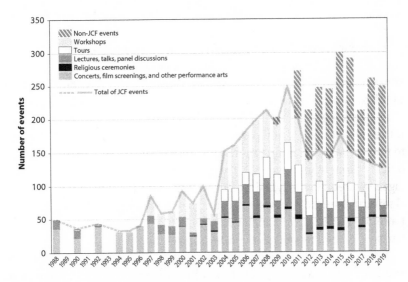

GRAPH 2. Kraków's Jewish Culture Festival: Events by Type, 1988–2019.
Source: Jewish Culture Festival in Kraków. Data for 1988–2009 are based on unpublished archival documents provided by the festival's administration. Data for 2010–19 were compiled from the festival's reports available on the festival's website. The festival was not held in 1989, and in 1991 a shorter event, Days of Jewish Kazimierz (*Dni Żydowskiego Kazimierza*), was organized. Like the preceding festivals, it featured concerts, tours, and lectures, but the details of the specific events are not available. The 1993 Days of Jewish Kazimierz was canceled (personal communication, Robert Gądek, deputy director of the JCF). "Non-JCF events" were organized by partner institutions such as the Jewish Community Centre in Kraków.

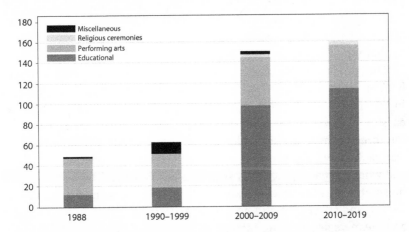

GRAPH 3. Kraków's Jewish Culture Festival: Average Number of Events per Year by Type, 1988–2019.
Source: Jewish Culture Festival in Kraków. Data for 1988–2009 are based on unpublished archival documents provided by the festival's administration. Data for 2010–19 were compiled from the festival's reports, available on the festival's website. The graphs include only events on the main program of the Jewish Culture Festival and not those organized by partner organizations during the festival (see graph 2). The festival was not held in 1989. As the 1991 "Days of Jewish Kazimierz" was unusually small and the 1993 edition was canceled, they are not included in the calculation of the annual average.

I conducted participant observation at the festival in 2010, 2014, and 2015, attending lectures, walking tours, and workshops during the day and concerts in the evening.[12] In 2010 I enrolled in a five-day minicourse on Yiddish. I was curious to see who would face an early-morning workshop after a late night out at the festival, especially since the payoff seemed rather meager. What could one hope to learn in five sessions? I arrived to find there was standing room only in the classroom. Extra chairs were quickly brought in (figure 30). The group mostly consisted of young adults (aged eighteen to thirty). Although more women than men were enrolled, significantly more men were present than in other specialized workshops I attended. Participants included a mix of locals and visitors from other parts of Poland, as well as a couple of foreigners.

What motivated these individuals to get up early, sit in a classroom, and learn the Yiddish alphabet on a beautiful summer day? Some were there to gain an impression of what Yiddish sounded like, as one young woman told me, using the past tense (*jak to brzmiało*). A small group of friends who knew some Hebrew were curious to see how much of that language was integrated into Yiddish. Another couple was eager to learn just enough to figure out whether some family documents they had found were written in Hebrew or Yiddish, and to find someone to help translate them. Others had enrolled to hear singing by the Makosz sisters, local performers, and learn some songs from their repertoire. As the days went by, many questions were broached about the mutual influence of Polish and Yiddish, and the class became as much about Jewish culture in Poland as about the Yiddish language per se.

The Jewish-cooking workshop held at Hotel Eden was equally popular. The room was packed, with people standing in the back and wedged in the doorways. I expected instruction in cooking, or perhaps a discussion of Jewish dishes and how they differ from similar Polish ones. But three of the five sessions led by the charismatic teacher and actress Hanna Kossowska ended up being entirely devoted to the rules of kashrut and what it meant, practically speaking, for cooking. The audience was mesmerized as the teacher explained the need to kosherize cookware, dishes, and silverware and how to do so. She described how to inspect and clean vegetables and instructed attendees to never mix dairy and meat during a meal. Many shook their heads or raised their eyebrows in disbelief when the teacher shared tips on how to ensure meat and dairy are kept apart in the refrigerator (lots of cellophane wrapping), in the dish-

12 For a full discussion of the fieldwork, see the methodological appendix.

FIGURE 30. Yiddish class offered through the Jewish Culture Festival in Kraków, in the JCC's preschool room. (Photo by Geneviève Zubrzycki, June 27, 2010.)

washer, and in kitchen cabinets. Some participants took copious notes and asked frequent questions. All seemed riveted by the teacher's anecdotes of creative problem-solving and of seeking and receiving advice from her rabbi.

What motivated people to attend? Some were there to learn Jewish recipes. Others were there out of curiosity, just to "see what it's all about." A few told me they were there to learn what it might mean for them to "cook Jewish," and perhaps even begin to keep kosher. Two women sitting in front me, sisters or cousins, chatted about their grandmother's cooking habits. "I'm telling you," one told the other, "I'm sure Babcia was Jewish. She was always careful to place meat in the very back of the fridge!"

Year after year the most popular workshops of all, for which it was difficult to obtain tickets, were the dance workshops. Sometimes they were offered in a school gym, at other times on the top floor of the JCC. Part of the class's appeal was its focus on participating more than on learning technique. The papercutting workshop was much quieter: eleven young Polish women and I were provided with patterns and tools to generate a simple papercut based on a traditional Jewish motif. All but me had some experience with Polish papercutting (*wycinanka*), but none were acquainted with the technique, styles, or compositions of the Jewish form. Concentration reigned for ninety minutes, and everyone left the event with extra patterns to practice at home. Walking tours were also very popular, often attended by locals eager to learn about the unknown Jewish history of their town.

The festival also offers two versions of a genealogy workshop: one in English, aimed mostly at North American Jews trying to find information on where their families came from, and the other in Polish, aimed at Poles who are aware that they have Jewish origins but know little about them and want to dig deeper, and at Poles who have some belief—sometimes well-founded, sometimes less so—that they are of Jewish descent and seek confirmation.[13] For the North Americans, the genealogists focus on providing a basic road map for research, explaining what was lost in the war and where one can look for available information. For the Polish groups, the genealogists focus less on the difficulties of finding original documents than on explaining how much effort was expended by Jews during and after the Second World War to conceal their origins—including baptizing children, keeping falsified identity documents, changing their names, intermarrying, and the like. Their first recommendation is therefore to start by interviewing family members, especially the elderly. Were there family rifts? Are there family members residing in Israel, France, Scandinavia, the United States, or Canada? If so, the instructors recommend establishing communication with those family members to learn how *they* tell the family story. Then they advise searching in family photo albums but also in boxes where photos might have been hidden from public view. Pay attention, they say, to the names of individuals identified on the back of photographs and those who might have signed a portrait with a dedication to a loved one. Look for letters, old ID cards, and life histories (*życiorysy*) that were provided to employers and might offer clues about birthplace, whereabouts during the war, and class origins. Of course the genealogists also instruct participants on which archival institutions to consult, but they advise doing so only after undertaking serious detective work to gain purchase on family histories.

In short, Kraków's Jewish Culture Festival has become a core institution in the dissemination of Jewish culture in Poland. It has not only grown in

---

13 I was told on several occasions (as a matter of fact and as gossip) that individuals converting to Judaism, a complex process that requires a great deal of time and effort, often start to look for matrilineal origins that would allow them to bypass the process.

FIGURE 31. Posters advertising the 24th Jewish Culture Festival in Kraków. Here, an Ashkenazi klezmer musician is juxtaposed with a Sephardic/Mizrahi all-women band. The stylized lion was adopted by JCF in 2013, when it rebranded itself with hipper, "offbeat" contemporary music and art forms in addition to its traditional ones like klezmer. (Photo by Geneviève Zubrzycki, June 27, 2014.)

size but also changed its focus over the years, shifting its offerings from narrow elite cultural forms in the early 1990s to more accessible, mostly Ashkenazi entertainment in the early 2000, and then expanding to include lesser-known (in Poland) Jewish cultures (e.g., Sephardic, Yemeni) and less familiar, offbeat musical styles in the 2010s—all while developing its educational mission (figure 31).[14]

Territorial Expansions and Local Variations on a Jewish Theme

The popularity of the Kraków Jewish Culture Festival has prompted the creation of many other festivals. Maps 1–4 show the territorial expansion of a variety of "Jewish Days" and festivals, spread across the country.

14 On the educational impact of the festival, see Kelman (2018).

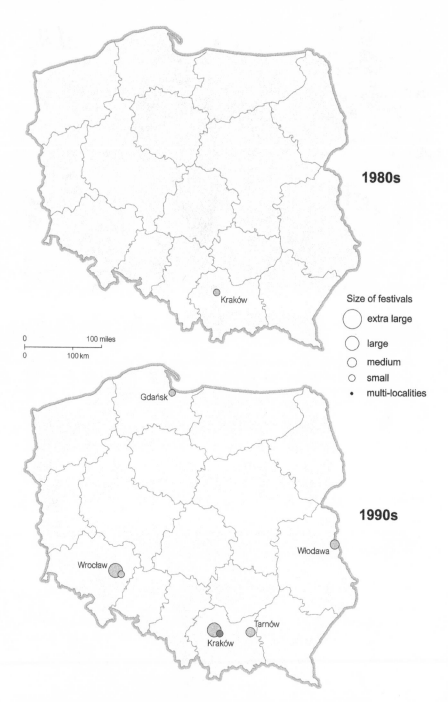

MAPS. Jewish Culture Festivals in Poland, 1988–2019. See appendix C for festival data used for maps. Cartography by Waldemar Spallek.

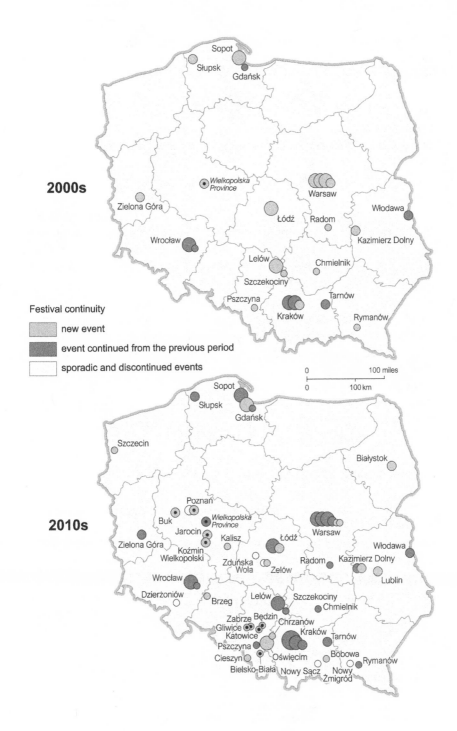

2000s

Sopot
Słupsk
Gdańsk

Wielkopolska Province

Zielona Góra

Warsaw

Łódź   Radom

Włodawa

Wrocław

Kazimierz Dolny

Lelów

Chmielnik

Szczekociny

Pszczyna

Tarnów

Kraków

Rymanów

Festival continuity

new event

event continued from the previous period

sporadic and discontinued events

0   100 miles

0   100 km

Sopot
Słupsk
Gdańsk

Szczecin

Białystok

Poznań

Wielkopolska Province

Buk

Jarocin

Łódź   Warsaw

Zielona Góra

Kalisz

Koźmin Wielkopolski

Włodawa

Zduńska Wola   Zelów

Radom   Kazimierz Dolny

2010s

Wrocław

Lublin

Dzierżoniów

Brzeg   Lelów   Szczekociny

Chmielnik

Zabrze Będzin Chrzanów

Gliwice

Katowice

Kraków

Tarnów

Pszczyna

Cieszyn   Oświęcim

Bobowa

Rymanów

Bielsko-Biała Nowy Sącz

Nowy Żmigród

The expansion accelerated in the 2010s. This is likely due in part to increased interest in Poland's Jewish past following the publication of Jan Gross's *Neighbors* and the debates about it, as well as funding promoting pluralism, diversity, and multiculturalism after Poland's entry into the EU in 2004. While festivals of Jewish culture are more prevalent and important in larger cities, they also occur in smaller towns, where they perform a significant educational function by teaching local populations the forgotten history of their towns and regions. Those festivals are also motivated in part by the hope of developing tourism and putting these towns on the map.[15]

Take, for example, the Jewish festival of Chmielnik, a small town south of Kielce that was 80 percent Jewish before the war. The event is produced locally and addressed primarily to the town's local population. Founded in 2003, the festival Encounters with Jewish Culture initially lasted two to three days. Following the election of a Law and Justice mayor in 2014, the festival was rebaptized the Festival of Cultures, and the Jewish portion shrunk to a single day. The new mayor, Paweł Wójcik, also reorganized the festival so that the Jewish-themed events took place on Saturday and the Polish-themed events on Sunday, with more resources allocated to the latter (Shapiro 2020).

In 2017, when I attended the festival, the Jewish events took place in the small street next to the former synagogue, now a museum, while the Polish events the following day took place in the town's main square. The Polish events included traditional folk and classical polonaise dances as well as demonstrations of noblemen's fighting styles. Accorded a more prominent site and better facilities, and benefiting from a sunny sky, they were much better attended than the Jewish events.[16]

The Jewish-themed events were a mishmash of educational programming and amateur, professional, and street entertainment. The Polin Museum had set up its Museum on Wheels in a building close to the main stage. In addition to the display of photographs of prewar Jewish life, a table with Jewish objects (a menorah, a dreidel, a loaf of challah, a shofar, kippahs, a kiddush cup, and examples of Hebrew letters) served as props for a Warsaw guide to teach about aspects of Judaism and Jewish culture.

15 On festivals of Jewish music in Poland, and how music performances facilitate the articulation of the unspeakable, see Shapiro (2020).

16 Both Shapiro's and Monika Murzyn-Kupisz's (2015) analyses of the Chmielnik festival are based on its earlier years, when the festival lasted longer, offered a fuller program, and involved prominent klezmer musicians and survivors returning to their hometowns. The contrast with the festival I observed could not be sharper.

The room received a steady flow of visitors seeking refuge from the cold wind who, once inside, listened attentively to what the speaker had to say, sometimes asking questions.

Schoolchildren and teens performed Jewish dances and songs on a stage set up on a small street. Overhead a clothesline was slung, with lace tablecloths hung on it to evoke a courtyard (figure 32). A few adults sang solos and acted out folk stories in simple skits for children. Between sets, a gala hosted by town officials recognized local students who had entered art and history contests. The event took place on the second floor of the synagogue-museum, where their work on the theme "Jews, Our Neighbors" was exhibited. Watercolors and papercuts depicted familiar scenes (an old Jew praying, the Western Wall) and motifs (the Star of David, menorahs, animals). Teachers, local dignitaries, and proud parents attended. The winners (seven girls, two boys) received certificates, history books, and an excursion to Brussels.

For most of the day, a young girl posed in a tableau vivant inspired by Aleksander Gierymski's painting *Jewess with Oranges* (1880–81) (figure 33),

FIGURE 32. Inhabitants of Chmielnik wait for festival events to start on a chilly June day. The street is decorated with traditional lace tablecloths to recreate the ambience of a courtyard. The stage is decorated with a menorah and white geese, traditionally associated with Jews. (Photo by Geneviève Zubrzycki, June 17, 2017.)

and teenage boys strolled through the festival area dressed up as traditional Orthodox Jews, with sidelocks and hats. One played a water carrier (figure 34). A photo stand-in board of an Orthodox Jewish family provided additional entertainment to the sparse crowd (figure 35).

The day concluded with a professional performance of the best numbers of *Fiddler on the Roof* (in Polish) at the local theater. In the row in front of me, two teenage girls dressed in their Sunday best held sheets of Hebrew letters and quizzed each other while waiting for the show to start.

A Study in Contrasts

The contrast between the Chmielnik festival's educational program and its organized street entertainment was striking. But it is not uncommon to encounter serious historical and cultural engagement next to the uncritical use of Jewish stereotypes.

FIGURE 33. A boy photographs teenage girls who participated in the program "Jews, Our Neighbors," after the ceremony in which they were awarded a certificate and history books. On the right, a young girl poses in a tableau vivant recreating Aleksander Gierymski's painting *Jewess with Oranges* (ca. 1880). The painting was stolen by German forces during the war and recovered only in 2011. It was restored and displayed at a special exhibition at the National Museum in Warsaw in the spring of 2014. (Photo by Geneviève Zubrzycki, June 17, 2017.)

FIGURE 34. Young man dressed as a traditional Orthodox Jew, with sidelocks and black hat, playing a water carrier. He walked around the festival area greeting spectators and posing for photographs for most of the afternoon. (Photo by Geneviève Zubrzycki, June 17, 2017.)

FIGURE 35. Local women take pictures of their children in a photo stand-in board. (Photo by Geneviève Zubrzycki, June 17, 2017.)

On my first visit to Chmielnik, in June 2014, the tension between the town's aspirations to rediscover its Jewish roots and the apparent lack of self-awareness of its main memory activist posed such a disjuncture. I spent an afternoon with Piotr Krawczyk, the local historian who had worked closely with Mayor Jarosław Zatorski to have Chmielnik's synagogue restored and transformed into a museum, the Świętokrzyski Shtetl.[17] He explained that he had always been interested in Jewish topics, but conceded that the creation of the museum was mostly related to efforts to promote a town that doesn't have much going for itself nowadays: "Some towns have a lake, others a castle. We have a synagogue." An EU grant funded 55 percent of the synagogue's extensive restoration, he told me, and the town and the Polish Ministry of Culture covered the rest. Mr. Krawczyk was extremely proud of that achievement and gave me the "grand tour." He was especially proud of the Plexiglas bimah conceived by Mirosław Nizio, whose architectural firm also designed the Polin Museum's core exhibition and the Museum of the Warsaw Uprising. He

17 The museum is named after the Świętokrzyskie province, in which Chmielnik is located.

discussed the bimah's bold design, its contemporary symbolism (light amid darkness, the victory of life over death), and the visual impact it makes on visitors: lit from above and below, the glass bimah is luminous, a jewel in the center of the otherwise dark museum space. My guide provided more detail about the bimah than about the actual content of the exhibition, which consists mostly of reproductions of prewar photographs of local Jews. He made sure to show me the bimah from different angles, including from the floor above, where a section of the wooden parquet was replaced by Plexiglas so that visitors could admire the glowing reproduction of the sacred object from above.

We finished the visit in an adjacent room designed to host special lectures or meetings. It was decorated with various contemporary portraits, including one of Leopold Kozłowski, "the last klezmer." A large canopy made from a prayer shawl covered the seating area.[18] Fragments of an original fresco on the wall were still visible, but Mr. Krawczyk directed my attention to an intricate folk diorama, made by a local woodworker, of a Jewish home and street scene. He then invited me to sit down and watch a music video by the local klezmer band, the Chmielnikers, which he projected on a large screen. The video was a klezmer-pop rendition of a traditional Yiddish song, showing Chmielnik's local population impersonating Jews at home, at school, and at synagogue shot in sepia tones. After it ended, my host told me he had a cameo role and asked whether I had recognized him. When I admitted I hadn't, he proudly revealed he was playing the rabbi (because he is the "father" of the synagogue and museum project).

I was taken aback by the impersonations, and puzzled by the tension between Mr. Krawczyk's museological endeavors, the video's crude cultural appropriation, and Mr. Krawczyk's apparent lack of self-awareness. The contrast between the two cultural objects the local activist had proudly shown me—the restored synagogue turned museum with its contemporary bimah, and the klezmer music video—was jarring. That disconcerting contrast is not, however, unique to Chmielnik, as a wide range of Jewish representations coexist in the Polish public sphere and are thus available to individuals to pick and choose from, and sometimes combine.

In Lublin, for example, the famous Grodzka Gate Theatre, an important cultural institution focused on the history of the region's Jewish heritage that organizes educational workshops and the artistic and educational

18 Born in 1918 near Lwów (now Lvi'v, in western Ukraine) into a family of klezmorim, Leopold Kozłowski-Kleinman was a pianist, composer, and conductor, and the main force behind the revival of klezmer in Poland. He died in Kraków in 2019.

festival Following Isaac Bashevis Singer's Traces, functions alongside Mandragora, a Jewish-style restaurant on the old market square.[19]

I had dinner with friends at Mandragora on a chilly Saturday evening in October 2014. We were in Lublin for an academic workshop on vernacular culture, and I had proposed that we include some cultural activities related to Jewish Lublin. We walked on the Jewish Heritage Trail and ended the evening at Mandragora. The restaurant is named after an exotic plant mentioned in the Hebrew Bible, used by Jacob and his wives as an aphrodisiac. It occupies a stately sixteenth-century corner building with an imposing round portal. A large banner stretched over the second-floor balcony bears a photograph of the restaurant staff dressed in traditional Jewish clothing, the women with white kerchiefs on their heads. The banner also bears a potpourri of Jewish icons—an archival photo of an old Hasidic man, apples, pomegranates, and menorahs—next to the name of the restaurant in Hebrew-styled Polish lettering. At street level, by the front door, a Singer sewing machine turned into a table is covered with a lace tablecloth, a samovar, and the menu to further entice passersby.

The restaurant's website describes it as "like a Jewish home, with a familial, friendly and loving atmosphere."[20] The interior is decorated in the style of a "traditional" bourgeois dining room of the prewar period. Old pictures, family portraits, mirrors, and clocks adorn the walls. A velvet chair in a corner of the main room, with a small table at its side, seems to await the patriarch of the family. Judaica can be found here and there—menorahs and kiddush cups, and the popular wooden figurines of musicians in Hasidic garb. Most striking is the large fresco painted on the back wall of the main dining room depicting dancing Hasidic men (figure 36).

When we visited on a Saturday night, the local diners were dressed to the nines for a special night out. Most were middle-aged Poles. There were no obvious tourists apart from our party of six—a group of young Warsaw-based academics and me. There was a klezmer band playing that evening, so the place was packed. We were lucky to get a table in the back of the main room, after insisting to the manager the day before that we could squeeze six around a four-top.

---

19 Named after the city gate that linked the Christian and Jewish sections of Lublin, *Brama Grodzka-Teatr NN* is a cultural and educational institution whose main mission is to teach the local community and visitors about the region's Jewish history and cultural heritage. See http://teatrnn.pl/brama-edukacja/en. For an analysis of the institution's commemorative performances, see Skórzyńska (2014) and Popescu (2017).

20 http://mandragora.lublin.pl/restauracja.

FIGURE 36. Young Polish men having lunch in the Jewish-themed restaurant Mandragora in Lublin. (Photo by Geneviève Zubrzycki, October 24, 2014.)

Most items on the menu were staples of Polish cuisine, such as cabbage or chicken soup, herring, potato pancakes, and pierogies. Some dishes were offered in "Jewish" variations—*po żydowsku*—with almonds and raisins, or garlic. Others were listed under their Jewish appellation ("Hanukah latkes, served ONLY in the fall and winter"). Also on offer were lamb, liver, and goose, alongside Mediterranean options like humus, and even one American dish, "corned beef" ("following recipes of East Central European Jews who emigrated to the United States").[21] I ordered the latkes to see if they differed from the potato pancakes available year-round at any Polish cafeteria, family or Polish-themed restaurant, especially popular on Fridays when observant Catholics do not eat meat. (They did not.)

21 Mandagora explains on both the Polish- and English-language pages of its website that the restaurant does its best to respect kosher rules, but it states on its English-language page that it does not have a kosher certificate. Its Polish page instead emphasizes "centuries-old recipes," notes that the offerings include a "Shabbat menu," and describes special holiday evenings such as Hanukah and Purim for the benefit of its gentile clients. See also its infomercial, performed by Szalom Chełm: https://www.youtube.com/watch?v=3juMJkX6qmY.

That night the klezmer band came from Chełm. They played Jewish standards like "Shalom Aleichem" and other surefire winners for this audience. Apart from refrains, most of the lyrics were in Polish. The crowd ate in silence, listening politely to the music until the bandleader encouraged them to clap along. Between tunes, the singer explained that Chełm, despite being a very small Polish town, was well-known in the Jewish world and that it even served as the setting for traditional jokes about fools.[22] Coming from Chełm, the singer said, was therefore special, since the town was a special place for Jews. That association seemed intended to give the band some street cred and Jewish legitimacy.

Outside observers like myself cringe at the Mandragora scene I describe above. Why? After all, servers and musicians at a variety of restaurants in Poland and elsewhere routinely don uniforms meant to suggest historical authenticity, and nostalgic restaurants, cafés, and products are hugely successful, in Poland and elsewhere (Baudrillard 1996; Berdhal 2010; Todorova and Gille 2010; Bach 2017).[23] Is it the kitsch nature of these cultural representations that causes discomfort? Or is there something especially problematic in non-Jews playing klezmer music and dressing up in faux Jewish attire for entertainment in a place where actual Jews were murdered just seventy-five years ago? Or is it the fact that among all these elements—the impersonation of individual Jews, the costumes, the simulated Jewish home—there are no Jews present? Are we left only with the appropriation of Jewish culture for its entertainment and commercial value?

Let us briefly consider another problematic commodity, that of the "Jew with a coin" (figure 37). A recent twist on the traditional folk-art figurines of Hasidic Jews, these objects made their initial appearance in the 1990s, becoming hugely popular only in the early 2000s. They are sold as good-luck charms in the form of refrigerator magnets, tiny plastic dolls one might slip into a wallet in order to avoid running out of money, or paintings typically hung at home to bring prosperity.

The phenomenon has become so popular in the last two decades that several scholars have investigated the meaning of the object and practices

---

22 See, for example, the short film *A Village of Idiots*, directed by Eugene Fedorenko and Rose Newlove (1999) (http://onf-nfb.gc.ca/en/our-collection/?idfilm=33250#nav-prix).

23 Jewish restaurants were among the first in a growing trend of "nostalgic" restaurants and businesses. Some now evoke nineteenth-century Galicia or interwar Warsaw. Czerwony Wieprz (Red Pig) in Warsaw presents a nostalgic take on the communist past. It has two menus: one for "party apparatchiks" and bourgeois with fancy dishes and expensive cuts of meat, and one for the budget-conscious "proletarians" with more affordable pierogies and the like (https://www.czerwonywieprz.pl/en).

FIGURE 37. A traditional wooden Jewish figurine and a "Jew with a coin," next to various Chopin knickknacks and amber souvenirs in the window of an upscale tourist shop in Warsaw. (Photo by Geneviève Zubrzycki, July 4, 2010.)

surrounding it. The anthropologist Joanna Tokarska-Bakir (2013) has proposed a Freudian interpretation, arguing that they serve to "exorcise" the ghosts of murdered Polish Jews. For Erica Lehrer (2014), the figurines are complex intersectional objects in which multiple vectors of memory converge. Paweł Dobrosielski (2015), on the other hand, shows that the "Jew with a coin" is a financial superstition that has evolved in reaction to the increasing sense of alienation experienced under neoliberal capitalism, as well as a cultural vernacular reaction to the feeling of alienation stemming from the difficult and complex Polish discourse on the Holocaust following the publication of Gross's *Neighbors* in 2000. Hanging a painting of the "Lucky Jew" in one's home therefore both alleviates financial anxieties and repudiates the new discourse on Polish participation in the Holocaust.

I describe my encounter with the Chmielnik museum curator and the Mandragora scene, and discuss the popularity of the Lucky Jew to show that various kinds of Jewish representations—besides those one can find at a museum or at a sporadic festival—are on offer in the Polish cultural marketplace. The revival of Jewish culture covers a broad spectrum of cultural styles and representations, involving different levels of human, financial, and cultural capital, evoking various degrees of sensibilities among non-Jews participating in it. Thus, one can encounter Jewish history by going to a local museum with a modest exhibition or by visiting the Polin Museum, with its expansive (and expensive) core exhibition; one can experience Jewish culture at a small festival or at the Jewish Theatre in Warsaw; and one can wear hip, pricey T-shirts with Hebrew inscriptions, or carry a "Jew with a coin" in one's bag. These different representations can be used by individuals in their own cultural bricolage. They also carry different meanings (conscious and unconscious) for those engaging with Jewish objects, persons, or practices.

What makes the Jewish turn in Poland such a rich and complex sociological problem to crack is precisely the sheer number of ways in which "Jews" and "Jewishness" are evoked and invoked, and the wide range of spaces where this occurs, sometimes involving self-critical reflection and serious historical investigation and at other times the uncritical use of stereotypes, often antisemitic to boot.

Religious Appropriation

The question of cultural appropriation brings up the issue of religious appropriation.

In March 2013, while in Kraków conducting interviews for this book, I heard from a non-Jewish interviewee about a "seder" planned for that week by local Christian evangelicals. Through acquaintances, I learned that the event was organized by Maryla and Irek Czubak, whom I have known since 2001 and had interviewed for my first book. I was thrilled to reconnect with them and to be invited to the event, titled Pascha 2013. It was held at the Franciscan monastery adjacent to the church in Kraków's old town, famous for its stunning art nouveau wall paintings and its stained-glass windows by the playwright, poet, and painter Stanisław Wyspiański. Over four hundred people were in attendance, seated at tables beautifully decorated with colorful linens and flowers, and featuring the seder plate, kosher wine, and plenty of matzoh. Some tables were filled by entire families or groups of friends, others by people who had purchased individual tickets. Several tables were occupied by orders of Catholic nuns, priests, or monks, recognizable by their different habits. Guests at my table were excited to "witness this important ritual," as a

FIGURE 38. Pascha 2013 (a Christian "seder"), organized by Protestant evangelicals, at the Franciscan monastery in Kraków. The other wing of the room was as full as the one pictured here. (Photo by Geneviève Zubrzycki, March 23 2013.)

woman in her thirties described it as we chatted beforehand. Programs on the table outlined the event and explained different parts of the ritual (figure 38).

Maryla was the host and master of ceremonies. After introducing an American messianic Jew as the "rabbi," she covered her hair with a lace shawl and lit the candles. The ritual moments of the seder were punctuated by entertainment: a choir and solo singers, klezmer music, and children's dance performances. Everyone was clearly well prepared: the children knew the songs and had rehearsed the dances to perfection.

The whole event was impressively well produced: over a dozen volunteers helped set the tables and welcomed and seated the guests, placing the VIPs at tables nearest the stage. A technical team made sure the sound and lighting were perfect and recorded the event for future DVD sales. Screens placed around the room provided a better view for people seated far from the stage where the rabbi and his translator sat.

This was the eighth Christian seder Maryla and Irek had organized. The events had become so popular that the couple started traveling to different Polish cities to hold seders and other Jewish rituals for Christians (interviews, March 27, 2013).[24] "This is important," Maryla told me when we met for tea the following day, "because talking about Jews and participating in Jewish rituals is the only way to get Polish Catholics and Protestants together in a room."

The audience was captivated, happy to witness a ritual that many might have seen in films or read about but that most had never witnessed in person. I kept asking myself whether participants thought they were witnessing a Jewish ritual and wondering if that mattered at all. Easter, that year, overlapped with Passover, and the Christian seder was on Maundy Thursday. Those present were learning about the ritual Jesus celebrated at the Last Supper, which would be commemorated the following day, on Good Friday. One could surmise that the event had educational value. Ritual borrowings are par for the course in religious life, and in other parts of the world Christian evangelicals and messianic Jews also observe forms of Jewish rituals in their assemblies. And yet I felt uneasy.

When I told my Jewish friends in Kraków about the experience, many referred to the event as "strange," not understanding what a "Christian seder" could be, but they were more perplexed than offended. One young man told me he didn't care, "since what they did at that Christian event clearly has nothing to do with us." For my Jewish interlocutors, the event was so far off from Judaism or "real Jewish culture," as another woman put it, that they could not relate to it by feeling offended or otherwise.[25]

I discussed cultural appropriation with many of my Jewish interviewees, typically by telling them that members of the North American public react very negatively to some of the Polish replications of Jewish culture that I analyze, invoking comparisons of "playing Indian" or minstrelsy.

---

24 A mash-up of several Christian "seders" can be seen on *Fundacja Polania's* YouTube channel at https://www.youtube.com/watch?v=2sABAkTMG-Y. Several videos of other holiday observances organized by the Czubak family are available on that platform as well. *Fundacja Polania* is dedicated to "the creation of a culture of hospitality and kindness toward national minorities in Poland, preserving the memory of Poles' and Jews' heritage of coexistence on our land, and provides support, help and hope to many poor, weak, hurt, and lonely individuals in Ukraine and Israel" (http://fundacjapolania.pl/o-fundacji-polania).

25 For their work at the Polania Foundation, the Czubaks received the 2020 Preserving Memory Award, presented every year since 1998 by JCC Kraków and the Galicia Jewish Museum to Poles working to preserve Jewish heritage. The award is sponsored by the World Jewish Congress and Jewish philanthropic organizations. While the award is for their memory activism and charity work rather than their events, if the latter were offensive to the individuals and organizations sponsoring the award, they most likely would not have conferred it on the Czubaks.

While many ordinary Polish Jews did not understand the references or the vehemence of these reactions, the chief rabbi of Poland, American-born Michael Schudrich, understood immediately and responded:

> Listen. I was young once and wanted to understand Native American culture, decimated by Whites, and went to a sweat lodge. I wanted to learn and understand. Here now, some young Poles go to synagogues, we lend them kippahs when they enter and teach them it's a sign of respect. It might happen that one guy keeps it or later buys one and walks around Warsaw or Kazimierz with a kippah on his head. Is he being disrespectful? No, they're just learning. And it's better for us to deal with people who are curious, who want to learn about us, than when they don't. It takes time. We have to teach them and be patient.

Several others expressed similar views. Jonathan Ornstein, for example, explained that he would of course prefer that Jewishness not be "marked"—that it should exist without being noticed, like the air we breathe. "But since that is not the case, it's better to live in a place where there's a desire to learn about Jews, Jewish culture, and Jewish history than in one where Jews face discrimination or violence." Ornstein also often emphasizes—as public intellectual Konstanty Gebert and others did in interviews—that he feels safer in the streets of Kraków and Warsaw than in those of Paris or London.[26]

Cultural appropriation generally refers to the process through which members of a dominant group not only adopt but also exploit, dilute, trivialize, or even degrade and desecrate elements of a subordinated group's culture. Often the result of colonialization or of ethnic, racial, or religious hierarchies, it always results from a power imbalance between the appropriating group and the one whose culture is being appropriated. A key problem of cultural appropriation is that the meaning of a given cultural artifact, symbol, practice, or skill is often lost or distorted when removed from its original context. It is for that reason that the appropriation can be experienced by members of the minority group as desecration. The object of the appropriation, moreover, can be stigmatized by the dominant group when used by its original owner but acquire cachet when used by the members of the appropriating groups. It is for these reasons that cultural appropriation has been fiercely denounced by minority groups

26 Personal interviews with Jonathan Ornstein (November 19, 2020), Konstanty Gebert (March 8, 2012), and Michael Schudrich (September 28, 2012).

for decades and brought to public attention in the last several years with controversies involving celebrities and other public figures, such as the Kardashian sisters braiding their hair with cornrows or darkening their skin with makeup or filters, or Miley Cyrus twerking at the 2013 MTV music video awards.[27]

But what about cases where imitations of religious or cultural forms and practices do not cause offense to those from whom they are appropriated? Should we define cultural appropriation based on objective distinctions (Jewish music played by non-Jews, for example, or Jewish cemeteries tended by Catholics) or subjective criteria (feelings of dispossession arising from having religious or cultural practices appropriated by others)? Is it a mix of both? Or is it less about who enacts a specific set of practices or has feelings about them than about the process and the power struggles involved in the appropriation?

In her insightful ethnographic study of klezmer in contemporary Germany and Poland, Magdalena Waligórska argues that cultural appropriation is not the right lens for examining what she sees as a dynamic process. Dismissing klezmer music played by non-Jews because they are not Jewish, and qualifying such a practice as one of simple cultural appropriation, she observes, misses the potentially important—perhaps even transformative—impact of "sites of cultural translation" such as klezmer (2013: 8). Considering the process as translation rather than appropriation makes it possible to read such performances as sites of enrichment and dialogue. While klezmer can reinforce some stereotypes about Jews—of the colorful, peaceful, multicultural shtetl, for example—Waligórska argues that it also has the potential to challenge such stereotypes, since playing and listening to klezmer music can be a political statement (2013: 274).

My own research shows that the cultural-appropriation paradigm is inadequate to capture the variety of processes at play in Poland's Jewish turn. At the most basic level, we should discern the straightforward theft of Jewish property during and after the war, so powerfully addressed in Sierakowski's speech in Bartana's film *Nightmares*; the lawful but no less problematic acquisition of Jewish objects one can find for sale today on-

---

27 For key statements on cultural appropriation, see hooks (1992, esp. 21–39), Ziff and Rao (1997), and J. O. Young (2010). For empirical analyses, see Deloria (1998) on "playing Indian," Brown and Kopano (2014) on White appropriation of Black culture, and Altglas (2014) and Lofton (2017) on the commodification of religious forms. See also Brubaker (2016) on cultural appropriation and "reverse passing." On philo-Sephardism and the appropriation of tradition, see J. Cohen (1999) and McDonald (2021).

line, in antique shops, and at flea markets;[28] the commodification of Jewish cultural forms; and sites of cultural translation, like the klezmer scenes observed by Waligórska. But how do we categorize festivals of Jewish culture that include critical reflections on Polish-Jewish relations, the history of interwar Poland, genealogical reckonings of hidden but recoverable Jewishness, and other pedagogical events? Or Jewish organizations staffed by non-Jews? Or non-Jews wearing Jewish symbols in commemorative solidarity or as political statements? Are these examples of cultural appropriation, sites of exchange or dialogue, or spaces for introspection and change?

The sheer variety of practices requires more refined conceptual tools to differentiate the various registers of engagement of non-Jewish Poles with Poland's Jewish past and Jewish culture.[29] Having already considered material reconfigurations and nostalgic imaginings of Poland's Jewish past, the discourses of cultural institutions and of people who patronize them, and the commodified representations of Jewishness, I now turn to the motivations of Poles who are closely engaged in Jewish cultural work and the meaning that this work has for them.

Stretching the Symbolic Boundaries of Polishness

Many Poles engage in daily, mundane activities that have Jewish connections. They enjoy Jewish music, from traditional klezmer to Israeli hip-hop; they eat in Jewish restaurants and drink kosher vodka—rumored to be "purer" and thus less likely to cause hangovers.[30] Some learn Jewish dances and perform them in schools and festivals, while others enroll in Jewish studies programs at Polish universities. A few volunteer in Jewish organizations like the JCC in Kraków or provide services to Jewish seniors,

28 During ethnographic observations at the Polin Museum, we heard one woman telling her friend about "a very old *hanukiah*" she had bought online and placed on the kitchen windowsill in her cottage. Her friend responded that she would "never buy such an item, because who knows where it comes from? It could come from stolen Jewish property." She explained that she would feel bad owning a "prewar Jewish object" knowing the history of Polish Jews. Her friend listened, an uncomfortable silence hanging in the air.

29 In a different but related vein, Ruth Ellen Gruber alludes to degrees of philosemitism (2002: 9) but does not expand on the distinction between them.

30 When I asked customers of Jewish restaurants why they had chosen that place, they typically responded, "Because the music is great" or "We like the atmosphere, the mood of the place." Unless Middle Eastern staples are served, food is not the primary attraction of these restaurants, since Ashkenazi dishes tend to be very similar to standard Polish fare. On the marketing of kosher and "Jewish-style" vodkas, see Ingall (2003).

and a small minority explore converting to Judaism. These practices imply different degrees and different registers of engagement with Judaism, Jewish culture, and the Jewish community. While it is safe to assume that most "passive" and occasional consumers of Jewish culture probably do so without deeper reflection or a conscious agenda, for others—non-Jewish Poles who actively participate in the revival of Jewish culture and support the revival of Jewish communal life—their engagement is deliberate, considered, and significant.

"Not a Fad!": Trangressing the Polak-Katolik

During my fieldwork in Kraków, I spent a significant amount of time at the JCC, an institution providing a wide range of services to the local Jewish community and their families as well as cultural activities for locals and visitors. I met many non-Jewish Poles volunteering there and carried out in-depth interviews with twenty.

All my interviewees were young women (the median age was twenty-three). This profile was representative of all the volunteers: very few are over thirty, and even fewer are men. Slightly over half (53 percent) were from large cities like Kraków, Wrocław, or Warsaw. Those from smaller towns typically had come to Kraków to study. Except for one highly motivated and mature high school student, two women in their thirties, and another one in her early fifties, all were enrolled in institutions of higher learning when they started volunteering.[31] All were Catholic: half of them observant, the others not.[32] One explicitly declared herself an atheist. Only one volunteer I interviewed had distant Jewish roots. A third of my interviewees, however, reported having looked for Jewish origins at some point.[33]

---

31 Most of my interviewees had started volunteering during their university studies and continued upon graduation, either on a regular basis or sporadically. Some volunteers also joined the staff of the JCC after graduating. These volunteers are not representative of Poland's population as whole, of whom only 17 percent have completed any higher education (Narodowy Spis Powszechny, https://stat.gov.pl/spisy-powszechne/nsp-2011/nsp-2011-wyniki /ludnosc-stan-i-struktura-demograficzno-spoleczna-nsp-2011,16,1.html).

32 Most practicing Catholics among the JCC volunteers and members of the Israeli dance group I interviewed associated themselves with Catholic movements related to what is called in Poland "open Catholicism," known for being more "intellectual" than ritualistic, associated with the progressive Catholic weekly *Tygodnik Powszechny*, and actively preaching the late Pope John Paul II's call for ecumenism and respect for "our older brothers in faith."

33 One young woman's search revealed that her grandmother was not Jewish but German— "unfortunately," she told me, laughing, aware of the irony of this discovery and perhaps also of her quest.

In the absence of familial or religious connections, what motivated those young, busy women to volunteer six to eight hours a week for a Jewish organization? One-third of my interviewees became volunteers because they were enrolled in a Jewish studies program and wanted contact with Jewish life; others did so because volunteer work was required for their university degree. Yet others came to the JCC through friends. A few dedicated their time for more personal reasons: Wera, for example, was a therapist in her early fifties with a passion for dance. After her Jewish fiancé died in an accident, she began volunteering at the JCC as a way to remain connected to Jewish culture and because "the JCC is a big family." Iza found out while in college that one of her great-grandfathers had been Jewish, which piqued her curiosity. She first volunteered at a Jewish cultural event, then signed up to work on a regular basis at the JCC. Daniela was from a very small village and had heard about the pogrom in Jedwabne as a teenager. She became so invested in learning more about the dark corners of Polish Jewish history that she convinced her parents to take the family on a trip to the infamous village. She then enrolled in Jewish studies and moved to Kraków shortly after graduating. Within a few weeks, she had become a volunteer at the JCC. She recalled:

> I remember it to this day, because it was an amazing feeling; for five, six years I had been reading exclusively about Jews, I would meet them once in a while at the Festival [of Jewish Culture], right? . . . and here [at the JCC] I have contact with people I've been *reading* about, contact with the whole history I've *read* about, and it's unbelievable. It's been a unique educational opportunity to witness Shabbat, meet the rabbi, listen to some lectures, and learn about Jewish holidays.

Not all volunteers have an academic interest in Jewish history. Ewa, an energetic woman studying nursing, was unusually busy but was looking for even more activities to keep her engaged outside of her studies. Her mother was interested in Judaism and Polish Jewish history, had heard of the JCC, and thus first introduced Ewa to the institution. Even after she graduated and started her career in nursing, I sometimes saw Ewa serving at JCC Shabbat dinners. Tellingly, all the volunteers I interviewed stayed on longer than they had initially planned, finding the experience fulfilling and the place and people uniquely welcoming. Iza, a master's student in computer science who had been volunteering for two years, told me, "The JCC—its members, staff, and volunteers—are like one big family." The conviviality and sense of community of the place were brought up, unprompted, by every interviewee. They referred to the great "ambience," the "unique atmosphere," and the "wonderful people" from abroad they met and learned from.

Most, however, viewed their work at the JCC as significant for reasons beyond conviviality. They saw it as part of something much larger: the renewal of Jewish life in Poland. For Daniela, institutions like the JCC and the Jewish revival more broadly "have enormous importance":

> Definitely and decisively. For Jews themselves, of course, because it's the renewal of [Polish] Jewry, in a new form, of course, because of historical conditions. . . . But for Poland as well; we're actually returning to our roots because Poland was never a cultural monolith. . . . So the renewal of Polish Jewry, I don't know, is a return to our roots.

Many of the volunteers I interviewed believed that the revival of Jewish communal life and Jewish culture had great value for the nation as a whole. Daniela, a practicing Catholic, also saw it as promoting individual emancipation and the building of civil society after decades of totalitarianism:

> Nowadays, we have the possibility of exercising freedom of choice. And the fact that there are so many conversions [to Judaism] is the result of the human search to define oneself, right? To decide for yourself. Ultimately, one has the possibility to decide. Other people—family members—cannot prohibit that. And citizenship, I mean, civil society, emerges from [that process]. If I want to be Jewish, I'm not stigmatized [for it], right? Because there are other people like me; I can turn to them, right? If I want to leave the [Catholic] Church, I'm also not stigmatized—I mean, yes, of course, for sure I'd be ostracized a bit by a conservative segment of society that does not tolerate otherness—but there are other people in similar situations and that would facilitate my making that choice. And that is good, because it makes us responsible for ourselves, for our own life.

From this vantage point, even acts like wearing Jewish jewelry or Jewish brands become significant. The clothing line Risk Oy was launched in 2014 by a Polish-Jewish-owned fashion house based in Warsaw. Initially targeted at young Jews, Risk Oy produces pricey T-shirts and hoodies with slogans such as "Thanks to my Mom" and "You Had Me at Shalom" (in English), adorned with a variety of Star of David designs and Hebrew inscriptions.[34] The owner of the brand told *The Times of Israel*: "What we really want ... is to rebrand Jewish identity. We want to show the modern, positive aspects of it. What we are doing is showing that being Jewish is cool and sexy."[35] Yet according to JCC Kraków's director, Jonathan Ornstein, there is really no need to rebrand Jewish identity since, as he has been insisting for years, "it's hip to be Jewish in today's Poland."[36]

Several non-Jewish volunteers at the JCC and non-Jewish members of a Kraków-based Israeli dance troupe I interviewed likewise commented that "Jewishness is fashionable" (*jest moda na Żydów*). One outspoken, well-traveled volunteer exclaimed: "A fad for Jews? Let it be, darn it! Better this than a fad for antisemitism, no?" Ilona, a smart, energetic woman then in her late twenties, explained in a conversation with me what the expression refers to, and what, according to her, the phenomenon actually means:

ILONA: [The expression] is sometimes used to describe [the Jewish revival], implying it's something superficial. It seems to me that even if [the phenomenon] takes some superficial forms, it has deeper meaning and it is completely nonaccidental. It's *not* superficial, [so] the word "fashion" [*moda*] is not a good term. I think there's a sort of awakening of collective consciousness that is sometimes manifested in superficial or folkloric forms, but it's really about something deeper. On the other hand, and perhaps it's a silly comparison, but it's also like in some milieus it's good to show up with a gay friend.

GZ: What do you mean? Why is that?

ILONA: Because Jewishness in our Polish reality is still associated with some kind of social stigma; this antisemitism kind of works, so this Jewish fad is actually an act of transgression. It's an act of rebellion and opposition, in a sense.

GZ: Against what?

ILONA: Against silence, against prejudices, against Radio Maryja. There was a period when I was involved in the campaign

---

34 "You Had Me at Shalom" is a play on the romantic line "You had me at hello" uttered by Renée Zelwegger to Tom Cruise in the Hollywood blockbuster *Jerry McGuire* (1996).

35 At: http://www.timesofisrael.com/polish-fashion-entrepreneur-makes-being-jewish-sexy/?utm_source=Newsletter+subscribers&utm_campaign=0c5a586595-JTA_Daily_Briefing_1_31_2014&utm_medium=email&utm_term=0_2dce5bc6f8-0c5a586595-25416689. On the Jewish fad, see the piece "I Love koszer" by Agata Jankowska in the popular magazine *Przekrój*, "Kocham Żydów" by Rita Osicka in the Polish edition of *Glamour*, and the brief blog entry "Judaizm jest trendy" (https://blogostan.wordpress.com/2011/11/05/judaizm-jest-trendy).

36 Personal communications, March 2011, March 2012, and March 2013.

against homophobia. I was fighting for multiculturalism in a different sense; to give voice to the weaker, to those in smaller numbers . . .

Supporting the revival of Jewish culture and the renewal of Jewish communal life in Poland can therefore be an explicit attempt by nominal Catholics to undermine the power of the Catholic Church and oppose the monopoly of the Catholic Right over the definition of Polishness (Zubrzycki 2013a).

For other religious minorities, too, the Jewish revival provides a counterweight to the heavy presence of Catholicism in Poland. Evangelical Christians I interviewed repeatedly emphasized that it was important for them to discover Judaism for theological reasons—in order "to go back to the source" and "get to know Jesus as a Jew"—but also because it might help diminish the force of Catholicism in public and political life. When I interviewed Natalia, a young Protestant woman who had majored in Judaic studies and art history, and mentioned that the right-wing Radio Maryja was organizing a protest in the following days, she responded:

Argh, I forgot that they still exist. . . . [But] let's leave these marginals in the margins! Radio Maryja, it's a bunch of old ladies—hopefully they don't have too many young followers. There's a chance, with Jewishness being fashionable, that it means that the young generation is more open, [and] that there will be more openness in the future.

It is significant that Natalia believes the hegemony of Catholicism and the Catholic Church can be effectively challenged by the promotion of Judaism and Jewishness rather than by other religious communities such as Protestants, Russian Orthodox Christians, Muslims, or Jehovah's Witnesses (which, while small, do exist in Poland). Martyna, a JCC staff member in her late twenties, reflected on precisely this point:

I think it's a question of worldview for the young generation now; young people—some at least, not all—like to identify themselves with and defend various minorities. That's especially the case for leftists, no? With sexual minorities, Jews, and sometimes with women. . . . But it's interesting that of all minorities, it's specifically focused on Jews somehow.

Why is Jewishness (like gayness) "fashionable" for some Poles? What does it signify for them? While Martyna didn't offer an explanation, an article published in *The Times of Israel* suggests some clues. In it the president

FIGURE 39. Screenshot from the Facebook page of Polish Jewish clothing brand Risk Oy showing a young man who wears the kippah "to share [the] statement that being [a] Jew in Warsaw is cool and safe. Non-Jewish Jew") (https://www.facebook.com/riskoyoy/photos /a.477556429025781/659502584164497/?type=3&theater).

of the Joint Distribution Committee (JDC) in Warsaw, Karina Sokołowska, suggested that the Risk Oy clothing line is popular in part because such clothing "is an attractive item for Poland's many philo-Semites." One non-Jew quoted in the story, a forty-year-old lawyer living in Warsaw, explained that wearing Risk Oy "is like taking part in a public discussion about Jews in Poland—that Jews live here and that Jews can live here." According to the company's Facebook page, another non-Jewish young man who worked at Risk Oy even wears a kippah in solidarity with Jews and to make a public statement that "it's cool and safe" to be Jewish in Warsaw (figure 39).

These comments are important on two levels. First, they emphasize that public discussions about Jews in Poland are concerned with the very identity of Poland and offer a critique of the still-dominant vision of the nation as ethnically Polish and Catholic; second, they demonstrate that this discussion is taking place not only in the pages of newspapers and the discourses of public intellectuals but also on the streets among hipsters and through the clothes they wear, the music they listen to, and the bars they patronize.

Several years prior, in 2004, the Polish NGO Foundation for Freedom (*Fundacja dla Wolności*) produced "I'm a Jew" T-shirts as part of a campaign that consisted of "spreading . . . slogans signaling the existence of . . . discriminated social groups in Poland," including Jews, atheists, and sexual minorities.[37] Hence liberal, leftist youth wore T-shirts and brandished posters in protests against clerical nationalists, subversively claiming to be Jews. Their display mocked antisemitic conspiracy theories of the Right claiming that Jews rule Poland. But they also called for a different kind of Poland, one in which the Right's distinctions between "real Poles," "bad Poles," and "Jews" would have no political traction.

The Jew as Indigenous Other

Still, all of these forms of engagement raise a single question: Why do those who wish to build pluralism focus specifically on Jews rather than on Silesians, Ukrainians, or Vietnamese? As I have noted, Jewishness carries a specific signification and symbolic capital associated with modernity, cosmopolitanism, and urbanity. Moreover, since Jewishness is the most direct contradiction of the *Polak-katolik*, progressive Poles like Ilona, who scorn the Catholic Right, and Aneta, who regards religious Jews walking around Kazimierz as a counterpoint to Catholic symbols and rituals, tend to support and participate in the Jewish cultural revival in Poland. And because Jews are mostly absent from the Polish landscape, they are therefore both nonthreatening and ready to serve as vehicles for one's fantasies: nightmares or dreams, depending on one's political orientation.

Yet another reason is that Jews, unlike other groups, are at once exotic and indigenous. Martyna, thinking aloud during our conversation, proposed that "maybe . . . there's a desire to know things that were once close and now are most distant? Ukrainians are not very distant, and they are Slavs." Jews are different; yet as Paulina, a born-again Christian enrolled in a sociology program told me in a conversation in 2012, Jewish culture "was nourished from the Polish soil and grew on these lands." Natalia, whom I cited earlier, put the idea in even more vivid terms:

On the one hand, [Jewish culture] is, let's say, "Oriental." But on the other hand, because it developed in Poland, despite everything it's somehow very much tied to Poland, right? It's kind of an exotic element in our environment. It's not something like . . . Swahili somewhere far off in Africa, but [rather] something that is different from Polish culture yet at the same time related to it, inseparable even.

37 Other T-shirt slogans that were part of the 2004 campaign included "I don't go to church," "I don't want to have kids," and "I'm gay." See http://www.tiszertdlawolnosci.tiszert.com.

FIGURE 40. Members of the dance troupe Kachol, rehearsing at the Popper Synagogue in Kraków's Kazimierz neighborhood. (Photo by Geneviève Zubrzycki, March 2011.)

Dancers in the group Kachol (figure 40) told me in individual conversations that performing traditional Jewish dances brings them (and, one presumes, their audiences too) closer to a different side of Polish history than other cultural forms exalted in Polish national mythology and its sensorium. At the same time, as Natalia's explanation suggests, the dances transport them to faraway, exotic, "Oriental" places that are also, paradoxically, more "Western" and cosmopolitan than Poland, like Tel Aviv or New York. It is that mix of the familiar and the exotic that attracts many to Jewish culture.

It is this duality that, according to another JCC volunteer, makes Jewishness so appealing to non-Jewish Poles:

> We could talk about [Jewish culture] as a foreign culture, different from Polish culture if we wanted . . . to separate, but we are still aware that we're talking about a culture that was here for centuries. But it's still something exotic, right? And yet, totally close to us. So it's easy to become interested in [Jews and Jewish culture] and become fascinated. It becomes fashionable.

Jewishness is therefore both "Other" and "ours." This observation emerged spontaneously in dozens of conversations and interviews. Another young woman who volunteers at the JCC told me, "Jewish culture is 'exotica' right here at home." For evangelical Protestants, Jews are familiar from the stories in the Hebrew Bible; for progressive Catholics, they are "our older brothers in faith." These various factors make the Jew an *indigenous Other*: different enough from Poles (unlike Silesians or Ukrainians) yet not too different (unlike Vietnamese).

Polish Jews also often display sufficient cultural capital to be admitted into the circle of Polishness, as one interviewee told me:

> We owe [Jews] for their contributions in the academic and scientific sphere where there were a lot of Jews, and in the administration here in Kraków. There were Jewish mayors, many well-known lawyers at Jagiellonian University, many architects . . . in music too. So they contributed a lot. In literature too! They were a big influence.

Julian Tuwim, Bruno Schulz, and Janusz Korczak are consistently invoked in discussions of the contribution of Polish Jews to Polish literature. When Olga Tokarczuk received the Nobel Prize for Literature in 2020, the public was also reminded that Poland could count many more Nobel laureates if it included Polish Jews who had emigrated from Poland at one point. In January 2021, the Polin Museum in fact inaugurated a series of events "dedicated to Polish Jews who made outstanding contributions to the arts, sciences, economics, politics, and other fields in the 19th and 20th centuries," a series that culminated in the opening of the new Legacy gallery, an extension of the museum's core exhibition.[38]

Multicultural Past to the Rescue

Many participants in the revival of Jewish culture have hopes of a more multicultural Poland. Dominika, a dancer in Kachol, told me that "it's Israeli multiculturalism that fascinates [her] more than Jewishness per se." This longing for multiculturalism is evident in the testimonies of many authors on the "I Miss You, Jew" website and something I have overheard countless times in other venues over the years. During a visit to the Polin

---

38 https://www.polin.pl/en/news/2021/01/15/launch-legacy-program and https://polin.pl /en/the-legacy-gallery. The Legacy Gallery presents the lives and achievements of twenty-six outstanding Polish Jews, among them David Ben-Gurion, Raphael Lemkin, Rosa Luxemburg, Arthur Rubinstein, Helena Rubinstein, Julian Tuwim, and Ludwik Zamenhof.

Museum, for example, a stylish woman in her early twenties, dressed in a retro outfit (black dress, white tights, black-and-white oxford shoes), lamented that she wished she lived in a "multicultural society," that she would have liked to "grow up amid Jews, Hindus, or Africans," and that she "really likes the atmosphere of London precisely because of that multiculturalism visible on the streets."

Several of my interviewees believed that reviving Jewish culture would allow Poles to become "authentically" multicultural and bring Poland back to its "true essence." Daniela observed that the renewal of Jewish life marked Poland's return to its roots (*powrót do korzeni*). Janusz Makuch, the cofounder and director of Kraków's Jewish Culture Festival, observed that

> Kraków was always a multicultural place, where cultural pluralism was often very obvious. . . . This national monotheism, religious monotheism, that was created after the Second World War is scorching me, hurting me. I really don't like this—so let's go back here to what is the basis of our spirituality, actually, since Jews were Polish citizens. (March 19, 2011)

The revival of Jewish culture contributes to the recovery of a truer national self and the reshaping of symbolic boundaries of the nation. Embracing pluralism and Jewishness not only helps to brand Poland as modern and European; it also gives Poland back its "true" shape. Festivals of Jewish culture throughout Poland therefore seek to educate Poles and tourists about the culture of Jews who once lived in Poland and contributed to Polish culture. The claim is not merely about mutual influence: it is rather that Jewishness is constitutive of Polish life.

That discourse has been seamlessly integrated by various groups involved in the Jewish revival. Ula, a woman in her late twenties who dances in the Israeli dance group as a hobby and is a practicing Catholic, told me:

> Well, basically, there has been a Jewish presence in our country [*u nas*] for eight hundred years, on our lands, here in Poland, so there is this influence that we don't remember anymore because there are almost no Jews left in Poland. There are very few. [But it's important to know that culture] so that we can better know ourselves. Our identity, who we are, what we have. . . . Not long ago I was talking with friends about hospitality, how Poland and Poles are known for their hospitality—kind of [laughter]—but that hospitality actually comes from *Jewish* culture!

The Polish heritage, various activists proclaim, is more than Catholic practices and folklore. It includes broad universalist values that shaped a long tradition of religious tolerance and civic openness that led to the flourishing of Jewish religious and communal life, prosperous Jewish towns and peaceful shtetls, and Polish civilization. As Janusz Makuch expressed it during another of our conversations:

> Whether people know it or not, it is a *fact* that Jews, for many, many centuries . . . made tremendous contributions to Polish culture. So when we're talking about Polish culture, we're equally talking about Jewish culture. Without the contribution of Jews, true Polish culture couldn't exist. Forget it! Literature, architecture, sculpture, history, intellectuals, music, economics, politics, food. So everything was intertwined and still is, thank God. What I'm trying to do . . . is to help Poles realize what is theirs. (March 1, 2012, conversation in English)

The recognition of the Jewish past and the presence of cultural markers in contemporary Poland allow public figures, teachers, and activists to plausibly argue for a civic, rather than ethnic or religious, definition of Polishness. Because in the postwar period the communist regime co-opted and corrupted civic discourse, that vision of the national community is often perceived as "foreign." Today's progressive nationalists must work harder to create a plausible and desirable civic national project. To render that vision of the nation legitimate and "truly Polish," they reach into the distant past and renarrate Polish history to emphasize ethnic and religious diversity, political openness and tolerance, and political freedom. They point to the large number of Jews who settled in Poland as evidence of the historical roots of a Polish civic nation. Poland's history of religious tolerance also allows them to articulate a discourse that historically sets Poland apart from other European nations, making Poles "European" *avant la lettre*, a discourse forcefully articulated by President Komorowski during his speech at the opening ceremonies of the Polin Museum.

That narrative of Polish exceptionalism is significant. I will return to some of its implications, but here I want to emphasize the link that cultural entrepreneurs, public intellectuals, artists, and ordinary citizens make between Jews and Poland's Europeanness. Laura, a woman in her early twenties who had volunteered at the JCC for two years when I met her, said that the presence of Jews in Poland would allow Poles to feel more at ease in the new Europe: "I'm totally for Jews living here, as it was before, as it was before the war. Then it would be more comfortable for us in Europe because we'd be more open, more understanding toward differences in general." At one point in Bartana's *Nightmares*, Sierakowski implores Jews to return . . . so that "[Poles] shall finally be European"—or rather recover the Europeanness Poland has lost with the disappearance of Jews from the Polish landscape. In this discourse, modernity, Europeanness, and multiculturalism, as well as a more authentic national self, are achieved through and thanks to Jews.

A conversation with another JCC volunteer, Maja, is most enlightening:

MAJA: Multiculturalism is important for Poland, for Poles, for Polishness. [It's important] to realize that Poland was once multicultural, . . . and that multiculturalism makes some things easier; it builds tolerance among people; it [promotes] thinking beyond oneself, about others; it teaches different things about the world, about life; it shows that one can live differently, like society evolves, in a word.

GZ: Does the Jewish revival play a role in that process?

MAJA: I think it does. It shows that people can learn a lot from others, and that . . . we need to consider that just like someone living without a hand or a leg, if there were Jews in Poland today—and there are not—well then, "Hello?!" we have to do something about that; either talk about this, write, investigate, read, and try to understand and not allow situations that led to [monoethnic Poland] to ever arise.

GZ: When you think about the future, what kind of Poland would you like to see?

MAJA: I'd like to see Poland like a multicultural mosaic; colorful, positive. I'd like to stop seeing sad, frustrated people, tired of living here and hoping to move to London, Paris, the US, or somewhere else. I'd like to see people who live well here, who have lots of different friends, who appreciate difference, who can learn from others and teach others too. Who travel and feel good everywhere, at home and abroad. Multiculturalism plays the most important role in building that Poland.

What is missing from Maja's and other interviewees' discourse on multiculturalism is a reflection on real, existing multiculturalism and its challenges, either in the European, North American, or Israeli contexts.

Maja's desire for a "multicultural, colorful mosaic" echoes Sierakowski's speech in Bartana's *Nightmares* when he mournfully exclaims that "with one color, we cannot see." Seeing requires more colors, and for many Poles, Jews provide it, metaphorically and literally. The posters advertising Kraków's Jewish Culture Festival from the early 1990s until the mid-2010s were unusually bright and colorful.[39] The use of color was intended to connote the lively and vibrant culture of Jews in opposition to the gray brutality of the Holocaust (and, later, of state socialism). The consistent use of rainbow colors was also meant to convey the diversity that Jews represent and bring to Poland, as Janusz Makuch told me in one of our conversations (March 1, 2012). While the festival abandoned that visual strategy in 2013, it has been adopted and deployed by multiple organizations fighting antisemitism and promoting Jewish culture and multiculturalism. Jews, whether in the past or the present, "real" or "symbolic," are imagined to allow Poles to build a multicolored, pluralist Poland against the monoethnic nation connoted by the white-and-red flag.

Perhaps in his *Nightmares* speech, then, Sierakowski's character should have declared to Jews that "there isn't an Other that is more *perfect* than you" instead of "an Other that is closer to us than you." That variation would have captured more accurately the kind of Other that Jews have become for many Poles: exotic but indigenous, modern, cosmopolitan, European, rich in cultural capital. And absent.

Conclusion: Registers of Engagement

Donning a Star of David pendant and going to a Jewish-style restaurant or a klezmer concert obviously does not entail the same time commitment and personal involvement as volunteering for a Jewish organization eight hours a week, learning Yiddish, or restoring abandoned Jewish cemeteries. But unless we consider the intentions and motivations behind individuals' practices, we cannot understand their signification and significance. In other words, to make sense of the Jewish revival, we need to adopt an interpretive sociological approach (M. Weber 1978) and focus on the meaning individuals give to their actions. My interviews and field observations lead me to identify six main registers of engagement with Jewishness and Judaism noticeable in individuals and institutions alike:

---

39 To view these posters, go to https://drive.google.com/drive/folders/1Fbkv6wmEq9k1q _BotlVhF0H4c4jqpmoh. In 2013, the festival abandoned the more folkloric and ludic designs in favor of a hipper, artsier aesthetic combination of black, white, and gold. At the same time, it adopted a stylized Lion of Judah as its logo.

Crude cultural appropriation, such as dressing up in Hasidic garb as a form of street entertainment during a festival or dressing waitstaff in traditional Jewish clothing in a restaurant to suggest authenticity. Individuals and organizations engaging with Jewish culture at this level lack awareness of how problematic the practice is, and how offensive it can be to Jewish individuals.

Casual engagement, denoting occasional consumption of Jewish cultural products, such as going to a Jewish-style café for its atmosphere or visiting a klezmer club because it's hip.

Romantic engagement, characterized by an uncritical, nostalgic view of Jewish culture and Poland's multicultural past. The anthropologist Agnieszka Pasieka (2014) argues that the "multiculturalization of the past" is problematic insofar as it conceals the complex dynamic of ethnic and religious hierarchies, discrimination, and power struggles common to stratified communities of all sizes, and which, in Polish society, placed ethnic Poles-Catholics at the top and Jews at the bottom. What I call romantic philosemitism in chapter 3 is precisely at this register of engagement.

Critical-introspective engagement involves deep reflection on blind spots regarding past and present Polish-Jewish relations and Jewish issues more broadly. It is most common in those with a high level of commitment to Jewish-related institutions and processes, like studying Jewish history and researching Polish-Jewish relations, working in a Jewish museum, or volunteering in Jewish or Jewish-related institutions.

Political engagement is less common but more visible, as in the cases of non-Jews wearing kippahs, yellow paper daffodils/stars on their lapels, or clothing with Jewish slogans in order to express commemorative solidarity or to make political statements in the public sphere.

Empathetic versions of appropriation, a type of engagement displayed by participants who feel a personal connection with the Jewish past and current revival, whether through family history, personal relationships, or individual commitments, and express this commitment through their lifestyle choices and acts.

These registers can be placed on a spectrum defined by degrees of reflection. The first three are unreflective—lacking consideration of a given practice's meaning or potential impact on Jewish individuals—while the last three are by definition reflective. Within the unreflective and reflective poles, the registers of engagement are not mutually exclusive: casual and romantic engagements can overlap, for instance, and political engagement can accompany empathetic versions of cultural appropriation. One register of engagement can also lead to another across the spectrum. An unreflective, casual engagement with Poland's Jewish past may evolve into a critical-introspective register of engagement. Some pairings, however, are unlikely. It is improbable that an individual engaging with Jewish culture in the critical-introspective register would also engage in crude cultural appropriation. At the level of institutions, however, this perplexing pairing is possible, as the case of Chmielnik illustrates. This typology, then, serves less to classify specific practices than to provide an interpretive framework for analyzing them. It seeks to avoid dismissing a wide range of Jewish-related activities by non-Jewish Poles as yet another case of undifferentiated "cultural appropriation."

This interpretive approach and typological framework reveal that Jewish-related discourses and practices in the fourth, fifth, and sixth registers of engagement serve to deconstruct identity and reconstruct it along new lines. Organizations like Kraków's Jewish Culture Festival not only bring non-Jewish Poles into contact with past Jewish presence in Poland but seek to instill an understanding that Jews and Jewish culture are constitutive of Polish culture. To rescue Poland from its present deformed, mutilated state, Jewishness must be recovered and reintegrated. In other words, to create a twenty-first-century Jewish presence in Poland is also to correct, broaden, and heal Polish national identity.

Polishness, then, is being consciously challenged and redefined by activists and artists, but also by ordinary people through graffiti art, walking tours of formerly Jewish spaces, commemorative marches, and the cleaning and restoration of Jewish cemeteries. Participants in those activities wish to undermine the political claim that Poland is essentially, primordially ethno-Catholic. Assimilating Jewishness by learning to cook Jewish foods or consuming them at a Shabbat dinner at the JCC, learning Yiddish songs and Jewish dances, or doing volunteer work to support Jewish individuals and organizations is a way to demonstrate that being Polish does not equate to being Catholic. Empathetic cultural appropriation is both a form of alliance with Jews and a form of resistance to the dominant, ethno-Catholic vision of Polishness. As Ilona succinctly expressed, the cultural revival can be "an act of rebellion and opposition . . . against silence, against prejudices, against Radio Maryja."

Evocative as these examples are, not all Jewish-oriented initiatives or their participants have the same level of investment or commitment, or the same sensitivity to the Polish-Jewish past, to postwar violence and persistent antisemitism. We should therefore pause to ask whether the revival of Jewish culture reaches enough audiences and provokes sufficient critical insight into notions of Polishness to spur significant change.

Will these initiatives remain elite practices by artists and activists that will never resonate en masse? How successful are the mnemonic recovery of immaterial heritage and the embodied practices undertaken to follow the footsteps of Jews who no longer live in Poland?

We should also ask what the empathetic appropriation of Jewish culture means to Polish Jews. If Jewish culture can save Poles from their nightmares and Poland's deafening ethnic and religious monotony, as Sierakowski claimed, what's in it for the Jews? And most importantly, how are they rebuilding their own culture and communities in Poland? These are the questions I take up in the next chapter.

CHAPTER 6

Coming Out

"NEW JEWS" AND THE RECONSTRUCTION OF JEWISH IDENTITY

"Whatever the number, double it and then add one," Chief Rabbi of Poland Michael Schudrich responded when I asked him how many Jews there were in Poland. "Because there's always one coming out of the closet." The "coming out" metaphor is commonly used in the Jewish community to describe the process of revealing one's Jewish origins to loved ones, coworkers, and sometimes also the world at large.[1] The reasons for hiding in the closet are many. For those who lived through the war, hiding their Judaism/Jewishness was a question of survival. Some survived by "passing," thanks to their so-called good looks (*dobry wygląd*, i.e., non-Semitic appearance), advantageous connections, and the resources to obtain false papers. After the war, fears of violence, discrimination, and social stigma pushed many Polish Jews to retain their assumed gentile identities, and many concealed their origins even to their spouses and children. Polish Jews who had survived as refugees in the Soviet Union often returned to Poland committed to socialism, casting off their ethnic and religious identifications in conformity with the socialist vision of a secular and postethnic society. Whatever the strategies and motivations of survivors' dissimulation or assimilation, many of their children—the "second" post-Holocaust generation—either were not aware of their Jewish origins or knew but were raised in families where Judaism was not a defining feature of identity.[2]

---

1 The English expression is either inserted into Polish (e.g., *mam koleżankę w trakcie coming outu* [I have a friend in the process of coming out]) or translated into Polish (e.g., *jeszcze nie wyszedłem z szafy w pracy* [I haven't come out of the closet at work yet]). The closet metaphor is especially powerful because stories of Jewish children hiding in closets and armoires, of wardrobes with false panels where Jews hid during inspections, have become a key Holocaust trope. See Justyna Kowalska-Leder's insightful essay "Szafa" (2017).

2 Some important leaders of the Jewish revival belong to that second group. See, for example, the memoirs of Stanisław Krajewski (2005) and Konstanty Gebert (2008). For a memoir and analysis of the second generation's trauma, see Hoffman (2004).

The stories of the secret suddenly being revealed to those who did not know it constitute an entire genre. The author Agata Tuszyńska, for example, learned only as a young adult that her mother was Jewish and had undergone traumatic wartime experiences. As she wrote in her auto-biographical account, *A Family History of Fear* (2005), "This book has been within me for years, like a secret, ever since I found out that I'm not who I thought I was—from the moment my mother decided to tell me she was Jewish." This revelation was a turning point in Tuszyńska's life. Still, it took time for her to integrate her mother's history into her own story and to embrace Jewishness as part of her identity. The revelation came as an even greater shock to Romuald-Jakub Weksler-Waszkinel, a Catholic priest who learned only in his thirties that his parents had adopted him as a baby from his Jewish birth mother, who wanted to save him from death.[3]

Members of the third generation—grandchildren of survivors—shared many more stories with me. One young woman realized her grandfather was Jewish when he had a stroke and woke up speaking Yiddish; others found documents proving a grandfather's change of name or a grandmother's pa-perwork seeking Holocaust survivors' compensation from Germany. Some learned of their grandparents' Jewishness from deathbed revelations or were told that a parent had been adopted by non-Jews during the war. Others had long harbored quiet suspicions pieced together from fragments and hints—a grandmother baking challah on Fridays, a grandfather getting phone calls from Israel—before finally confirming their Jewish origins through deliberate research.[4] In short, discovering one's Jewish origins is a not a rare occurrence in Poland today. For some—those who are told of their heritage in confidence, and those who find out by chance or through their own research—a better metaphor might be that of facing a skeleton in the family closet. They may decide to slam the door shut and move on, or choose instead to investigate the past, embracing the possibility of building a new identity in the present. And still others, who knew they had Jewish roots but did not accord much weight to that part of their identity, are now acquainting themselves with aspects of Jewishness and Judaism that were unavailable to them until recently. All these "new Jews," as they are often referred to and even call themselves, re-cover Jewish identity by digging into their family history to find branches

3 See footnote 40 on page 23.

4 These stories of "discovery" were shared by interviewees and community leaders. Many more are available in Irena Wiszniewska's book of interviews with Polish Jews (2014) and Katka Reszke's analysis of the third post-Holocaust generation's narratives (2013). See also documentary films such as *Torn* (2011) and *H.I. Jew Positive* (2013), by Ronit Kertsner; *We Are Here*, by Francine Zuckerman (2013); and *The Return*, by Adam Zucker (2014).

of the family where Jewishness and Judaism remained underground or bloomed abroad. They are hungry for knowledge. Many attend festivals of Jewish culture, take history classes, read about the history of Polish Jews, and visit museums. Some seek guidance from rabbis, while others join secular organizations like the JCCs in Kraków or Warsaw. Each year, a few who meet the Birthright Israel criteria join a group to visit Israel.[5]

The number of Polish Jews living in Poland is very small. In the 2011 Polish census, only seven thousand residents of Poland indicated "Jewish" as their primary or secondary identity (Główny Urząd Statystyczny 2015). Based on that number, Sergio DellaPergolla (2020: 311) estimated that Poland's "core Jewish population"[6] in 2019 was approximately 4,500, and that thirteen thousand individuals had at least one Jewish grandparent or a Jewish spouse (thereby satisfying the criteria of Israel's Law of Return and being eligible for Israeli citizenship). While these are only estimates, it is certain that the number of Jews living in Poland today is a minute fraction of what it was on the eve of the Second World War, and that Poland's Jewish population is minuscule even in comparison with that of its neighbors.[7]

DellaPergolla's 2019 demographic snapshot fails, however, to show the slow but steady growth of Poland's Jewish population since the fall of communism. In 1990 Zvi Gitelman estimated the total Jewish population of Poland to be five thousand. Fewer than half were registered with the official *Gminy*. Ten years later, in 2000, the number of Jews officially registered with *Gminy* or receiving aid from the American Jewish Joint Distribution Committee had tripled to approximately 7,500, and between ten thousand and fifteen thousand additional Poles had shown interest in rediscovering their Jewish ancestry (Gruber 2000). These numbers could grow significantly, as community leaders believe that tens of thousands more Poles have some Jewish ancestry.[8]

---

5 Because of the Holocaust's long-term impact on the Jewish communities of Central and Eastern Europe, criteria for eligibility to the Birthright program in this region are different from those of other diasporas: having at least one Jewish grandparent instead of one Jewish parent suffices. At the time of my participant observation in a Polish Birthright trip (2017), the program was restricted to those between the ages of eighteen and twenty-six. In 2018, Birthright raised the maximum age to thirty-two.

6 This measure "includes all persons who, when asked in a sociodemographic survey, identify themselves as Jews, *or* who are identified as Jews by a respondent in the same household, *and* do not profess another monotheistic religion" (DellaPergola 2020: 323).

7 For comparative purposes, in 2019 the "core Jewish population" of Russia was estimated to be 165,000, that of Germany 118,000, Ukraine 48,000, and Hungary 47,300 (DellaPergolla 2020: 265).

8 Interviews with Rabbi Michael Schudrich (September 28, 2012). Jonathan Ornstein estimated that as many as one hundred thousand Poles may have one Jewish grandparent (interview, March 26, 2021).

That growth is neither the result of natural increase nor (as was the case in Germany) of immigration, but of a cultural shift. It was accelerated by a confluence of fast-moving currents: the fall of communism and the lifting of certain taboos; the influx of foreign financial and human resources facilitating the creation of new Jewish schools, student clubs, and community centers; the public debate over Poles' role in the Holocaust; the rediscovery of Poland's Jewish past; a movement that transformed Jewishness into a positive category in Center-Left and progressive circles; and the coming of age of the third post-Holocaust generation.[9]

What the 2019 demographic snapshot also blurs are the people and their stories, and the dynamic nature of the Polish Jewish community. As Miriam Gonczarska, a Jewish activist and progressive-Judaism leader, told the journalist Irena Wiszniewska, "Development is not only a matter of numbers. Social engagement evolves through time: someone moves abroad, comes back, moves to a different city, retreats [from social life] because of children or a heavy workload. Development is not always visible in numbers, but it always is at the level of consciousness" (2014: 30). It is on this level of consciousness, an awakening in those who choose to explore their Jewishness, and on the diverse processes of individual discovery and cultural reappropriation that I focus in this chapter.[10]

Recovery and Renewal: Building a New Community

Since the fall of communism, and particularly since the mid-2000s, Jewish institutions in Poland have expanded significantly, with the opening of JCC Kraków in 2007, JCC Warsaw in 2013, Hillel Polska in 2017, and the introduction, in 2008, of annual Limmud meetings—three-day

9 According to the "Hansen effect" in migration and immigration studies, the third generation is typically inclined to search for roots that the first generation left behind and the second tried to ignore. See D. Weber (1991).

10 I am aware that basing my analysis on people whose discovery of Jewish origins motivated them to explore that identity provides only a partial portrait of the impact of those revelations on different individuals. My goal in this book is to understand the meaning of Jewishness to those who embrace it (Jewish or non-Jewish), and, among those for whom it becomes a salient feature of their identity, to study how they recover and reappropriate Jewishness and/or Judaism in their lives. When I asked Jewish interviewees how their siblings or cousins reacted to learning of their Jewish origins, they reported a wide range of reactions, from acceptance and embrace to indifference, disapproval, and denial, and sometimes even conflicts and family rifts. Needless to say, there are many Polish Jews for whom Jewish identity is a given, and who are therefore not engaged in that process of self-discovery.

meetings or "festivals of Jewish learning" organized by and for Jews.[11] These secular institutions are important; they provide opportunities to explore Jewishness for those who are not religious while also offering hospitable venues for observant Jews. On the religious front, too, the menu is expanding: while the Orthodox movement remains dominant in Polish Judaism, there are now several Reform communities (in Warsaw, Kraków, Gdańsk, and Konstancin-Jeziorna), and Chabad Lubavitch has representatives in Warsaw and Kraków. Official religious communities (*Gminy*) continue to operate, as do other organizations such as *TSKŻ* (the Social-Cultural Association of Jews in Poland).[12] These institutions provide tools for the renewal of Judaism in the country and the relearning of Jewish culture for those just discovering Jewish roots and nurturing their growth.

Led by smart, dynamic community organizers, institutions like the JCCs in Kraków and Warsaw have become the center of Jewish secular life. They offer spaces where Jews of all stripes and nationalities, together with their mostly non-Jewish staff and volunteers, build a new kind of Polish Jewish world. The JCCs allow those who grew up in Poland's monoethnic and monoreligious postwar society to acquaint themselves with Jewish culture through a variety of classes, workshops, and rituals.

JCC Kraków, for example, provides a wide range of services to its 750 local members and their children, from a preschool to a seniors' club, and offers Hebrew and Yiddish classes, cooking workshops, book clubs, public lectures, Shabbat dinners, and day trips, as well as travel excursions across Poland and beyond.[13] The JCC is a colorful and welcoming place that its members, staff, and volunteers often call a "home away from home." At once hip and familial, the atmosphere keeps people coming back. Members learn how to celebrate holidays they have never celebrated at home;

---

11 *Limmuds* are learning meetings organized by and for Jews, where all courses, seminars, and workshops are taught and animated by members of the community, with rare exceptions. The first Limmud Polska took place in 2008, with approximately 350 participants; it now attracts over one thousand. Meetings take place in a hotel outside Warsaw and are the occasion of large communal get-togethers where the atmosphere is resolutely festive. I attended the 2016 meeting. For accounts of the institutional renaissance and communal renewal of Jewish life in Poland by participants, see Gebert and Datner (2001), Krajewski (2005), Gebert (2008), Penn, Gebert, and Goldstein (2009), and Penn (2014). For a striking photographic essay, see Fishman (2018).

12 *Towarzystwo Społeczno-Kulturalne Żydów w Polsce (TSKŻ)* was founded in 1950. For a timeline of the creation of various institutions, organizations, and initiatives, consult appendix B.

13 Membership is extended to Jewish persons, regardless of citizenship, and to their spouses on request. Non-Jewish members may retain membership after divorce or the death of their Jewish spouse (interview with Jonathan Ornstein, March 26, 2021).

they discover new rituals and new foods, establish new domestic habits, and learn to live with and in a new calendar and cycle of observances.[14] The JCC has a genealogist on staff to help members recalibrate their place in family histories. It organizes weekly (kosher) Shabbat dinners led by the local Orthodox rabbi.

Directed by the charismatic, American-born Jonathan Ornstein, the JCC has become the organizing center and the heart of Kraków's Jewish community. JCC Kraków is a microcosm of the complexities of the renewal of Jewish life in contemporary Poland, pressed into service on multiple levels and in multiple media. It serves a diverse group of Jews: elderly and young, "old" and "new," as well as foreign Jews living in Kraków. It negotiates communal issues with older organizations such as the official Jewish Gmina. It also works closely with Jewish-focused cultural institutions such as the Jewish Culture Festival and the Galicia Museum, also located in Kazimierz, Kraków's Jewish neighborhood.

One of the JCC's missions is to "change both the world's perception of Poland and Poland's perception of the Jews." Ornstein has extended his role of community builder in Kraków to become a sort of ambassador of Poland's Jewish revival via public speaking throughout North America, and by creating new transatlantic commemorative initiatives like Holocaust Survivor Day and the Ride for the Living. That latter event brings Poles— Jewish and non-Jewish—together with non-Polish Jews from Western Europe and North America to cycle the one hundred kilometers "from the gates of Auschwitz-Birkenau to JCC Kraków," thereby "commemorating the Holocaust and honoring the rebirth of the Jewish community in Kraków."[15] The ride reverses the historical itinerary of Polish Jews from their hometowns to Nazi camps. It also disrupts and complicates the narrative promoted by the March of the Living, when Jewish teenagers from around the world come to Auschwitz-Birkenau on Yom Hashoah (Holocaust Remembrance Day) to commemorate the victims of the Holocaust, and then travel to Israel to celebrate Yom HaAtzmaut (Israel Independence Day) (Zubrzycki 2006: 127–31). In that narrative, Poland stands for death and Israel for life. The Ride *for* the Living focuses instead on Jewish life

---

14 On the importance of calendars for identity-group formation, see Eviatar Zerubavel's classic article on Easter and Passover (1982); on time and collective memory more broadly, see his *Time Maps: Collective Memory and the Social Shapes of the Past* (2003).

15 https://ridefortheliving.org. The Ride for the Living originated to commemorate the survivor Marcel Zielinski, who at eleven years old walked back from Auschwitz-Birkenau after its liberation by the Soviet army to Kraków, his hometown. Now living in Montreal, Zielinski is an avid cyclist, hence the choice of a bicycle ride.

in Poland in the present.[16] The JCC's Shabbat dinner marking the end of the Jewish Culture Festival gathers some six hundred guests from Poland and abroad and has become another signature event that celebrates and promotes Poland's Jewish revival.

This renewal of Jewish life is built from hard cultural work. It requires the creation or recreation of ties between diverse individuals and institutions, and the expansion and solidification of social networks and alliances. "New Jews" in Kraków have access to several different Jewish spaces: the secular JCC; the *Gmina*; the Chabad-led Izaak Synagogue; and the Reform movement, which meets at the Galicia Museum. Despite their significant differences, one may encounter the same people in all of these places, as individuals try to map their place in a complex ecology. They seek answers to a question perhaps more complex than it first appeared: Who are my people now? And where? At the first Purim ceremony I attended, in 2011, the reading of the Megillah (Book of Esther) took place at the Remuh Synagogue. It was followed by a parade through the streets of Kazimierz, with a local television-station crew in tow, and ended at the JCC, where many partied late into the night. The following day, almost everyone reassembled at the Izaak Synagogue for brunch; later the JCC seniors and their friends met at the Klezmer Hois Restaurant for dinner and a musical program (performed by non-Jews).[17] All these events and venues contribute to a process of creating, celebrating, and promoting Judaism and Jewish culture across a range of aesthetics, media, materials, and institutional forms.

A Tale of Two Seders

If the issue of who makes up the Jewish community is an ongoing domain of cultural work, another vexed problem is the issue of what is properly Jewish, and how to make it so. These challenges are not unique to Poland, of course, but in that country's post-Holocaust context, the cultural work required is especially intense. While holidays are typically celebrated at

16 For years the JCC spread a large banner addressed to March of the Living participants visiting Kazimierz: "Hey, March of the Living! Come inside and see Jewish LIFE!" After groups started to visit the JCC on a regular basis, a revised banner replaced the old one: "Thank you, March of the Living, for coming in and seeing Jewish life."

17 Purim is a holiday held in spring to commemorate the defeat of a plot by the Persian Empire official Haman to kill the Jews. It is celebrated with the wearing of masks and costumes and eating of hamantaschen, triangular pastries meant to resemble Haman's ears.

home with family and friends, in Poland today many Jews celebrate holidays such as Passover or Purim at communal organizations. Many individuals have been cut off from those rituals and traditions and must learn them anew; others have no Jewish loved ones to celebrate with at home. I recount here two seders I attended in Kraków, the first at the JCC, the second at the official *Gmina's* headquarters, to highlight different models of, and visions for, the community.

Unlike the Christian "seder" I discussed in the last chapter, which was a well-rehearsed performance rather than a communal experience or a religious ritual, the seder I attended at the JCC-Kraków was slightly chaotic but a vibrant affair joining a mix of generations and families.

A few days before the beginning of Passover in 2013, the JCC's director, Jonathan Ornstein, decided it was time to buy china and silverware for the JCC to set out for festive communal meals, replacing the disposable items they typically used. But the new tableware needed to be kashered before use. It was not a simple undertaking, as the process involves immersion in a mikvah, or ritual bath, and everything had to be carried from the JCC to the Eden Hotel, which then housed the only mikvah in town. I accompanied Jonathan and a volunteer, holding doors open as they lugged box after heavy box through the hotel's narrow lobby and down in a cramped elevator to the small mikvah area.

At the dinner, guests gasped in awe as they took their places at long tables set with the new porcelain dishes. JCC members and their families, Jewish American expatriates, the United States consul, a few scholars, and a couple of journalists were in attendance. More guests arrived than the main room could accommodate, and more tables were set up in the reception area (figure 41). A second room was taken over by the JCC's younger crowd, the seder led by Aleks, a twenty-something JCC member who took his role very seriously. Kraków's head rabbi, Rabbi Boaz, was at home in Israel for the holiday but had sent his oldest son to lead the main seder. The young man was obviously knowledgeable, but he was inexperienced at leading a crowd, especially one unfamiliar with the ritual. Few in the room knew what to do or say when. Boaz Jr. had his work cut out to capture and keep the guests' attention. Yet the atmosphere was festive, and the ritual morphed into a collective affair, with a translator and other guests helping to guide their neighbors through the ritual. Toward the end, Pan Muniek, a senior JCC member, Holocaust survivor, and one of the few remaining native Yiddish speakers in Kraków, got up and sang a Yiddish song. Boaz's son concluded the event by inviting everyone to sing "Hatikvah," the Israeli national anthem. Only a few were familiar enough

FIGURE 41. Passover seder at the Jewish Community Centre in Kraków. (Photo by Geneviève Zubrzycki, March 25, 2013.)

with the anthem to join in, though, and the participants slowly dispersed while volunteers and the most active members remained to clean up and debrief. The following day, a full-page article on the JCC seder appeared in the Israeli daily *Maariv*, to the community's delight.

That evening I accompanied Jonathan, his partner Kasia, and a few other JCC members to a very different seder: the *Gmina*'s seder on the second night of Passover. This one was small, formal, and solemn rather than festive. It had gravitas but no communitas; in fact, there was a certain tension in the air, as relations between the JCC and the *Gmina* were strained. The *Gmina*'s president, Tadeusz Jakubowicz, was accompanied by his daughter, the vice-president. Her partner, serving as *Gmina* manager, led the seder, accompanied by Itzhak Horovitz, an ultra-Orthodox cantor, *mashgiach*, and restaurateur who filled the room with his powerful baritone.[18]

Upon the conclusion of the Barekh—a prayer offered after meals— Elijah's cup was set aside and, as is customary at the seder, the door to the dining area was opened. The seder leader loudly declared that the door

18 A *mashgiach* supervises and certifies the kosher status of an establishment.

was open only to let the prophet Elijah enter, and theatrically recited in Polish verses from the Psalms and Lamentations that are often softened or replaced with less violent alternatives: "Pour your wrath upon the nations that did not know You and upon the kingdoms that did not call upon Your Name! Since they have consumed Ya'akov and laid waste his habitation" (Psalms 79:6–7). "Pour out Your fury upon them and the fierceness of Your anger shall reach them!" (Psalms 69:25). "You shall pursue them with anger and eradicate them from under the skies of the Lord" (Lamentations 3:66). The room was silent. Many attendees lowered their heads and exchanged side glances. The silence was broken by Horovitz singing the last hymns and songs, and then the "Hatikvah."

We left soon after. Once out on the street, the small group of JCC members erupted with comments, interpreting the recitation of those verses as an aggressive rejection of goyim that was inappropriate in the Polish context. Someone said it was a terrible "faux pas"; but several exclaimed that it was far beyond a faux pas or a passive-aggressive message. They saw it as an obvious insult to those present and to the broader Jewish community, since most have non-Jewish family members and loved ones. This kind of brazen exclusion, someone else added, not only was uncalled for and offensive to the non-Jews present at the seder but even hypocritical, since the *Gmina* president's own family is mixed.

Both seders highlight significant issues in the renewal of Jewish life in Poland. The first is the rediscovery and reappropriation of Jewish traditions in communal settings, thanks in great part to support from foreign organizations and foundations. This is not without its own challenges. A young foreign rabbi once confessed to me that he felt a bit uneasy in his role in Poland, which he felt was part of a "quasi-colonial" program, with foreigners—mostly Americans—teaching Polish Jews how to be Jewish. This situation does not go unnoticed among Polish Jews, since nearly all rabbis in Poland are American- or Israeli-born. In an interview with a journalist, a Yiddish-language activist, who had learned as a child from his dying maternal grandmother that she was Jewish, explained that

the majority of Jews in Poland discovered their roots and are just now building their identity. They're learning to be Jews according to models worked out by different institutions. Whether they are religious or secular, these are strongly associated with Israel or the United States—that is, institutions that are more or less Zionist. At the Shalom Foundation there are three flags hoisted: the Polish, the Israeli, and the American flags. That bothers me. And not only me. (Quoted in Wiszniewska 2014: 104, my translation)

The fact that most Jewish institutions are typically sponsored by foreign foundations—again, mostly American—and private donors, and often belong to transnational organizations, like the JCC, Hillel, or Chabad, sometimes leads to tensions. In one public meeting, for instance, a young Polish Jewish academic challenged an American-born, Poland-based Jewish activist's representation of Jewish life in Poland, asking who had authorized him to speak in the name of "Polish Jews."[19]

The second issue both seders bring out is that of tensions between older forms of communal associations, such as the *Gmina*, and new organizations like the JCC. They have different styles of leadership and decision-making, unequal access to local resources, and different models of interaction with non-Jews and non-Poles. The JCC's inclusive membership and its general familial atmosphere explains why there were five times as many guests at its seder than at the *Gmina's*, with many young families with children and plenty of young adults present. There is little doubt that this form of community best corresponds to the needs of the third and fourth generations of Polish Jews. Yet both seders illustrate the complex relations that both bridge and divide different groups within the Jewish community, as well as the perceived hierarchies of Jewishness and the zones of its making and manifestation.

Hierarchies of Jewishness

Hierarchies of Jewishness are not officially recognized in secular communities, yet different categories are often unofficially acknowledged (Cukras-Stelągowska 2016; Lorenz 2016). Some of the categories used by my interlocutors included "halachic Jews" (those who are Jewish through matrilineal descent), "Jewish on both sides," "new Jews," "converts," and "wannabes" (in English). While people of all categories are—for the most part—welcome in the community, the issue of who fits where is contested and debated among friends and the topic of a constant stream of gos-

---

19 Of course this type of challenge could have been made to a Polish Jew as well, as national origin is not the only issue dividing members of a diverse community. I found non-Polish-born representatives of Jewish institutions to be typically well integrated into their local Jewish community, as well as into Polish society more broadly. They also play an important role in explaining the Polish context and the situation of Polish Jews to North Americans and Israelis.

sip and rumors. Once, for example, friends shared over beers the news of a community member recently engaged to a halachic Jew. All agreed that this was a "big deal"; that issue settled, they moved to more detailed questions about the fiancée's family: Was she "really" Jewish through her mother's lineage, or was her mother a convert?

People's claims of Jewish heritage are sometimes questioned: "Ach, what are you talking about? He's no Jew at all! He was going through the conversion process, it's hard, it takes time, and then there's the circumcision thing . . . and then all of the sudden, it 'turns out' that his maternal grandmother was Jewish?! Yeah, right." For converts to Judaism, their status in these hierarchies may depend on who prepared them for conversion and where the conversion ritual took place—Israel being the gold standard.

A person's place in the hierarchies is also affected by whether they married a Jew or someone with Jewish origins. One evening, for example, a JCC member shared with me her frustration with the Kraków's Religious Jewish Community (*Gmina Wyznaniowa Żydowska*), which had denied her formal membership because she was no longer a Polish citizen (her family had been stripped of Polish citizenship when they left the country in the late 1950s). She now had an apartment in town and was active at the JCC, organizing various meetings and activities. She expressed her sense of injustice by complaining about the "half-Jews" and "fake Jews" who were members of the *Gmina*, about those "married to goyish women and raising Catholic families," yet excluding her, a fully Jewish woman.

Tensions also exist between models of Jewishness—one based on ancestry and culture, for example, versus one based on religious orthodoxy.[20] During my fieldwork, I witnessed a conflict between two young men studying with the rabbi and competing for his attention. Janek was raised in a Jehovah's Witness family in a small provincial town, was enrolled in Judaic studies at the university, and was in the process of converting to Orthodox Judaism. He was effortlessly cool and well-liked, and his English was so good that he often translated Rabbi Boaz's Dvar Torah (a commentary-dialogue on a passage of the Torah) for English speakers attending JCC Shabbat dinners. Aleks was slightly younger and had Jewish roots. He was more reserved and less at ease in social settings. Both young

---

20 Anxieties about the inclusion of too many converts and their potential "takeover" are sometimes expressed (Lorenz 2016), and conflicts between groups also arise over issues such as how "authentically" Jewish members are and whether a community is (too) inclusive of gentile family members.

men wore kippahs and tzitzit and half-grown sidelocks.[21] One afternoon they had a heated argument. It was not clear exactly what it was about, but a couple of days later, during a Purim event at Klezmer Hois, Aleks complained to me about Janek's condescending attitude toward him, constantly telling Aleks what to do and how to do it. Aleks was furious that his Judaism was not properly recognized and respected by a convert, simply because he was not halachically Jewish and had not yet gone through an official conversion: "But I grew up speaking Yiddish with my grandma! And he's going to tell *me* how to be a real Jew, just because he's further along in his Orthodox conversion?"

Great Expectations

What is the future of Polish Jewry? That question or some variation thereof is asked of Jewish community leaders at every public meeting with non-Jewish Poles or foreigners. During the 2010 festival, in a conversation between the JCC director Jonathan Ornstein and the Polish Jewish philosopher and activist Stanisław Krajewski, an audience member asked what was the ultimate goal of the Jewish revival. Ornstein responded that the goal was to help Polish Jews to recover their identity and choose their own paths as Jews. The JCC, he said, offered a secular setting where they could do so. If the path for some was to make aliyah—that is, to emigrate to Israel—then that was what he supported. For Krajewski, though, the prospect of making aliyah posed the key dilemma. The institutional renaissance, cultural revival, and religious renewal taking place in Poland were important developments. Yet, he reasoned, the more observant one became, the more difficult it was to live in Poland. But when observant Jews left for Israel, the Polish Jewish community was weakened again. The goal, Krajewski argued, was for the renewal to create the conditions for Polish Jews to remain and thrive *as Jews* in Poland.

For Rafał, who knew from his youth that his grandfather was Jewish and decided to convert in the 1990s, the style of the youngest generation of new Jews poses challenges for building a long-term Jewish community:

Today people have completely different notions on how to be a Jew. In Poland it's *trendy* and *cool* to have Jewish origins. But doing some-

---

21 Tzitzit are fringes on the corners of the prayer shawl (tallit); the term also commonly refers to the fringed undervest worn by some observant men.

thing with it—by registering with the *Gmina*, participating in religious services, leaving for Israel—is too embarrassing. To be an active Jew, for those twenty-somethings, is some kind of oddity. . . . I can understand people who cut themselves off from their roots, considering their Jewishness a closed chapter . . . . But I don't feel special respect for individuals who desire Jewishness because it is *multi-kulti* and allows them to distinguish themselves. . . . I see a kind of instrumentalism in that attitude. . . . But then there are no miracles: if we wish for some Jews to be [here, in Poland], there must be Jewish institutions, Jewish marriages, and Jewish children. (Quoted in Wiszniewska 2014: 87; italics denote terms used in the original Polish)

Rafał converted to Orthodox Judaism and was circumcised in his adulthood. In the end, after having lived in Israel and encountered different forms of Judaism, he found his religious home in the Polish Reform movement.

While new Jews of the third or fourth post-Holocaust generation have multiple paths of practice on offer, they are not all equally viable options. On a walking tour of Kazimierz, I spoke with Marta, a twenty-something woman from Kraków who volunteered at the Jewish Culture Festival, and an American tourist. Marta told us that her father had recently learned that his mother was Jewish. He didn't care much about the revelation, but Marta was taken with it and eager to discover her "new identity." For her, that one Jewish grandparent seemed to matter more than the others, and more than years of living as a Pole. She felt torn, however, because she could not imagine wearing a wig (to comply with the Orthodox requirement that married women cover their hair). "Oh, honey," the American tourist responded, with a benevolent smile, "I'm Jewish, and I'm not wearing any wig. . . . If you were in the US, you'd just go see another rabbi." While Marta did indeed have other options—join a Reform synagogue or develop a secular Jewish identity—those, she told me later, didn't seem "really Jewish." "I don't quite feel it with Rabbi Tanya," she said, referring to the leader of Kraków's Reform congregation.[22] It wasn't immediately clear to me what she meant by that, but several months later, during a Purim party at the JCC, Marta and her friend were encouraging each other to be brave enough to talk to Rabbi Gluck, who was based in Brooklyn and visited Kraków a few times a year. He looked the part of the archetypical

22 Rabbi Tanya Segal is a Russian-born Israeli and an artist and performer. Her Reform congregation meets at the Galicia Museum, not having been granted access to any of the seven synagogues in Kraków by the *Gmina*.

rabbi: male, elderly, sporting a long white beard, black satin coat, and fur hat, and bearing an honorary title straight from the eighteenth century (chief rabbi of Galicia). Maybe he would be able to help Marta get over a painful breakup and move forward on her (Jewish) path? Wisdom, it seemed to her, could come only from the most traditional Jewish authority. Hence her dilemma: to become a "real Jew," she believed, she would have to take the Orthodox path, a path she nevertheless was ambivalent about—and which she ultimately did not take.

As Irena Grudzińska-Gross wrote in her preface to a collection of interviews with Polish Jews of the second and third post-Holocaust generations, "Their search is not a return to the culture of their ancestors, but something else, new. It is the discovery of fragments, pieces, from which one's own history is constituted" (2014: 8). And that process of discovery is arduous and confusing. For those who choose the Orthodox path, it can feel infantilizing, as they are forced to relearn how to be and act in the world, but also reassuring because the rules are clear.

I gained a glimpse of those difficulties when I witnessed what appeared to be an impromptu wedding ceremony of two middle-aged couples in the courtyard of the JCC during the Jewish Culture Festival. It wasn't clear exactly what was going on, even to the JCC director and staff. Several men conferred on the part of the lawn closest to the synagogue wall, putting together a chuppah. Rabbis arrived. Many in the small crowd were, like me, accidental witnesses to the ceremony. The story circulating was that the couple had come to Kraków during the Jewish festival to get "remarried as Jews." The brides, I was told, were waiting inside the JCC building until the men were ready for the ceremony to begin. "They're not from here," a member of the JCC told me. The first groom, a middle-aged man with a long gray beard, wore a black hat and a *kittel* over his black suit and sports shirt, and waited under the chuppah, surrounded by two Kraków-based Orthodox rabbis and a few others visiting from the US for the festival. Local Jewish men held the chuppah.[23]

Finally a plan for the ceremony coalesced, and the event got underway. The first bride emerged from the JCC building, making her way through people gathered on the steps. She wore a long white Indian cotton skirt and a white long-sleeved T-shirt, her hair tied in a chignon adorned with tiny white flowers. Her face was covered by a simple bridal veil. She was accompanied by two local women who guided her through the ritual. She

---

23 A *kittel* is a white coat worn by religious Jews over their regular clothes on religious occasions. Because it symbolizes purity, it is sometimes worn by bridegrooms.

FIGURE 42. Wedding in the courtyard of the Jewish Community Centre during the Jewish Culture Festival in Kraków. (Photo by Geneviève Zubrzycki, June 28, 2010.)

walked toward her groom as the latter, camera in hand, snapped a picture of her (figure 42). He beamed. She appeared frazzled, leaning on the other women to direct her. The ceremony itself was quick. As it concluded, the groom removed his borrowed *kittel* and passed it to the second groom, who took his place under the chuppah. The second bride emerged from the JCC. She was slightly older, in her late fifties. She wore what seemed to be her street clothes—a long beige linen skirt and sweater—and a white shawl over her hair. The only clearly bridal symbol was the bouquet of yellow roses clasped in her hands. After the second ceremony was over, both brides were ushered a few feet away for a joyous round dance with four other women. Everyone clapped and snapped pictures, while the brides were clearly confused, neither of them smiling. They seemed to be following the cues given to them and embarrassed by everyone watching.

Conversion requires humility and courage since converts typically must learn everything anew.[24] What pushes them to embark on this journey?

---

24 This is certainly not unique to Jews in Poland, of course. On *baalei teshuva*—secular Jews who return to Judaism, often Orthodox—see Davidman (1991).

A Journey into (Polish) Jewishness

In 2017 I was fortunate to observe thirty young Poles negotiate their Jewishness during a ten-day Birthright trip to Israel. Founded in 1999 by a group of philanthropists led by the North American billionaires Charles Bronfman and Michael Steinhardt, Birthright Israel is a Zionist program that offers every eligible Jew a free trip to Israel. Its primary goal is "to ensure the future of the Jewish people by strengthening Jewish identity, Jewish communities, and connection with Israel via a trip to Israel for the majority of Jewish young adults from around the world." It also seeks to "motivate young people to continue to explore their Jewish identity and support for Israel and maintain long-lasting connections with the Israelis they meet on their trip."[25]

I flew to Warsaw the day before the group's departure for Israel. We met for the first time for an afternoon of formal introductions, icebreaker games, practical information about the trip, a briefing on safety guidelines and rules, and a rudimentary lesson in common Hebrew expressions. There were two pairs of siblings; a handful of other participants were acquainted because they belonged to the same social circle at home. A few had been to Israel before to visit extended family, and two women (from two different families) spoke Hebrew because they had an Israeli parent. The participants had converged from the four corners of Poland— from large cities such as Warsaw, Kraków, Wrocław, Gdańsk, Szczecin, and Łódź, as well as from smaller towns such as Częstochowa, Luban, and Radomsko. The youngest participant was eighteen, the oldest twenty-six. The two Polish *madrichim* (leaders) were recent participants in the Birthright program. One was from Warsaw and had deep roots in the Jewish community; the other was a "new Jew" from Wrocław who had only recently discovered his Jewish heritage. I introduced myself to the group as a sociologist conducting research on identity and was given the status of "staff" on official documents and on my ID badge.

Strangers in the "Homeland": Ten Days of Birthright Israel

Birthright trips are typically timed so that groups celebrate Shabbat in Jerusalem. Arriving in Israel on a Monday, we immediately traveled north

---

25 https://www.birthrightisrael.com/about-us. For a detailed description and analysis of Birthright Israel's mission and educational goals, organizational structure, and role in the identity formation of young American Jews, see Saxe and Chazan (2008). See also Kelner (2010); and Taylor, Levi, and Dinovitzer (2012).

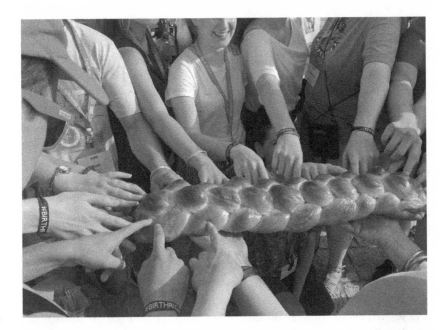

FIGURE 43. Shehecheyanu ceremony on the Haas Promenade, Jerusalem, to welcome the Polish Birthright group. (Photo by Geneviève Zubrzycki, July 20, 2017.)

to Tiberias, where we stayed three days, visiting the Golan Heights, rafting down the Jordan River, and exploring Tzfat, known as the birthplace of Kabbalah. By Thursday afternoon, all were eager to finally reach their "true destination," Jerusalem. Many hoped for a better hotel, some were planning roommate swaps, and everyone seemed excited at the prospect of an evening out on the town in Tel Aviv on Saturday night, after Havdalah, the ceremony marking the conclusion of Shabbat and the beginning of the new week.

We arrived in the late afternoon on Thursday and were welcomed on the Haas Promenade, overlooking the city, by an American-born, Jerusalem-based Birthright representative. Our arrival in the holy city was celebrated with a Shehecheyanu blessing, a prayer for first occasions, over challah and accompanied by festive tam-tam players (figure 43). Our host explained the significance of arriving in Jerusalem: "Your parents and grandparents dreamed of being here and of you making it here, and here you are!"—a line that was repeated frequently over the following days.[26]

26 Our Israeli tour guide and the two Israel-based Birthright representatives we met during the trip spoke to us in English. All special workshops, small-group exercises, and rituals were conducted in Polish by our two Polish *madrichim*. When IDF soldiers joined us for those special activities, someone would typically translate into English for them.

The young participants were giddy, some dancing, others taking in the breathtaking panorama, snapping photos and selfies.

A visit to the Western Wall was planned for the following morning, but it was not certain we would be able to go. A week earlier, two Israeli Border Police officers had been killed and two others injured by Arab Israelis just outside the Temple Mount. The Israeli police immediately closed the area, and the grand mufti of Jerusalem was detained after asking the faithful to defy the orders and march on the Al-Aqsa Mosque for the Friday prayers. In the days that followed, protests erupted on the Temple Mount, and new security measures were implemented, restricting access to the holy site and leading to more protests, violence, and retaliation. As a result, we didn't know whether Birthright would agree to let us go to the Old City, nor whether we'd be allowed in. The uncertainty only intensified our anticipation.

We were already seated in the bus early on Friday morning when we finally received official authorization to go. After passing through the security checkpoint, we quickly crossed the Armenian Quarter to reach the Jewish sector of the Old City. As we approached the Western Wall, our Israeli guide stopped and instructed us to close our eyes. She played soothing music on a small speaker, and then asked the five Israel Defense Forces (IDF) soldiers who had joined our group the day before to slowly guide us to an area from which we would be able to see the wall below us. As we opened our eyes, our guide instructed participants to "take it all in: this, the most sacred place–which your parents, grandparents, and great-grandparents hoped to see for themselves, and hoped their descendants to see one day." The response from the group was mixed. Some giggled, others were just impatient to move to the site. One young man later told me the whole scene was way too much, that the guide was "trying too hard with these theatrics." A couple of young women and one young man seemed moved by the experience. The guide told me, "It does not matter whether it works for all, a few, or just one. If I reach only one, then that's the one that matters at that time."

As we descended toward the wall, women and men were instructed to separate. Several women from our group commented on how small the women's section was compared to the men's, and on how "casual" the scene was, with random plastic chairs dotting the area. Participants were told they could write a prayer and wedge it between stones, and most did. An Orthodox woman nearby was praying and wailing, sparking curiosity and concern among the Birthright group. Two women in the group told me they felt "the weight of history" and the "spiritual energy" of the site.

Others later told me they felt uncomfortable, out of place, more confused by the site and scene than moved by it, even that they did not belong. "Perhaps because I'm not religious? This feels so foreign to me," one of them speculated aloud as we walked back toward the bus.

We had free time that afternoon at the Machane Yehuda open-air market. I walked through the busy alleys with Monika, a smart and bookish woman. Over lunch, she described how her confusion had mounted as the days went by on the trip, as she struggled to understand where Jewishness and Judaism should fit into her life. Three months later, when Monika and I sat down for an interview in Warsaw, she shared more of her trajectory. She had been a religious seeker for a while, and that search had taken her to different places, including being baptized in the Roman Catholic faith at eighteen—out of infatuation for a boy, she said. She now realized she had followed the wrong path and was turning to her Jewish ancestry in the hopes of finding meaning there. For her, the Birthright experience was not "a good time" or a "free trip," but a rather stressful experience related to her quest for identity. She liked the structure the trip provided for social interactions and was very upset when we returned to Poland, as she felt she'd be unlikely to remain in contact with other participants. Three months after the Birthright trip she remained unsure whether she had found what she sought. Still, the experience had been significant for her, and she had begun participating in activities offered at Hillel-Warsaw.

National Scripts versus Diasporic Ties

After the market visit, we returned to our hotel and met as a group to reflect on the day's events and on the meaning of Shabbat. The plan was for the women to light Shabbat candles in the hotel lobby and then for everyone to join other national groups in the ballroom for a festive dinner. Birthright encourages meetings between groups from different countries to foster cross-national diasporic ties. Our Polish group was matched with a Russian one, a pairing that perplexed most and frustrated many. "Why are we having dinner with Russians? We have nothing in common with them," I could hear Tomek say, rolling his eyes. "Whatever," he added, in English.

At our tables in the ballroom, we waited for the group from Russia to join us. Unlike our group, the Russian group attended synagogue, we were told, so they were probably just a bit late. Since the blessing of the challah and the kiddush, a blessing recited over wine preceding the meal, was not supposed to happen until members of both groups were present, we waited . . . and waited. The group grew impatient, wondering what was taking the Russians so long. Other groups had already performed the ritual and were eating, talking, and laughing. Then the organizers realized that the Russian group had actually arrived before us but had elected to sit at tables closer to the buffet. Many already had food heaped on their plates. Outrage ensued. "OMG, I can't believe it! They totally dissed us!"

Our guides tried to make the best of an awkward situation. We stood and approached the Russian group. No empty seats were left at their tables, so the Poles remained uncomfortably on their feet as the two groups' guides hurried to configure a new plan. Given the lack of a common language, the blessing was recited in Russian for the Russian group and in English for the Polish group. Then the Polish group stomped back to their original table at the other end of the room, visibly peeved. One woman who was fluent in Russian recounted to her girlfriends the interaction she had had with one young Russian man, seated with his plate full, who asked her, "So how many of you are there in Poland? Ha! There's more of us in Moscow alone!" Her friends gasped. "Do you think it's true they don't speak English," one asked, "or it was just so that they wouldn't have to hang out with us?" Either scenario made the Russians deplorable.

If the intent of mixing national groups was to foster a stronger shared Jewish identity, this incident achieved the opposite, at least on the Polish side: it highlighted differences, reinforced stereotypes, and solidified national identification. Jewishness receded, and the experience was perceived in the context of a bitter history marked by Russian domination of Poland. At least in this case, national resentments proved stronger than ethnoreligious commonality.

Reconciling National and Jewish Identities

Another incident the following day reinforced the salience of national identity. As we visited the Mount Herzl Cemetery in Jerusalem, moving from Yitzhak Rabin's grave to that of Michael Levin, an American *oleh* killed in the Second Lebanon War, we passed the Memorial for the Jewish Soldiers Fallen in the Service of the Polish Army during the Second World War.[27] Dedicated in 1988, the monument was hard to miss with its imposing size, the bronze figure of the Polish crowned eagle, the monument's name inscribed in English and Hebrew, and the nineteenth-century motto

27 An *oleh* is a Jewish immigrant to Israel.

of the Polish legions, "For Our Freedom and Yours," in Polish (figure 44). Yet our guide bustled past it without slowing down or pointing it out. Several members of the group, including Ola, a schoolteacher, were puzzled, distraught, and then disgruntled.

Word finally reached the guide at the front of the group that a quorum in the back was upset. We had a lot to see, she explained. We couldn't stop everywhere, and if people had comments or requests, they should make them directly to her. One woman responded that as Polish Jews, the memorial was obviously important to them, and worth learning about. "Fair enough," our guide responded, and slightly annoyed—and pressed for time—we hurried back to the monument. Once at the site, everyone read the inscriptions and posed for photos (figure 44). Some left written prayers.

Like the previous evening's incident with the Russian group, this incident ignited a sense of national belonging, of Polishness. Ola later commented: "Come on! How could we ignore this monument but then gather by the tomb of some American martyr? How could I let this go?" I was myself puzzled by what I initially perceived as our guide's faux pas. The standard tour—bookended with the graves of two martyrs for Israel, the

FIGURE 44. Birthright participant posing in front of the Memorial for the Jewish Soldiers Fallen in the Service of the Polish Army during the Second World War, Mount Herzl Cemetery, Jerusalem. (Photo by Geneviève Zubrzycki, July 23, 2017.)

statesman and the soldier, the *sabra* and the *oleh*—made perfect sense from a Zionist perspective.[28] But this was not the first Polish group the guide had led, and she had been chosen for her understanding of the Jewish situation in Poland. Her failure to tailor the visit to a Polish group by taking in the Polish monument was a missed opportunity, since recognizing and validating Polish Jewish identity could nurture an emergent Jewish identity in Birthright participants. Instead, they reported feeling alienated, marginalized as "not Jewish enough," or dismissed by members of other Birthright groups as "anomalies" for staying in Poland. One participant jokingly told me that she felt out of place in Israel because, "after all, I'm not American."

When I conducted follow-up interviews with participants of the trip several months later, Ola brought up the monument incident again:

> It's then that it hit me personally, because I understood then that they really—sorry to say—don't give a shit about Poland [*mają w dupie głęboko*], and that we [the Polish Birthright group] were [only] "okay" Jews for them. But I'm also Polish. . . . For me, a Jew does not need to be from Israel. He can be French, American, or whoever. And I think we should respect that. Uriel [one of the IDF soldiers attached to the group] asked me why I wanted to go back to the monument. He didn't understand. You know him, he's open, without prejudices. But he had such an image of Poland! Auschwitz, Sobibór, Treblinka and nothing more. I explained why it mattered [to visit the monument], I explained the meaning of the eagle with a crown, and he listened.[29] He didn't know anything about Poland. Zero. He only knew that there was an uprising in the ghetto, he knew about Marek Edelman—but [Edelman] was so-so, since he wanted to stay in Poland and therefore was not a very good model. There was Irena Sendler, a good Pole, you know; Bartoszewski. Those names, he knew. Okay. But otherwise, nothing. He knew nothing about Poland. So I explained to him what happened after the war—under another occupation, our eagle without the crown. And he said—"Okay, now I get it. I understand, because I feel the same about my country. You know what, let's take a picture together [at the monument]: if it's important for you, it's important for us too."

28 A *sabra* is an Israeli-born Jew.

29 When the communists came to power, they removed the crown from the Polish coat of arms. The crown then came to signify Polish sovereignty, since state socialism was perceived as an imposition by a foreign power and as Poland's loss of independence. After the fall of communism, the crown was returned to the white eagle's head.

For Ola, having her Polish as well as her Jewish identity recognized in Israel was important. It is part of who she is.

Incompleteness and Cultural Competency

Polish youth were keenly aware that their Jewishness and Judaism were seen as "incomplete" by their Israeli counterparts, but they also felt the same disdain from other diaspora groups, particularly Russians and Americans. At the Independence Hall Museum in Tel Aviv, we listened to a recording of David Ben-Gurion proclaiming the establishment of the state of Israel on May 14, 1948. As "Hatikvah" was played in the archival recording, everyone rose, but while groups of Americans joined in the singing, the Poles remained silent, unable to hum the melody, let alone sing the words of the Israeli national anthem.

Interactions with Jews from other countries thus confronted the Polish Jewish youth with their lack of Jewish cultural fluency. Unlike North American participants, they didn't know "Hatikvah." They couldn't relate to the repeated statements that they were fulfilling their parents' and grandparents' dreams of going "home." In after-hours parties with other Birthright groups we shared hotels with, one participant told me she repeatedly had to explain that yes, there were Jews in Poland. They made her feel like "an alien," she said, "as if a Polish Jew living in Poland was totally weird."[30]

The participants' interactions with the IDF soldiers who were integrated into our group on the fourth day of the trip were more productive. That aspect of the program created a more tangible bond with Israel than the imagined dream of the "return to the homeland," the refrain our Israeli guide so often repeated. The conversations, casual exchanges on the bus, challenging debates, and shared meals and outings with the soldiers were the closest encounter with the "real" Israel that the young visitors had.

During one evening workshop, participants were organized into small groups and given cards bearing statements of values, beliefs, and practices. Each group was asked to decide which was the single most important in order for a Jew to be a Jew. The cards included practices such as "Marrying a Jew," "Believing in G-d," "Speaking Hebrew," "Serving in the IDF,"

---

30 This feeling of alienation from other diaspora Jews was commonly expressed by Polish Jews during my fieldwork in Poland. Many expressed annoyance for being regarded as an "oddity" or "aberration." One middle-aged man once told me he was exceedingly frustrated to have to justify living in Poland instead of making aliyah, and that he now routinely responds to American Jews, "Why aren't *you* moving to Israel?"

FIGURE 45. Cards for Birthright group exercise on core Jewish values. (Photo by Geneviève Zubrzycki, July 22, 2017.)

"Belonging to a Jewish organization," "Commemorating the Holocaust," "Raising a Jewish family," "Taking an active part in the Jewish community," and "Visiting Israel" (figure 45).

The discussion that followed was thoughtful and animated. While the IDF soldiers in our small group regarded speaking Hebrew as an essential feature of being a Jew, for Poles this was not a tenable criterion. "Hebrew might be a precondition to be *Israeli*," Kamil said, "but not Jewish! These are different things. Besides, you'd cut the world Jewish population by more than half if that was a criterion for Jewishness. Same for serving in the IDF or visiting Israel. Those are out!" The Israelis conceded that those features were too narrowly Israeli, and that even some Jewish Israelis didn't serve in the army and were still very much Jewish. One self-described socialist IDF soldier then interjected, half-jokingly, that if the Jewishness of ultra-Orthodox (most of whom don't serve in the army) was not in question, maybe their Israeliness should be. Some Poles in the group did not understand the allusion, and the conversation moved on.

Both the Israelis and Poles rejected religiosity as the core of Jewish identity, "since many, many Jews are secular." Ironically, one Polish man considered marrying a Jew important, even though he was in a long-term relationship he described as "very happy" with a non-Jewish Pole, but the other Poles in the group reacted strongly against that: "If this were an essential criterion, we wouldn't be here today playing this game," said one woman whose father was an Israeli Jew and whose mother was (non-Jewish) Polish. Commemorating the Holocaust, likewise, was not identified as essential. One of the Israelis posed it as a question to the Poles, who acknowledged that it was important but could not be the basis for building a Jewish identity. In the end, consensus was achieved around the card "Taking an active part in the Jewish community." This choice seemed to encompass other options, such as "Having Jewish friends" and "Celebrating Jewish holidays," and it could facilitate meeting a Jewish partner. One other small group selected the same option, while a third chose "Raising a Jewish family."

Back Home: Retrospective Impressions of Israel in Poland

By the end of the trip, two romantic couples had formed, one lasting for a while after the return to Poland. Others kept in touch via social media, small get-togethers, and participating in Hillel-sponsored post-Birthright events in Warsaw. While three participants indicated that they had considered making aliyah, or at least returning to Israel for study or professional development, to my knowledge none have yet done so.

During that field trip I remained as invisible as possible, participating in activities, games, and discussions but keeping to the side (see appendix A). I did not take notes during events, to avoid distracting participants or, worse, inducing self-censorship or performative reactions to being observed. I did, however, talk with participants during the long bus rides, meals, and hikes, and I conducted follow-up interviews with a third of the participants three and nine months after the trip. My main objective during those interviews was to learn how they retrospectively narrated their own experience of the Birthright trip: whether, for example, they regarded it as a watershed event, dividing their lives into "before" and "after," whether they saw it as significant, and what they felt had been the key moments, if any. The responses varied greatly.

Karolina, a bright and beautiful student in a demanding program at a top university, is Jewish on her father's side. With him, she has attended a progressive synagogue since childhood. Karolina reported that the trip had dramatically changed her:

> Before the trip we'd go to the synagogue with Dad on holidays. It was important to us, but after returning from Israel, from Birthright, something changed in me . . . and I felt that . . . that it's [my] religion, and it was when I saw all those places in Israel that I understood what my Dad also feels. He visited Israel several times and repeated to us from childhood that we must go there, that it is simply our place. . . . And it turns out that he was right, because it changed how [I] feel.

Karolina spoke of the trip as a "transformation" (*przemiana*), one she said other participants also experienced:

> It was like a spiritual trip . . . ; we were by the Western Wall, and those feelings were induced by that place and by seeing all those people who are praying incredibly intensely. For those believers, devoted, going there is something normal. And for us it was so . . . For us it was the first time we felt some kind of a bond with all those people; that nevertheless that place is our place too, in some sense, and it was incredible. So for sure, during Birthright there were many such moments when one would feel connected to history, religion, with those people who survived all those terrible events like Masada, for example. It's terrible, and I think that until you are there to see it, you can't feel it to the same extent.

Her later report stood in contrast to her remarks during the trip, when she commented on the chaos and dirty streets, the heat, and her overall impression that aside from Tel Aviv, Israel was a Second World country.

For Ola, the trip was important from the very beginning:

The trip made a big impression on me. You know, I experienced Israel spiritually. I was a bit surprised by it myself then, because you know, I've talked about the Holocaust often, about my grandmother. I've talked about this a million times. I've written about this. I've talked about this at the university. And when we sat down [as a group on the first day], I don't know why, but I broke down and just bawled. To this day I don't know why. I don't know if I actually cried for all those in my family who perished in the camp—like they say—but that's how I interpreted it.

Unlike Karolina, Ola did not grow up in a Jewish environment. She found out about her Jewish roots when she discovered documents compiled by her grandmother to apply secretly for reparations from Germany. Ola was shocked by the discovery, and with those documents in hand she began to dig deeper into her family's history before, during, and after the war. She ended up writing her master's thesis on the topic. Her sister, on the other hand, was not interested in the discovery and was puzzled—and even annoyed—by Ola's fascination with that side of the family's history. She initially resisted signing up for the Birthright trip, but finally agreed to accompany Ola. For her, too, it was a meaningful experience, partly because it brought her closer to Ola.

For Monika, who had just finished her master's degree, the Birthright experience was deeply unsettling:

Well, I've got a problem, after Birthright. I [need to figure out] who I am and what to do with myself. Because on the one hand I'm a baptized Catholic—and worse, baptized by choice, with full cognizance of what I was doing—and then I discover, that . . . the Jewish world I didn't have much contact with during my entire life feels closer to me than Christianity and that Catholicism around which I've lived my whole life. You know, I could abandon Catholicism and convert to Judaism, but I have no idea if Judaism could be "it," whether I'd feel that "this is it." Maybe my place is elsewhere, maybe it's in between those two religions, yes? I'm processing that. And I discussed it briefly with the rabbi . . . , explaining the situation, and I asked him if it's possible to be at once a baptized Catholic and a Jew. His response? "It is, since you are." But I have a problem.

Even though the rabbi affirmed Monika's experience and the possibility of a dual identity—both Catholic and Jewish—the duality remained unsettling for Monika.

For others, the most important aspect of the trip was the friendships it created. Igor, an unusually poised eighteen-year-old, told me he felt the same after the trip as he did before it: "Polish with some Jewish roots. I have strong values, passed down to me by my parents; my values and my identity were established long ago. There's no way a trip would change that, would change who I am, nor would I want it to." A practicing Catholic who knew that his paternal grandfather was Jewish and had visited family in Israel, Igor explained that he was no more, yet also no less, interested in that side of his heritage than in the Polish-Catholic one. Mostly he was impressed by how well the trip was organized and by our guide, and he was grateful for the great friends he had made and kept in touch with. He was now pushing his younger brother to go on a Birthright trip himself as soon as he turned eighteen, and he planned to start attending Hillel in Kraków "for the people," who he thought were "a smart, interesting crowd."

For Paweł, in his mid-twenties, whose Jewish roots were never hidden, the Birthright experience had been positive, but it had neither been life-changing nor affected his identity in any transformative sense. As he told the group at our last workshop the night before our departure from Israel, he was first and foremost a cosmopolitan: for him, national, ethnic, or religious identifications simply didn't matter.

Kamil's story was a bit more complex, as was his relationship with his Jewish identity. Also in his mid-twenties, Kamil grew up with knowledge about his mother's Jewish roots, but that knowledge was fraught: as a young adult, his mother had found out in a deathbed conversation with her own mother—Kamil's grandmother—that the latter was Jewish. This discovery launched Kamil's mother on a difficult journey to learn the family's history and rebuild her identity. The rest of her family, however, refused to acknowledge the revelation's authenticity and significance, and marginalized her. While Kamil had gone to a Jewish high school and celebrated his bar mitzvah, he still felt his mother's pain at not being able to fill in all the blanks, even more so now that she had passed away. The Birthright experience helped him feel validated in his quest and more determined to solidify the friendships he had made on the trip. He considered it important to build Polish Jewry, a goal his mother had labored toward.

National identity remained important to many of the Polish Birthright group. Though the organizers labored to instill and inspire a diasporic, pan-Jewish solidarity, young Polish Jews were constantly aware of the Israeli and American inflection of the program. Often they were made to feel inadequate or insufficiently developed in their Jewishness. Yet this feeling pushed many toward serious reflection on the question of what exactly Jewishness requires. Though it remains to be seen how many participants in this specific Birthright tour will volunteer their time to the JCC, Hillel, or other centers for relearning how to practice Jewishness in Poland, several at least have already done so.

Conclusion: The Social Construction of Primordialism

Many of the "new Jews" I interviewed displayed an understanding of identity as primordial. Statements like "It turns out I'm Jewish," or "I found out that I'm actually Jewish, even though I know nothing about Jews" were commonplace.[31] At the same time, they demonstrated that identity is constructed and takes hard work.

Katka Reszke (2013) has analyzed the narratives of third-generation adults who, like her, discovered Jewish roots and worked to recover a Jewish identity. She found a remarkable uniformity in the narrative frameworks they deployed to make sense of "the discovery" and of the tropes they mobilized to activate a new identity. One is that of a lingering "hunch," of always having felt "different," "not quite," or sensing that "something was missing," a feeling that is validated by the subsequent revelation or discovery. It is impossible to tell whether those early feelings of difference are real, or retrospectively created and projected onto the person's past, as is common in converts' narratives and processes of identity reconstruction (see Smilde 2007). Perhaps those who have embraced a new Jewish identity upon learning of Jewish ancestry felt "different" for other reasons but then latched on to the ethnoreligious account once it became available to them.

This chicken-and-egg question is ultimately unanswerable, and from a sociological perspective it hardly matters. What does matter, and what, felicitously, is also available to sociological inquiry, is how Jewish ancestry can be reframed and integrated into a primordialist understanding of one's "true identity." As Reszke is quick to point out, despite these narrative frameworks, "Jewish culture in contemporary Poland is not a returning phenomenon. It is a new construct, which very much relies on its past renderings and aspires to be rooted, to be a continuation" (2013: 12). Irena Grudzińska-Gross has made a similar observation based on the discourses of Polish Jews about how they experience their Jewishness: "The assumption

---

31 "No i okazuje się, wyobraź Sobie, że jestem żydowką!" or "Po śmierci Babci, dowiedziałem się, że tak naprawdę jestem żydem. A nic nie wiem o żydach."

that from a palimpsest of the past one can recreate something real, authentic, direct, dominates. That it is only a question of effort, of consistent pursuit" (2014: 13).

Grudzińska-Gross rightfully points out that "the conviction that it is possible to reach some kind of kernel is an illusive dream [*kwiat paproci*]" (2014: 13). Yet this dream is one that many hold dear. The readiness of some of my interlocutors to embrace their Jewishness on the basis of having one Jewish ancestor clearly shows the power of biological understandings of ethnic identity, but also of cultural imaginaries where even partial and remote Jewish ancestry seems to matter more than "Polish" or other religious or national origins.[32] Identity and life story can be based on the "discovery" of a grandparent's Jewishness, for example, which takes precedence over the origins of the other three grandparents and one's own Polish identity, which was taken for granted until then. Constructing that Jewish self, however, requires significant cultural work: solving genealogical mysteries, learning new languages, adopting new traditions and rituals, and sometimes even formally converting. The process entails cultural *reappropriation*: acquiring new cultural and religious competencies to replace those lost in the twentieth century's historical caesura and its aftermath.

In *Ancestors and Relatives: Genealogy, Identity, and Community*, the sociologist Eviatar Zerubavel observes that

> by selectively highlighting certain ancestors (and therefore also our ties to other individuals or groups presumably descending from them) while ignoring, downplaying, or even outright suppressing others, . . . we tactically expand and collapse genealogies to accommodate personal as well as collective strategic agendas of inclusion and exclusion. The way we construct genealogies thus tells us as much about the present as it does about the past. (2012:16)

What does the embrace of their Jewish past by a growing number of Poles tell us about the present? For one thing, it suggests that the social, cultural, and political context has changed: such "discoveries," "recoveries," and "reappropriations" were difficult or impossible three decades or so ago.

---

32 This is not unique to the Polish case, of course. Biological understandings of Jewishness are common, since the category can be both an ethnic and a religious one. For analyses of biological discourses and essentialist views of identity among American Jews, see Tenenbaum and Davidman (2007); for a comparative analysis of ascription and choice among different religious groups in the United States, see Davidman and Cadge (2006).

It also suggests that Jewishness has acquired a symbolic value that it did not possess a generation ago. When one's identity construction is dependent on the context in which individuals and groups evolve, however, it also means that the process of renewal can be stalled, and perhaps even reversed.

CHAPTER 7

Conclusion

MEMORY, MYTHOLOGY,
AND NATIONALISM

Three years after Poland amended the statute of its Institute of National Remembrance and enacted the so-called Holocaust speech law, the scholars Barbara Engelking and Jan Grabowski were found liable in a civil case brought against them by ninety-four-year-old Filomena Leszczyńska, who sued the historians for offending the memory of her long-deceased uncle. Ms. Leszczyńska's lawsuit was supported by the Polish League against Defamation, a nationalist NGO based in Warsaw.[1] At issue was an account Engelking and Grabowski cited in a chapter of their two-volume study on the risks incurred by Jews hiding in the Polish countryside during the German occupation (2018). According to witness testimony, in 1943 the plaintiff's uncle, Edward Malinowski, had denounced a group of Jews hiding in the woods to the Germans, leading to their murders. As part of the judgment, the scholars were ordered to publicly apologize for the defamation of Malinowski's memory. They appealed, and on August 16, 2021, the Warsaw Court of Appeal ruled in their favor, overturning the previous decision. In her opinion, the appeal judge, Joanna Wiśniewska-Sadomska, stated that "freedom of speech is one of the pillars of democratic society and a condition for its development. It cannot be restricted to opinions that are considered favorable, perceived as benign, or neutral." She added:

> It is difficult to share the view according to which the court in a civil proceeding would adjudicate the credibility of historical findings and sources, or that it would instruct historians about which sources they should base their findings on, and which of those sources deserve greater credibility. Such action, according to the Court of Appeal, would

---

1 The organization's full name, in Polish, is *Fundacja Reduta Dobrego Imienia—Polska Liga Przeciw Zniesławieniom.*

constitute an unacceptable form of censorship and interference in the freedom of research and scientific work. . . . The court is not the proper place to conduct historical debate.[2]

This judgment is important not only because it provides an unexpected denouement to a tortuous story about academic freedom and freedom of speech, nor solely because it sets a clear precedent for cases that are likely to follow, but also because it squarely situates the specific lawsuit (and the Holocaust speech law itself) in the broader context of Poland's war over its collective memory and identity. The university and the courtroom are not the only spaces where history is debated, national mythology questioned or defended, and identity affirmed or contested. The fight over the past and for national identity in the present is being fought in multiple spaces. The Jewish turn I have analyzed in this book is one such crucial space.

Philosemitism and Polishness

Resurrecting the Jew has sought to reveal the various expressions and meanings, as well as the impact and limits, of Poland's multifaceted Jewish turn. I have considered the macro, meso, and micro levels of this phenomenon and examined how its structural-institutional, ideational-discursive, and material-emotional aspects are interrelated.

Mythology, Narrative Shock, and a New Sensorium

The fall of communism in Eastern Europe in 1989 brought about a widespread reexamination of the past. In Poland, that process set in motion a significant wave of historical revisionism concerning the Second World War and its aftermath. When that movement questioned Polish martyrological mythology, it shook Poles to their core. That existential narrative shock led to what Michael Rothberg (2009) has called in a different context "multidirectional memory": acknowledgment and soul-searching in some, denial in many, nostalgic visions of the past shaping the articulation of

2 My translation. For a full (unofficial) transcript of the decision, see https://oko.press /niedopuszczalna-forma-cenzury-uzasadnienie-wyroku-ws-engelking-i-grabowskiego -slowo-w-slowo/.

present political projects in yet others. The key to understanding the cultural and political dynamics of Poland's collective memory and amnesia of its Jewish past, then, is national mythology. It is national mythology that makes certain memories of the war (and other historical periods) plausible and desirable while diminishing and effacing others.

Because it is embodied in a densely layered national sensorium, national mythology seems not only historically true and important: to individuals, it appears real and close. Any attempt at redefining national identity therefore requires alteration of that sensorium. The commemorative objects, discourses, practices, and institutions I analyzed in *Resurrecting the Jew*—from paper mementos and street art to commemorative marches, monuments, and museums; from individuals performing and consuming Jewish culture to guardians of Jewish memory tending Jewish-heritage sites—all serve to expand Poland's national sensorium and could potentially facilitate the redefinition of Polish national identity.

In a society characterized by an exceptionally high ethnoreligious homogeneity, and where the dominant understanding of Polish national identity is based on ethnicity, progressive nationalists have a limited repertoire of political symbols and stories from which to draw in order to articulate an alternative civic vision of the nation and overcome the narrow and ideologically loaded notion of the *Polak-katolik*. Some elements of civic discourses have been compromised because of their use by the former socialist state, while some have been absorbed into the ethno-Catholic narrative. Yet others seem like imports from outside, from the European Union or "the West." Instead of emphasizing the ideological heterogeneity of Poland's current population, then, civic nationalists locate pluralism in an ethnically and religiously diverse past, characterized by a Jewish presence, and create tangible, visible, countable Jewish markers in the public sphere.

NGOs, left-leaning politicians, public intellectuals, memory activists, cultural entrepreneurs, *engagé* artists, and ordinary citizens contest the dominant ethno-Catholic understanding of Polishness by participating in memory work such as graffiti art, walking tours of formerly Jewish spaces, commemorative marches, or the cleaning and restoration of cemeteries. Through embodied activities such as learning how to "cook Jewish" and how to serve and consume Jewish foods, learning Yiddish, practicing Jewish decorative arts, performing Jewish music and dances, and donating time and energy to Jewish individuals and organizations, ordinary citizens participate in a broadly understood Jewish revival that undermines the dominant view of Poland as essentially, primordially ethno-Catholic. Jewish presence—whether in its historical or contemporary incarnation—is invoked to trump Poland's ethnoreligious homogeneity. Paradoxically, then, ethnicity remains the means through which civic nationalists attempt to transcend ethnonationalism, tragically limiting their own chances of success.

The Limits and Risks of Philosemitism

Philosemitic discursive, material, and performative practices do not necessarily whitewash history to erase traces of antisemitism. Many of my interviewees developed an interest in Jewish history and culture after learning of the violent crimes committed against Jews by ethnic Poles before, during, and after the Second World War. The Jewish turn itself gained momentum in the wake of the debates over the participation of ethnic Poles in the Holocaust, following the publication of Jan Gross's *Neighbors* in 2000, and after Poland's accession to the European Union in 2004. These discursive and performative strategies are not purely instrumental: it is not the case that cultural entrepreneurs lack genuine interest in Jewish culture or Judaism or that participants in Jewish-related cultural initiatives do not care about the memory of those murdered in the Holocaust. Rather, in their artistic creations, beliefs, discourses, and actions—and alongside and through their cultural investments in Judaism—they weave their individual identities and private aspirations into a vision of Poland made cosmopolitan in and through Jews. They articulate their own imagined futures unfolding in a different form than the one promoted by Poland's motto *Polonia semper fidelis*.

Yet as crucial as that progressive agenda is, it presents significant risks. One is that this process of "resurrection" feeds a naive, complacent, or even manipulative "redemptive cosmopolitanism" that could curb critical self-examination (Meng 2012). That risk is especially significant given the Law and Justice Party's multipronged efforts to quell processes of reckoning with Polish antisemitism and to sacralize Polishness as a heroic, martyrological virtue beyond criticism.

Polish philosemitism also poses risks for Jews themselves. The resurrection of Jewish culture is primarily made by Poles, for Poles, and in the name of Polish culture. Jews are included in the national narrative and into an expanded conception of the national self precisely because they are considered to be different, Poland's internal "Other." Paradoxically, the liberal inclusion of Jews within the symbolic boundaries of the nation, in order to expand notions of Polishness, entails the continued Othering of Jews. In order for a multicultural, diverse Poland to exist, the Jew must remain irremediably Other. For Poland to become plural and inclusive, distinctions between citizens based on ethnicity and religion are highlighted, legitimized, and even celebrated. And we know that distinctions serve to maintain more or less rigid hierarchies (Bourdieu 1984; Pasieka 2015).

This paradox is important for scholars and memory activists alike to ponder. How can it be transcended, overcome, or resolved? How can Jews be given their history and legacy, their due place in Poland's past and present, without being Othered? How can Poles rediscover Jews and Jewish culture without exoticizing and fetishizing them, and without reproducing so-called intrinsic differences? And how can this be achieved without making Jews disappear into a civic narrative of "Polish citizens" that erases them from the national landscape altogether (Irwin-Zarecka 1989; Zubrzycki 2006)? In other words, how can Polish Jews and Jewishness be normalized as distinct, yet Polish, without being instrumentalized?

Part of the answer is for Poles to work even more diligently at problematizing the Catholicity of Polishness. While there is a rich scholarship undertaking this agenda (e.g., Bjork 2008; Porter-Szűcs 2012; Pasieka 2015), much remains to be done on the ground—in school curriculums, museums, and public spaces. In recent years, many Poles have undergone the complex process of apostasy (the formal renunciation of Catholicism) to avoid being included in statistics that legitimize the Catholic narrative of the nation (Centrum Badania Opinii Społecznej 2018; Zubrzycki 2020; Sadłoń 2021). Another strategy is to insist that ideological, political, and sexual diversity are legitimate forms of national pluralism. This strategy's effectiveness is limited for reasons I discuss above, but recent developments in the public sphere, with women's and LGBTQ rights movements gaining visibility and undermining the patriarchal model of society promoted by the Catholic Church, could shift the ways in which Poles think about diversity. It is when Polishness is secularized—that is, when the equation between Polishness and Catholicism is broken—that a broader range of significations of national identity will be possible, and Jews will stop being the Other against or through which different visions of Polishness are articulated.

Polish Jews' own identities and trajectories also face significant challenges. "We are here," the Holocaust survivor Marian Turski poignantly declared at the ceremonial opening of the Polin Museum of the History of Polish Jews in 2014. Collective identity is always a thorny issue, but Turski's "we" is perhaps even more elusive than usual because the articulation of a Polish Jewish "I" is itself an especially complex process in the wake of the Holocaust. Polish Jews occupy a liminal position in the Polish and in the Jewish diaspora's imaginations; an internal Other in one case and an anomaly in the other, as the continued presence of Jews in Poland complicates a Zionist narrative in which Poland is cast as Egypt and Israel as the Promised Land. Polish Jews, moreover, are heirs of a rich and diverse civilization that has been all but annihilated, of which they are now recovering traces together with, and sometimes thanks to, non-Jewish Poles. The fact that many, until recently, in fact identified as "non-Jewish Poles" makes individual and collective identity building especially difficult.

What Does the Case of Poland's Jewish Turn Teach Us?

While Poland's Jewish turn is distinctive, it has lessons and implications well beyond Poland. This study shows how a symbolic category—in this case the Jew, or Jewishness—can serve as a foil against which an exclusive national identity is constructed, as well as the means through which an inclusive, expanded national identity can be articulated. The process of expanding the symbolic boundaries of the nation through the Other, however, is potentially fraught because that Other, whether real or symbolic, remains subject to manipulation by the dominant group. The symbolic power exerted to "articulate the principles of vision and division," to quote Bourdieu (1991), is thus still violent, even when it is used in progressive projects.

Resurrecting the Jew shows the ways and the extent to which dominant modes of imagining the nation shape not only formal membership rules such as citizenship (Brubaker 1992) but also symbolic membership in the national community. That the nation is generally imagined in ethnic terms in Poland (as it is elsewhere in Central and Eastern Europe) explains why some nonethnically Polish residents and citizens may never fully "belong." It also explains why and how some members of the dominant ethnonational group are symbolically excluded from the national community for their political leanings, religious affiliation, sexual orientation, or gender identity by being "ethnicized"—that is, by being turned into ethnonational Others. Further, it explains why proponents of a civic vision of the nation cannot rely on abstract principles to promote their project, since the civic nation is antithetical to ethnoreligious conceptions of the national community.

To understand not only formal political modes of inclusion via citizenship but also the logic of symbolic exclusion in nationalist discourses and practices, we must pay attention to the ways in which a given nation is imagined. That observation helps us to understand other cases. France, where I sit as I draft these concluding pages, is the archetype of civic nationhood, where inclusion into the national community is premised not on blood but on adherence to the social contract (Renan 1996 [1882]; Schnapper 1994). How, then, can the French Right, and recently even Emmanuel Macron's centrist government, legitimately exclude ethnic and racial Others whom it perceives as threatening? It does so by ideologizing them: that is, by turning Arabs and Africans into Islamist zealots who threaten the republic by infringing upon secularism, a sacred tenet of the French social contract (cf. Scott 2007; Bowen 2007).

We know from the scholarship on nationalism and everyday life that national identity is constructed not only at the level of elite discourse and institutional (re)arrangements, official policies, or state-sponsored institutions such as museums, educational programs, or NGO outreach actions, but also through memory work, cultural initiatives, and everyday practices undertaken by ground-level actors in a variety of venues. As I have shown in these pages, these everyday practices do not always serve to reify and reproduce an existing identity but can also deconstruct and reconstruct identity along new lines. Polishness is being challenged and redefined by activists and artists, as well as by ordinary people in their mundane activities.

This study thus sheds new light on processes through which symbolic boundaries of national identity are negotiated and redrawn. I identified three main, diachronic, and overlapping processes at play: "softening," "stretching," and "reshaping." In order to expand the notion of a given national identity, dominant visions must be undermined. In the Polish case, softening is achieved discursively by tunneling holes in the ethno-Catholic fortress. Symbolic boundaries are stretched by materializing traces of the Jewish past and by making visible the contemporary Jewish presence. The stretched boundaries of Polishness are then reshaped and legitimized by Poles participating in cultural work that indigenizes the figure of the Jew and firmly roots Jewish culture in Polish soil, thereby naturalizing an alternative to the dominant model of Polishness that ties it to Catholicism. In that narrative, it is the historical, pluralistic Poland that is the "true" Poland while postwar Poland is an anomaly, a casualty of the Nazis and communists, now taken hostage by the Catholic Church and the Right.

Cultural Appropriation and Registers of Engagement

Resurrecting the Jew complicates the issue of cultural appropriation by attending to the multiple registers of engagement with Jewish culture by non-Jews, ranging from crude cultural appropriation, to critical-introspective engagement, to empathetic versions of cultural appropriation. Some registers may overlap, and across a longer history one form of engagement could lead to another: Someone who casually engages with the klezmer scene, for example, may move to more reflective registers of engagement as her interest in Jewish history deepens as a result of her musical taste and social encounters. Likewise, someone who participates in a march commemorating the victims of the Holocaust, a political act, may develop a taste for Jewish cuisine and restaurants, a "casual" register of engagement.

The feelings of members of a minority group about a dominant group's engagement with their culture must always remain in focus. But considering the motivations of individuals engaging with the culture of other groups, and the personal meaning their practices have for them, remains essential if we are to gain any understanding of the phenomenon. This conceptual development should be helpful in studying cultural appropriation in different contexts. Consider, for example, the borrowing by dominant groups of minority groups' musical or dance forms, religious practices, fashion, body postures, and speech patterns, or attempts by majority groups to revive the culture of vanished (or almost vanished) groups they often are responsible for annihilating, like the Armenians in Turkey or Native communities in settler societies.

In the end, *Resurrecting the Jew* reiterates the case for interpretative sociology: it is only by paying attention to the multiple, varied motivations and meanings of the Jewish turn that we can appreciate its full significance. Without such an approach, we might remain stuck in bewildered incomprehension, or limited to its normative valuation. Multi-sited, multi-method analysis of discursive representations, material and visual culture, and performative practices makes possible the peeling back of various layers of Poland's Jewish turn to show how the phenomenon is related to the structure of Polish nationalism on the one hand, and the politics of history on the other.

Perhaps most importantly, however, *Resurrecting the Jew* invites readers to consider the limits of testifying to vanished or diminished communities. These limits are imposed by the stubborn fact of loss. At issue, in other words, is not the simple commemorative logic of recollection and recovery, reflection and redress—a matter of simply reattaching a severed limb to a now healthier and rehabilitated national body. Rather, what is at stake is the problem of the phantom limb itself: How do we represent that which remains lost? How do we reincorporate that which is no longer? What does it mean to rewrite a national history, and imagine its future, when those who have been excised and that which has been erased can never return to full presence? In contrast to the conventional ambitions of historical commemoration, it is this far more elusive and disquieting fact that the contemporary Polish activists, cultural entrepreneurs, and volunteers who animate these pages seek to engage.

Methods, Data, and Analytical Strategies

Resurrecting the Jew is based on multiple types of data collected between 2010 and 2020. This appendix provides detailed information on these data, their sources, and how they were collected and analyzed.

Interviews

I conducted over one hundred interviews for this project. Approximately one-third were with public figures identified in the sources and references. The other two-thirds were carried out with participants integrally involved in the Jewish turn, both Jewish and non-Jewish. Some are non-Polish, but all interviewees were residing in Poland during the period of the study. Interlocutors include members of the Jewish communities in Kraków, Warsaw, and Wrocław; members, staff, and friends of various Jewish organizations in those cities (see list below); staff and volunteers at JCC-Kraków and the Jewish Culture Festival in Kraków; dancers in Kachol, a troupe specializing in Israeli dance; participants in a Birthright trip to Israel; and editors of a Wrocław-based Jewish publication. I conducted formal interviews with many more individuals met at social events, or via references from other interviewees, through a process known as "snowball sampling."

All interviews were conducted in Polish, unless my interlocutor was a native speaker of English or, in rare cases, their English was more fluent than my Polish. Interviews were audio-recorded with interviewees' permission and lasted between 45 and 120 minutes.

Interviews followed a loose script: I first introduced myself and then presented my study as one on national identity and the ongoing Jewish revival in Poland. I asked my conversation partners to introduce themselves, specify their age, where they were from, and whatever additional biographical information they wished to share. For Jewish interviewees, I tried to avoid asking questions that might elicit a "story" that had already been worked out and followed a set script (I discussed this issue in the preface). For non-Jews, after these general introductions I asked what brought them to a specific organization (JCC, a museum, and the like). After discussing their personal motivations and experiences, I typically asked what they thought motivated the Jewish revival, how they explained the phenomenon, what it meant to them personally, and what it might mean more broadly. While I followed up on interesting statements, asking for clarifications or further elaboration, in most interviews I left space for participants to compose their own free-flowing oral histories during which I interjected as little as possible. Sometimes I repeated things I had heard or read as prompts, asking interviewees to explain a statement to me or whether they had an opinion on a given topic. In general, I concluded the interview by asking interviewees to describe where and how they imagined themselves five and ten years hence. Interviews were transcribed by native speakers of Polish, and I analyzed them in the original Polish. I personally translated all interview extracts I quote in the book. Finally, unless interviewees were speaking to me in their official capacity, I employed pseudonyms to protect their anonymity.

Many more conversations occurred in the course of everyday fieldwork, and provide important complements to formal interviews. These included informal exchanges with patrons, owners, and staff of Jewish-style restaurants and cafés; with visitors at festivals and public events; with museum visitors and guides; with students in Jewish studies programs; and with members of various Jewish communities during ritual events and social occasions. Even mundane conversations with seatmates on trains, fellow shoppers in grocery stores, and acquaintances made through old friends provided rich data. Such conversations were obviously not taped, yet they often provided important insights occasionally cited in the text. Likewise the gossip, rumors, and putative "scandals" reported to me from myriad different sources. I rarely attempted to determine the factual basis of such rumors; more relevant for this study were the forms in which those fragments were told, circulated, evaluated by their receivers, and to what effect.

Participant Observation

The fieldwork for *Resurrecting the Jew* built on extended periods of living in Poland in the 1990s and early 2000s, and this twenty-year research experience provided me with the deep knowledge of the sites that is requisite to rigorous ethnographic fieldwork. I built on a dense and extensive network of friends and colleagues known for over two decades, as well as important new relationships specifically related to this project.

Among those new connections, the most significant was with the Jewish Community Centre in Kraków. I was privileged to be welcomed in the life of the JCC by its director, Jonathan Ornstein, who introduced me to the center's members, staff, and volunteers. All generously shared their ideas, ideals, and opinions in formal interviews and informal conversations over the years. Since I began the fieldwork in the summer of 2010, many have married, some have had children, several have graduated and moved on; still others have made aliyah and started new lives in Israel. New faces appeared, yet many familiar ones remained. The JCC itself has expanded its membership and programming both in service of its members and as offerings to the public, and established itself as the core institution of Jewish life in Kraków.

In between research trips to Poland, I followed various organizations on social media, collected news reports and opinion pieces published in traditional media, and remained in touch with many interviewees on email and other social media platforms. This online ethnographic work was important as it allowed me not only to follow Jewish life as it was unfolding while I was in the United States but also to easily reintegrate into communities during my field trips.

Organizations

I observed and documented the work of, participated in the activities of, and /or interviewed members of the following organizations:

- Jewish Community Centre-Kraków
- Jewish Community Center-Warsaw
- Jewish Culture Festival in Kraków
- Hillel-Warsaw
- Hillel-Kraków
- Joint Distribution Committee (Warsaw)
- Forum for Dialogue Among Nations (Warsaw)
- Klub Przymierze
- Limmud Polska
- Chidusz (Wrocław)

Documentary Evidence

In addition to field research, I collected a variety of documents available to the public, or shared with me directly by relevant organizations, artists, and private individuals:

- Films (fiction and documentary) and visual art initiatives.
- Novels, autobiographies, investigative reports.
- Published surveys and opinion polls on antisemitism, the memory of the Holocaust, and religiosity.
- Legal briefs and bills, as well as commentaries and debates about them in the national and international media.
- Activity reports by the *Fundacja Ochrony Dziedzictwa Żydowskiego* (*FODŻ*) (Foundation for the Preservation of Jewish Heritage in Poland) detailing Jewish-heritage efforts, as well as cases of antisemitic vandalism for each year.
- Brochures and information from Polish-government websites and private tourist agencies detailing information on Jewish-heritage points of interest.
- Parliamentary debates and press releases related to declaring the Year of Korczak (2012), Year of Tuwim (2013), and Year of Sendler (2018).
- Press releases in Polish newspapers about contemporary cultural initiatives related to Jewish heritage.

In what follows, I present details on the data, sources, and methods employed in specific chapters.

Chapter 2 is based on three types of data:

1. **Official commemorative initiatives** such as monuments, commemorative plaques, mnemonic mementos, as well as marches of memory.
2. **Artistic mnemonic projects** such as street-art murals and smaller graffiti, temporary architectural installations, visual commemorative "happenings," and Mi Polin's Mezuzah Project.
3. **Special events** such as Kraków's 7@nite, when the Jewish Quarter's seven synagogues are opened to the public, or the lighting of the *hanukiah* in Warsaw on the first night of Hanukah.

The specific cases I selected for this chapter were chosen because they are *exemplars* of different types of mnemonic engagements with Jewish absence. Many are situated in Warsaw. Because the city had a large number of Jewish sites before the war and because of the extent of its wartime destruction, Warsaw has a significant concentration of mnemonic recovery projects. It is also the country's capital and thus has been the home of significant Jewish social and educational institutions. The phenomenon is also noticeable in Kraków, Łódź, Lublin, and Wrocław, to name only a few other key sites included in this study. Moreover, mnemonic engagement is not an exclusively urban phenomenon. A multitude of local initiatives in small towns and villages throughout Poland seek to educate residents about their communities' past Jewish presence.

Chapter 3 is based on the analysis of Rafał Betlejewski's "I Miss You, Jew" project. I collected four types of data:

1. Betlejewski's own **discourse** on Jewish absence; how he described the project on his website, in published interviews, and during my own conversation with him.
2. **Visual evidence** of community-based "happenings" organized throughout Poland; photographs and videos posted on the website and YouTube.
3. **Discussions and debates** in the public sphere about the project.
4. **Testimonies** and comments posted on the website.

Testimonies were especially important for my analysis. I downloaded all 349 testimonies and comments posted on the website as of December 15, 2012. Some authors wrote more than one testimony, and I determined that 301 distinct individuals participated. Two research assistants and myself analyzed all the entries and the comments (when applicable), and built an analytical grid based on that initial review.

The goal of the grid was to establish basic characteristic of participants/authors, including their gender, age group, socioeconomic status, religious affiliation, and whether they live in a small town or a large city. Some characteristics were provided by authors in their testimonies; others we inferred from cues appearing in the testimony, or from the writing style. When it was impossible to determine authors' characteristics with confidence, that information was left blank.

The analytical grid was also intended to identify who and/or what was being remembered in the testimony (a person, an event, or a place), and whether the memory was the author's own or one transmitted to them by family members, read in books, or learned in school. Finally, I identified recurring themes and tropes in order to establish the types of memories participants shared.

Once that basic content analysis was concluded, I focused on discourse analysis: how authors expressed their feelings and opinions; the relationships they drew between stories they told; the language used and the tone employed in the testimony. Aside from rare exceptions, all testimonies were in Polish and the analysis was conducted in that language. As is the case for interviews, I translated all testimony extracts I quote in the chapter.

Chapter 4 is primarily based on **ethnographic observations**. In addition to attending the ceremonial opening of the Polin Museum of the History of Polish Jews and observing visits of its core exhibition over half a dozen times, I hired two advanced doctoral students (Polish) to conduct participant observation at the museum's core exhibition. From December 2014 through September 2015, they conducted a total of 104 visits to the museum. These consisted of joining guided tours, following individuals and small groups visiting on their own, as well as "tagging along" with small focus groups they created. Given the subject of this study, I instructed the research assistants to observe primarily Polish and/or Polish-speaking groups and visitors. They also attended public lectures, roundtables, and workshops offered on a regular basis by the museum.

I met with the research assistants in Warsaw in October 2014 to discuss research objectives, observation strategies, and practical matters, and again in March 2015 to discuss preliminary findings. The research assistants informed me at that moment that following guided tours was not as fruitful as we had envisioned, since both the guide and the visitors have headsets to hear the guide's comments that hinder questions and comments from the visitors and discussion among visitors (because visitors' headsets do not have microphones). Since they had already observed a significant number of such tours and had managed to identify the typical narratives provided by tour guides, I directed them to refocus their observations on small ad hoc groups visiting on their own. An afternoon at the museum, then, could be spent in a single gallery of the exhibition, observing visitors walking through a single space; or following a small group as it perambulated different galleries of the exhibition. We also built an analytical grid to facilitate cross-observational comparisons: specific sections of the exhibition where a given observation was conducted; descriptions of visitors observed, including gender, age group, likely socioeconomic status, and demeanor; comments visitors would make to each other about information relayed or about the space; specific artifacts, information panels, or interactive objects that generated interest by visitors in a given section. In their reports, the research assistants also noted where visitors took selfies, tended to stop and linger, or galleries that visitors typically sped through or skipped. They recounted recollections and experiences they overheard visitors sharing with their companions, as well as their own emotions and reactions, both to the exhibition and to the visitors and guides observed.

Throughout that nine-month period, the research assistants were supervised by Dr. Agnieszka Pasieka, whom I hired to oversee the assistants' work plan, note-taking, and reports, as well as to coach them to sharpen their observational skills. I received biweekly notes and reports from the research team.

In addition to the Polin Museum, I visited Schindler's Enamel Factory Museum; the Galicia Jewish Museum; the Warsaw Uprising Museum; the Świętokrzyski Shtetl museum; the Marek Edelman Dialogue Center in Łódź; and the Ulma Family Museum in Markowa.

Chapter 5 considers a variety of institutions and ad hoc groups, as well as individuals who are significant participants in the revival of Jewish culture in Poland. Most actors involved in these events were non-Jewish Poles.

My **ethnographic work** at Kraków's Jewish Culture Festival was extensive given this festival's importance, longevity, as well as the large number and varied types of events it offers. I attended over half a dozen editions of the festival between 1990 and 2004, when I lived in Poland or returned in the summers when I was a doctoral student or completing the research for my first book. My previous experiences of the festival provided a useful comparative vantage point for my analysis of it today.

Specifically for *Resurrecting the Jew*, I participated in the festival in 2010, 2014, and 2015. Most important for my research were the multiple workshops, lectures, symposiums, and walking tours offered to participants. Some are offered several days in a row (e.g., Yiddish, Hebrew), others once or twice. In 2010, I attended as many events as I could in a day, for the duration of the festival. Registration was required for individual events and a fee collected for each. In 2014 and 2015, I received a special festival badge allowing me to access events without preregistration. This allowed me to visit many more events, since during any given time slot, two or three might be scheduled. During those three editions, I participated in the following workshops:

- Yiddish language (daily)
- Hebrew language (daily)
- Jewish cuisine (twice)
- Rules of kashrut (twice)
- Hasidic songs (six times)
- Jewish dances (four times)
- Papercutting motifs and techniques (twice)
- Walking tours of Kraków (famous Jews of Kraków, famous rabbis, Kraków synagogues and cemeteries, Jewish women)
- Finding hidden Jewish traces in Kazimierz

I also attended public lectures, roundtable discussions, and book launches during the festival, and conducted several interviews with its cofounder and general director, Janusz Makuch, as well as with the festival staff in subsequent research trips, typically in early spring when the schedule for a new festival edition is ready but the organizational frenzy has not yet started.

The fieldwork was complemented by **documentary evidence** on the festival to trace its evolution in time and growing popularity, as well as its reception in the Polish press. I consulted the following sources, publicly accessible on the festival's website or shared with me directly by its management:

- Festival programs from 1988–2019
- Official annual reports issued by the festival committee that summarize sponsorships, organizers, partners, types and numbers of performances, and participant demographics
- Grant applications submitted by Kraków's Jewish Culture Festival to various funding agencies
- Over 1,536 articles from approximately 180 different news sources spanning twenty years of media coverage of the Kraków Jewish Culture Festival

Finally, I attended smaller cultural events, such as a Christian "seder" organized by Polish evangelical Protestants (2013); meetings and award ceremonies of *Klub Przymierze*, the Kraków Association of Christians and Jews (2012, 2017); the Gala of the School of Dialogue (2016); as well as the Day of Jewish Culture in Chmielnik (2017).

Another major source of data for chapter 5 comprised **interviews** conducted with volunteers at the JCC, the Jewish Culture Festival, and with dancers of a troupe of Israeli dance.

During my multiple visits at the JCC-Kraków in 2010 and 2011, I noticed the role of young volunteers, mostly women, who worked in the reception area, served Shabbat dinners, and occupied other similar functions. After learning about their investment in and dedication to the organization, and following many informal conversations with a few of them, I decided to include volunteers in the study. I was interested in their motivations for volunteering in a Jewish organization, their personal trajectory and what brought them to the JCC, the meaning of their work, as well as their long-term life plans and vision for the kind of society they hoped to live in or eventually raise children in.

I composed a brief informational bulletin that was posted at the JCC reception, describing the study in general terms, explaining that participation was voluntary, unpaid, and promised anonymity. After receiving positive responses, the JCC offered a private room where I could meet individual volunteers, who then signed up for an interview slot when it was convenient for them. I provided pastries and other refreshments, briefly introduced myself to those who did not already know me, outlined my research, asked whether I could tape our conversation, and then asked my interlocutor to introduce her/himself, where they were from, how long they had been volunteering at the JCC, and what had brought them there. From there, we had open-ended conversations that touched upon varied topics: the Jewish revival, family life, Polish national identity, the political climate, and life goals and expectations.

I learned about Kachol, a company that performed Israeli dances, from JCC volunteers who were members of the troupe. They introduced me to their artistic director, who invited me to attend their rehearsals at the Popper Synagogue in Kazimierz. After visiting on several occasions, I interviewed several of their members before or after rehearsals. With these subjects, too, the interview was open-ended. I sought to learn who they were, what attracted them to Jewish dance styles, and what motivated them to invest a significant part of their free time in this activity.

Finally, I frequented "Jewish" cafés, restaurants, and clubs, sometimes alone, often with Polish Jewish or non-Jewish Polish friends. Patronizing these sites was significant as it allowed me to analyze how Jewishness is represented in those physical spaces, "packaged" in menus and soundtracks, advertised on signboards and websites, and experienced by patrons.

Chapter 6 is based on **participant observation, ethnographic interviews,** and **formal interviews** with members of various Jewish communities from

2010 to 2019. My most intense and sustained fieldwork was in Kraków, but I also attended communal events in Warsaw, conducted interviews in Warsaw and Wrocław, and participated in a Polish Birthright trip to Israel in 2017.

In Kraków I joined the daily life of the JCC during my frequent research stays. I participated in Shabbat dinners, seders, Purim parties, and multiple public events. In addition to these communal events, I was invited to religious services, private celebrations, and small gatherings in bars after Shabbat dinners and parties in homes.

Thanks to the JCC director Jonathan Ornstein and his wife Kasia Leonardi, I was invited to communal events taking place in other Jewish organizations in Kraków such as religious services at the Tempel and Izaak Synagogues, or a seder at the Jewish Religious Community in Kraków (*Gmina Wyznaniowa Żydowska w Krakowie*) (2013). Ornstein introduced me to Kraków-based rabbis (see list of interviews), as well as the teams of JCC-Warsaw and the Joint Distribution Committee in Warsaw.

I joined the Kraków delegation to Limmud Polska (2016), a three-day annual gathering for members of Jewish communities and their families taking place at a hotel/conference center outside Warsaw. The event is both educational—with lectures, roundtables, and workshops—and social, as participants share meals and Shabbat rituals. Registration is required and limited to members of the Jewish community. I was able to attend thanks to the recommendation of the organizers. What is perhaps most interesting about the gathering is that it is organized by and for community members: all classes, workshops, and lectures are by members who share their expertise and experiences. I attended roundtables on growing up Jewish after the war; on March 1968; on raising Jewish children; on the legal framework for the return of Jewish communal property and Jewish-heritage preservation; and then shared meals with participants, attended the Havdalah ceremony, movie screenings, and joined in informal social events and gatherings.

As a general rule, I did not take notes during participant observation so that my presence and actions would not distract participants I observed, affect their self-awareness, or influence interactions and conversations that participants might have among themselves and with me. I took field notes or tape-recorded observations when alone at the end of the day. Exceptions to that research practice included when I was attending a workshop, a class, or a discussion forum where other attendees were themselves taking notes, and where my doing so was therefore neither conspicuous nor distracting.

A significant section of chapter 6 is also based on my participation in a Polish Birthright trip to Israel in July 2017. Being neither Jewish nor in my twenties, I needed permission from the board of Birthright Israel to join a Polish group on the twelve-day trip. I submitted an outline of my research, a copy of my curriculum vitae, and was interviewed by the organization's vice-president. After being personally vetted and having my request accepted by the board, I was connected with the tour organizer to pay my participation fee, and with Polish organizers to coordinate my travels with the group. We prepared my integration into the group by email and Skype meetings.

I flew from the United States to Warsaw two days before our departure for Israel and attended the first meeting of our group, when participants encounter each other for the first time. That first meeting was meant to provide essential information about the trip and its pedagogical goals, describe expectations and rules of conduct, and get to know each other through formal "icebreakers" and games. I introduced myself to the group as a researcher from the University of Michigan writing a book on the Jewish revival in Poland. Birthright had given me the status of staff, so I easily blended into the small group of older adults that included two Polish Birthright "graduates," the guide, and the Israeli security/medical aid. We typically sat in front of the bus, along with participants most invested in hearing the guide's commentaries. Like the other "staff" members I did not share a room with the participants, but shared all meals and participated in all activities with them.

The guide was Israeli and the official tours were in English; all other activities were in Polish. I spoke Polish with everyone but the guide and the medic, with whom I spoke mostly English but sometimes in French in private conversations with the guide, who was a native speaker like myself.

Birthright trips are intense. The schedule of visits is heavy, and when not on the bus and touring, participants are actively taking part in group workshops, discussions, and other planned activities. I participated in everything except the unofficial after-hours social gatherings, which often lasted late into the night.

Participants felt comfortable around me, and I had many informal but significant conversations during the long bus rides, meals, hikes, and sightseeing. I took care to keep these interactions "casual" and pursue only questions likely to arise in the normal course of a conversation between fellow travelers, unless unusual lines of conversation were initiated by my interlocutors. In other words, I did not conduct directed interviews during the trip. I also refrained from taking notes in front of participants.

I sought to maintain a relatively invisible presence, in order not to shape or intrude on the experience of the individual participants. For all, it was an occasion to make new friends and discover a place that only a few had previously visited. For many of them, the trip was a meaningful personal experience, sometimes with strong emotional resonance. For some, the experience included religious dimensions, while for others it was a moment of political awakening. My role was to witness all this without interrupting the course of these individual paths, protecting the anonymity of participants as well as respecting their boundaries. I took notes or recorded my observations late at night, once I was back in my room.

I then returned to Poland in fall 2017 and spring 2018 to conduct formal interviews with approximately one-third of the participants (in Warsaw, Kraków, and Wrocław). I selected these individuals based on their active participation in the trip, the personal connections I had established with them during the trip, and access (i.e., currently living in Poland). Finally, I attended reunions for the group organized by Hillel-Warsaw in 2018–19, became Facebook friends with several participants, and remain in touch with them via social media.

Jewish Life in Poland, 1945–2021

1945   JANUARY 27: Auschwitz-Birkenau is liberated by the Soviet army.

The American Jewish Joint Distribution Committee is granted the right to function in Poland again. It is constrained to temporarily discontinue its operations in 1950.

AUGUST 11: Kraków pogrom. After rumors spread that Jews in the city had killed dozens of Polish children over a few weeks, mobs attack Jews in Kazimierz, Kraków's Jewish Quarter. At least one person is killed, many are injured, and the Kupa Synagogue is set on fire.

1946   APRIL 16: A small plaque commemorating the heroes of the Warsaw Ghetto Uprising is unveiled.

JULY 4: Kielce pogrom. Following rumors of a Polish boy's kidnapping by an unknown man suspected to be a Jew, a mob attacks Jewish refugees housed in a communal building. The pogrom was the deadliest event in postwar Polish Jewish history, leaving at least forty-two Jews dead and forty wounded. It propelled as many as a hundred thousand Jews who remained in Poland after the Second World War to leave the country.

1947   Establishment of the Jewish Historical Institute (*Żydowski Instytut Historyczny* or *ŻIH*), which publishes the quarterly review *Biuletyn Żydowskiego Instytutu Historycznego*. It is the largest repository of Polish Jewish heritage in the world.

This timeline does not constitute an exhaustive list of events relating to Jewish life in Poland; it is necessarily incomplete. The use of quotation marks indicates that the text comes from the organization described.

Establishment of the Oświęcim-Brzezinka State Museum at the site of the Auschwitz and Birkenau death camps, on the basis of a law "on the remembrance of the martyrdom of the Polish Nation and other Nations."

1948   APRIL 19: Unveiling of Nathan Rapoport's Monument to the Ghetto Heroes. It has been visited by numerous world leaders and prominent figures, including West German chancellor Willy Brandt in 1970, Pope John Paul II in 1983, and Barack Obama in 2013.

1949   Establishment of the Religious Association of Judaism in Poland (*Związek Religijnego Wyznania Mojżeszowego w Polsce*). This association is not recognized by the socialist state as the legal heir of prewar Jewish communities (*Gminy*), prohibiting it from recovering communal property.

1950   Founding of the Social-Cultural Association of Jews in Poland (*Towarzystwo Społeczno-Kulturalne Żydów w Polsce* or *TSKŻ*) to replace other Jewish organizations that had been dissolved.

1951   The *Yiddish Buch* (Yiddish Book) publishing house starts reediting Yiddish classics.

1955   The State Yiddish Theater (*Teatr Żydowski im. Estery Racheli i Idy Kamińskich*), revived in Wrocław immediately after the war, is relocated to Warsaw, where Yiddish-language plays are performed to this day.

1956-60 As part of the Thaw following Stalin's death, about fifty thousand Polish Jews leave the country for Israel.

1958   A Jewish museum is opened in the Old Synagogue (*Stara Synagoga*) in Kraków's former Jewish Quarter, Kazimierz.

1968   MARCH: Widespread antisemitic campaign sponsored by the Communist Party, partly aimed at suppressing the student movement and purging academia and the party. A massive exodus of Polish Jews follows: between 13,000 and 25,000 Jews leave in the years 1968–70. Those who remained (est. 5,000–20,000) often adopted alternative identities and concealed their origins, sometimes even from their children and family members.

1978 Founding of the "Flying Jewish University" (*Żydowski Uniwersytet Latający, ŻUL*) by Konstanty Gerbert and others a decade after the March 1968 student protests and the government-sponsored anti-Jewish campaign. The Flying Jewish University was part of the broader social initiative of Flying Universities under communism, and aimed to teach both Jewish and non-Jewish participants about lesser-known parts of Polish history and to explore taboo subjects and topics censored by the communist regime.

OCTOBER 16: **Election of Cardinal Karol Wojtyła, archbishop of Kraków, to the Holy See.**

DECEMBER 10: Isaac Bashevis Singer, a US-based, Polish-born author writing in Yiddish, is awarded the Nobel Prize in Literature and becomes widely read in Poland.

1981 Establishment of the Citizens' Committee on Jewish Cultural Monuments, an organization focusing mostly on the preservation of Jewish cemeteries. It is the first organization dedicated to protecting Jewish heritage to obtain legal status since 1950, when the Social-Cultural Association of Jews in Poland (*TSKŻ*) was established.

1983 Reopening of the Nożyk Synagogue in Warsaw after its restoration.

1984-93 Establishment of a Carmelite convent in Oświęcim, in a building that, while being outside the Auschwitz-Birkenau Museum per se, overlooks the former camp and was used to store Zyklon B during the war. After protests from (non-Polish) Jewish groups objecting to the presence of the nuns at the site, an agreement is reached and ratified in Geneva in 1987 between representatives of the Catholic Church and European Jewish leaders. The accord stipulates that the convent will be moved from the proximity of Auschwitz by 1989. After the nuns fail to move by that date, tensions escalate. In July 1989, a group of Jews from New York, under the leadership of Rabbi Avraham Weiss, occupy the grounds of the convent and are forcibly ousted from its premises. The

Carmelite nuns finally relocate in 1993 when John Paul II personally intervenes in the conflict by asking them to leave.

1985 Claude Lanzmann's film *Shoah* premieres in Paris. Parts of the film are shown on Polish television, provoking impassioned discussions. Amid outrage over the representation of Poles as complicit in the Holocaust, *Shoah* is denounced by the party-state, the Catholic Church, and ordinary citizens for being anti-Polish and offending Polish honor.

1986 OCTOBER 1: Founding of the Interdisciplinary Center of History and Culture of Jews in Poland (*Międzywydziałowy Zakład Historii i Kultury Żydów w Polsce*) at Jagiellonian University in Kraków. In 1998, the center became a department (*Katedra*) and began offering an undergraduate degree in Jewish history and culture. It also offers a master's degree since 2001, and a doctoral degree (through the History Department) since 2002. In March 2012, the Department of Jewish Studies (*Katedra Judaistyki*) was transformed into the expanded Institute of Jewish Studies (*Instytut Judaistyki*), now located in the Kazimierz Quarter of Kraków.

1987 JANUARY 11: Jan Błoński publishes "Poor Poles Look at the Ghetto" in the Catholic weekly *Tygodnik Powszechny*. The essay engages Czesław Miłosz's poems "Campo di Fiori" (1943) and "A Poor Christian Looks at the Ghetto" (1943) to discuss Polish moral responsibility for the Holocaust. It provokes a significant discussion in intellectual circles about wartime Polish-Jewish relations.

Establishment of the Shalom Foundation by Polish Jewish actress Gołda Tencer. The foundation's main goal is to preserve the heritage of Yiddish culture. Since 2004, it organizes the "Singer's Warsaw" Jewish Culture Festival and manages the Yiddish Culture Centre, which holds annual Yiddish-language workshops and periodic meetings of the Jewish Books Book Club.

1988 The March of the Living is organized for the first time. Jewish youth from all over the world march from Auschwitz to Birkenau, three kilometers away, to commemorate the murder of six million Jews during World War II.

1989 Establishment of the Lauder-Morasha Kindergarten in Warsaw, the first Jewish pedagogical institution since 1968. Its enrollment has grown from an initial seven children to about sixty today.

JUNE 4: The first semifree elections in postwar Poland, following the agreement reached at the Roundtable Talks in February, take place. Solidarity emerges as the clear winner and establishes the first noncommunist government, led by Tadeusz Mazowiecki.

1990 JULY 4: Unveiling of a plaque commemorating the Kielce pogrom at the site where forty-two Jews were murdered by Poles in 1946.

Establishment of the Mordechai Anielewicz Center for Research and Teaching of the History and Culture of Jews in Poland at the University of Warsaw's Institute of History (upgraded to a department in 2001). Since 2014, the institute offers a bachelor's program in Jewish History and Culture, and since 2017 a master's program.

Establishment of the Grodzka Gate Theatre in Lublin, a cultural institution focusing on cultural and educational programs related to the Polish Jewish past.

Establishment of the Polish Council of Christians and Jews.

DECEMBER 9: Lech Wałęsa is elected president for a five-year term.

1991 At its November congress, the Religious Association of Judaism (*Związek Religijnego Wyznania Mojżeszowego*) adopts a new name, the Union of Jewish Religious Communities in Poland (*Związek Gmin Wyznaniowych Żydowskich w Rzeczypospolitej Polskiej*) and registers that change in 1993.

Establishment of the Association of Children of the Holocaust in Poland (*Stowarzyszenie Dzieci Holocaustu*), for survivors who were thirteen or younger in 1939 and for those born during the Second World War.

1992 First issue of the bilingual Polish-Yiddish monthly *Słowo Żydowskie/Dos Jidisze Wort* published by the Communal-Cultural

Association of Jews in Poland. It replaces *Folks Sztyme*, which was published from 1946 to 1991.

A monthly youth journal, *Jidele*, is also issued this year (published until 2000).

Founding of the Polish Union of Jewish Students (*Polska Unia Studentów Żydowskich*), known as *PUSZ*.

1993 MARCH–MAY: Filming of *Schindler's List* over the course of seventy-two days in Kraków. The film premiered in the United States on November 30 and received seven Oscars, three Golden Globes, and numerous other awards. Soon afterward *"Schindler's List* tourism" is developed in Kraków.

Establishment of Jewish studies at the University of Wrocław. Initially a research center (Centre for the Culture and Languages of the Polish Jews), it began offering a two-year program in 2003 and a bachelor's degree in 2013. In 2016, the Centre for the Culture and Languages of the Polish Jews was transformed into the Department of Jewish Studies, and in 2017, it was officially renamed the Taube Department of Jewish Studies following a generous donation by of the American Taube Foundation.

SEPTEMBER 19: **Parliamentary elections won by left-wing parties (the Democratic Left Alliance and the Polish People's Party).**

NOVEMBER 24: Opening of the Center for Jewish Culture in Kraków's Kazimierz neighborhood, upon the civic initiative of the Judaica Foundation established two years earlier. The center organizes diverse events dedicated to the promotion of Jewish culture, from book readings and film screenings to conferences and seminars.

1994 The Lauder-Morasha Elementary School is established in Warsaw by the Ronald S. Lauder Foundation.

An exhibition of prewar photographs of Polish Jews, *And I Still See Their Faces* (*I wciąż widzę ich twarze*), is enthusiastically received in Warsaw.

1995   Formation of the Polish Association for Jewish Studies (*Polskie Towarzystwo Studiów Żydowskich*), officially registered in February 1996. From 1997, it began publishing the academic journal *Studia Judaica*.

NOVEMBER 19: Aleksander Kwaśniewski defeats Lech Wałęsa in the presidential election, assuming the office for two consecutive terms (1995–2005).

1996   APRIL: The White Stork Synagogue Choir (*Chór Synagogi Pod Białym Bocianem*) is formed in Wrocław under the leadership of Stanisław Rybarczyk.

1997   FEBRUARY 17: The Polish Episcopal Conference declares February 17 the Day of Judaism in the Catholic Church (*Dzień Judaizmu w Kościele Katolickim*). It is held annually on that day, on the eve of the Week of Prayer for Christian Unity.

FEBRUARY 20: The Act of 20 February on Relations Between the State and Jewish Religious Communities in the Republic of Poland is ratified. It effectively reactivates several Jewish religious communities including those of Bielsko-Biała, Gdańsk, Katowice, Kraków, Legnica, Łódź, Szczecin, Warsaw, and Wrocław on May 11 of that year. The law also allows for partial restitution of Jewish communal property seized by the state after the war. However, to date there is no law regulating the restitution of private property to former Jewish owners or their descendants.

The Warsaw Jewish Religious Community is reactivated around the Nożyk Synagogue, which holds daily, Sabbath, and holiday services. The Union of Jewish Religious Communities in Poland is headquartered in Warsaw, where it oversees the Nożyk Synagogue, the Jewish Welfare Department with its Volunteer Center, a Jewish school and a kindergarten, as well as a kosher canteen, seniors' center, and a youth club.

APRIL: With support from the Ronald S. Lauder Foundation, the first issue of *Midrasz*, a monthly publication dedicated to Polish Jewish culture, art, history, and religion appears. Konstanty Gerbert, a renowned Polish Jewish public intellectual and activist, served as its editor-in-chief from 1997 to 2000. A year later *Mi-drasz* organizes the first annual Jewish Book Days (*Dni Książki Żydowskiej*) in Warsaw.

SEPTEMBER 21: Parliamentary elections are won by the conservative Solidarity Electoral Action (*Akcja Wyborcza Solidarność*), which forms a coalition government with the post-Solidarity Freedom Union (*Unia Wolności*).

OCTOBER 17: The Constitution of the Third Republic of Poland comes into effect. It was adopted by the parliament on April 2 and approved by a referendum on May 25.

1998   FEBRUARY: Rumors that a large cross (the "papal cross") that had remained in the former Carmelite convent's garden would also be relocated ignite a yearlong "war of the crosses" just outside the Auschwitz-Birkenau Museum. Throughout the summer and fall, self-defined Poles-Catholics bring crosses to the site to protect the "papal cross," defend Catholic Poland, and commemorate Polish victims of the camp. By the time the Polish army removes them in May 1999, there are a total of 322 crosses at the site.

First issue of the bimonthly Jewish children's religious magazine *Szterndlech*.

Establishment, in Gliwice, of the Forum for Dialogue Among Nations (*Forum Dialogu Między Narodami*). It moved to Warsaw in 2004 and was renamed Forum for Dialogue. Its mission is to "provide a space for Poles and Jews to meet and to get to know one another despite historical divisions." The forum sponsors educational opportunities for schools that attract 1,200 students annually who work on projects focusing on the Jewish history of their towns and region.

DECEMBER 18: Establishment, via parliamentary legislation, of the Institute of National Remembrance–Commission for the Prosecution of Crimes against the Polish Nation (*IPN*). It began to function as an independent institution in 2000. As its name indicates, its primary goal is to investigate the repression of, and political crimes against, Poles between the beginning of World War II and the end of the communist era.

1999 Founding of Beit Polska Religious Association; and of Beit Warszawa Jewish Cultural Association in Warsaw.

Opening of the Lauder-Morasha Middle School (*Gimnazjum*) in Warsaw.

MARCH 12: Poland joins NATO.

2000 MAY: Publication of the original Polish-language book *Sąsiedzi: Historia zagłady żydowskiego miasteczka* by Jan Tomasz Gross. The book provokes an important debate among historians, public figures, and the population at large.

AUGUST 31: The Institute of National Remembrance opens an investigation of the 1941 massacre of Jews in Jedwabne. The highly publicized two-year investigation of Polish, German, and Soviet documents revealed similar pogroms occurring in nearly twenty localities in July and August 1941. The results were published in two volumes (*Wokół Jedwabnego*) in 2002.

OCTOBER 1: The Department of Jewish Studies (*Zakład Kultury i Historii Żydów*) is launched at Maria Curie-Skłodowska University in Lublin. It offers specialized courses since 2008.

2001 MARCH 15: An old monument in Jedwabne is removed. Originally unveiled in 1963, its inscription falsely stated that "Here, the Gestapo and Nazi gendarmes burned alive 1,600 people on 10 July 1941."

APRIL: Publication of the English translation of Gross's *Sąsiedzi* as *Neighbors: The Destruction of the Jewish Community in Jedwabne, Poland* (Princeton University Press).

JULY 10: A ceremony is held for the sixtieth anniversary of the pogrom in Jedwabne. A new monument is unveiled and President Kwaśniewski apologizes for the crime, making it the first apology by a Polish head of state for crimes committed by Poles against Jews during the Second World War. Catholic bishops of Poland decide not to participate in the event.

AUGUST 21: Founding of the Poland-Israel Center for Civic Education (*Centrum Edukacji Obywatelskiej Polska-Izrael*) in Białystok, an institution whose aim is to preserve local Jewish heritage and ensure the accuracy of information presented about Polish Jewish history.

SEPTEMBER 23: Parliamentary elections are won by the Center-Left coalition of Democratic Left Alliance and Labor Union.

2002   MAY: Premiere of *The Pianist*, a film directed by Roman Polanski that tells the story of Polish Jewish pianist and composer Władysław Szpilman, based on his autobiographical book under the same title. The film received multiple accolades, including three Academy Awards.

JULY: Inaugural International Summer Seminar on Yiddish Language and Culture organized in Śródborów near Warsaw by the Center for Yiddish Culture and the Shalom Foundation. The workshop, which hosts participants from Poland, Europe, North and South America, has been held annually since.

SEPTEMBER: First of the six "Karski Benches" commemorating Jan Karski, designed by Polish sculptor Karol Badyna, is unveiled in Washington, DC, on the Georgetown University campus where Karski obtained his PhD in 1952 and taught until his retirement in 1984. Karski's family protested because Karski himself was against monumental commemoration of his actions.

The Foundation for the Preservation of Jewish Heritage in Poland (*Fundacja Ochrony Dziedzictwa Żydowskiego, FODŻ*) is established by the Union of Jewish Religious Communities in Poland and the World Jewish Restitution Organization.

2003   JULY 2: The Polish Center for Holocaust Research is established as part of the Institute of Philosophy and Sociology of the Polish Academy of Sciences, under the direction of Professor Barbara Engelking. "It is the first and so far the only research institution in Poland dealing exclusively with Holocaust studies," its website indicates.

The Jewish Heritage Initiative in Poland (JHIP) is established by the Taube Foundation for Jewish Life & Culture with a mission to "strengthen the institutional life of Polish Jews." "Since then, the JHIP has disbursed more than 450 grants totaling over $30 million to more than 100 cultural and communal programs and organizations," its website announces.

The Jewish Agency for Israel in Poland assumes responsibility for Taglit-Birthright Poland.

2004   JANUARY: Establishment of Israeli dance group Kachol in Kraków's Old Town Youth Culture Center, located in the Jewish Quarter. Kachol organizes dance workshops, lectures, concerts, film screenings, and thematic trips aimed at "get[ting] to know Israeli culture through art."

APRIL: Opening of Kraków's Galicia Jewish Museum, established to "commemorate the victims of the Holocaust and celebrate the Jewish culture of Polish Galicia, presenting Jewish history from a new perspective."

APRIL 15: Publication of Anna Bikont's *My z Jedwabnego*, a book-length investigation of the Jedwabne pogrom and its cover-up. The book was translated into French in 2010 and into English in 2015 (*The Crime and the Silence*). It won the European Book Prize in 2011.

MAY 1: **Poland joins the European Union.**

AUGUST 4: Official dedication of Survivors' Park in Łódź (*Park Ocalałych*) on the sixtieth anniversary of the liquidation of the city's ghetto.

Establishment of the Polish Jews Forum (*Forum Żydów Polskich*— http://www.fzp.net.pl), an online platform "for Polish Jews and Poles" whose mission is information exchange about "Jewish life, culture, religion and history." Today, the forum also has a

Facebook group with fourteen thousand members and a Twitter account with over 7,200 followers.

Founding of Cholent Jewish Association (*Żydowskie Stowarzyszenie Czulent*) in Kraków. Initially a student organization providing space for reflection on the meaning of Jewish identity in Poland, it expanded to a national-level project whose aim is to facilitate intercultural dialogue and support the rights of ethnic minorities.

2005 JANUARY 27: On the occasion of the sixtieth anniversary of Auschwitz-Birkenau's liberation, the United Nations declares January 27th International Holocaust Remembrance Day.

APRIL 2: **Death of Pope John Paul II.**

APRIL 22: Official unveiling of the second "Karski Bench" in Kielce, Poland.

JULY 1: Founding of the Jewish Research Center (*Centrum Badań Żydowskich*) at the University of Łódź, a research institution dedicated to the history of Polish Jews, with a specialization in that population in central Poland.

SEPTEMBER: **Parliamentary elections are narrowly won by the right-wing Law and Justice (*PiS*) with 26.99 percent of the vote. The Center-Right party Civic Platform follows with 24.14 percent of the vote.**

OCTOBER: **Lech Kaczyński is elected president. He was in office until his death in the Smoleńsk air crash on April 10, 2010.**

2006 Establishment of the Bente Kahan Foundation in Wrocław, initially with the goal of restoring the White Stork Synagogue; the foundation's activism now centers on promoting human rights and cultural tolerance through the perspective of European Jews.

The Foundation for the Preservation of Jewish Heritage in Poland establishes the Chassidic Route (*Szlak Chasydzki*), a trail spanning twenty-nine towns featuring synagogues and other Jewish monuments in southeastern Poland.

JULY 1: Publication of Jan Tomasz Gross's *Fear: Anti-Semitism in Poland after Auschwitz: An Essay in Historical Interpretation* (Random House and Princeton University Press). The book is immediately reviewed and discussed in the American, German, and Polish press. Heated debates about the book ensue in Poland.

JULY 4: On the sixtieth anniversary of the Kielce pogrom, President Kaczyński declares that it was "a crime and a disgrace . . . bringing shame and tragedy to Poles and Jews, who survived the Nazi Holocaust in such small numbers." He asserts that "there is no justification for this crime" and "no room for antisemitism or racism in democratic Poland."

Article 132a is added to the penal code stipulating that "anyone publicly accusing the Polish Nation of participating in, organizing, or being responsible for communist or Nazi crimes is subject to up to three years' imprisonment." In the public sphere, Article 132a is nicknamed "Gross's Law" as it was specifically tailored to target the Polish-born, US-based scholar Jan T. Gross, who published that year *Fear: Anti-Semitism in Poland after Auschwitz*. Article 132a was repealed in 2008; a new law restricting speech on the Holocaust was adopted in 2018.

DECEMBER 18: President Kaczyński hosts representatives of the Jewish community in Poland for the lighting ceremony on the first night of Hanukah. The ceremony now takes place every year.

2007   The Polish Union of Jewish Students (*PUSZ*) is dissolved and succeeded by the Jewish Youth Organization of Poland, known as ŻOOM (*Żydowska Ogólnopolska Organizacja Młodzieżowa*).

FEBRUARY 11: Opening of the Synagogue Chachmei Lublin Yeshiva in Lublin after extensive renovations undertaken by the Warsaw Jewish Religious Community.

JULY: The Polish state radio's *Kol Polin* (Voices of Poland) service starts broadcasting in Hebrew.

SEPTEMBER 9: Reestablishment of the Polish chapter of the international association *Żydowskie Stowarzyszenie B'nai B'rith w Rzeczypospolitej Polskiej* (or *B'nai B'rith—Loża Polin*), which originally operated in Poland from 1922 to 1938.

OCTOBER 1: Antonina Wyrzykowska, who hid seven Jewish escapees from the Jedwabne pogrom in a cellar for two and half years, receives the Commander's Cross of the Order of Polonia Restituta from President Lech Kaczyński. Wyrzykowska was also honored by Yad Vashem with the title Righteous Among the Nations in 1976.

OCTOBER 21: Parliamentary elections following an early dissolution voted by the Sejm are won by the Center-Right Civic Platform. Donald Tusk is named prime minister.

NOVEMBER 11: The third "Karski Bench" is unveiled in New York City, near the intersection of Madison Avenue and 37th Street, now known as "Jan Karski Corner."

DECEMBER 21: Lech Kaczyński becomes the first president of Poland to visit a synagogue since World War II.

2008 JANUARY: Publication of Jan T. Gross's *Strach——Antysemityzm w Polsce tuż po wojnie: Historia moralnej zapaści*, the Polish translation of *Fear: Anti-Semitism in Poland after Auschwitz*, originally published in English in 2006.

APRIL: Establishment of the Jewish Community Centre of Kraków (*Centrum Społeczności Żydowskiej w Krakowie*). In its first five years, its membership surpassed six hundred, and it attracted on average over eight thousand visitors per month. By 2021, it had over 750 members.

APRIL 16: Establishment of Beit Polska, which incorporates Beit Warsaw, Beit Tricity, and Beit Konstancin. In 2009 it was added to the national Register of Churches and Other Denominational Congregations.

JUNE: Establishment of the Covenant Club (*Klub Przymierze*), the Kraków Association of Christians and Jews, whose mission is to "overcome stereotypes, alleviate existing tensions, popularize models of cooperation and strengthen the friendships of Poles with different faiths and origins."

SEPTEMBER: Yael Bartana's short film *Nightmares* (*Mary Koszmary*) is released and screened in various cultural centers throughout Poland. It is the first film of the trilogy *And Europe Will Be Stunned*.

Establishment of the Irena Sendler Memorial Award by the Taube Foundation for Jewish Life & Culture. The award "honors Poles who contribute to the preservation of Jewish heritage and the renewal of Jewish culture in Poland."

Founding of the Jewish Theatre in Kraków—Midrash Theatre (*Teatr Żydowski w Krakowie—Teatr Midraszowy*), in the Jewish Quarter, Kazimierz, on the initiative of Rabbi Tanya Segal.

First Limmud Polska gathering, a weekend-long educational and cultural initiative sponsored by the American Jewish Joint Distribution Committee, drawing several hundred participants from communities around the country. Between 2008 and 2018, nine Limmud meetings were organized. In 2019, local editions replaced the large national meeting.

2009   JANUARY: The Jewish Historical Institute (*Żydowski Instytut Historyczny* or *ŻIH*) is renamed after Emanuel Ringelblum and formally established by the Ministry of Culture and National Heritage as a new institution of culture.

MARCH 10: Establishment of the Brama Cukermana Foundation in Będzin, a town in Silesia, in order to preserve the Jewish House of Prayer in Cukerman's Gate.

MARCH: Founding of the Progressive Jewish Community of Kraków 'Beit Kraków' (*Postępowa społeczność żydowska 'Beit Kraków'*), whose structures were formalized in 2011. Its founder and leader is Rabbi Tanya Segal, the first woman rabbi in Poland.

APRIL: The Higher School of Hebrew Philology in Toruń (*Wyższa Szkoła Filologii Hebrajskiej w Toruniu*) is founded by the Franciscan Order. The school offers courses in Hebrew and Jewish studies. It was closed in 2016 because of lack of interest from local students.

JUNE: Establishment of the Taube Center for the Renewal of Jewish Life in Poland by the Taube Foundation for Jewish Life & Culture. It is the only Jewish American foundation to have an office in Poland.

JUNE: Yael Bartana's short film *Wall and Tower* (*Mur i wieża*) is released. It is the second film of Bartana's trilogy *And Europe Will Be Stunned.*

AUGUST 19: Fourth "Karski Bench" is unveiled in Łódź's Survivors' Park (*Park Ocalałych*).

NOVEMBER 30: Fifth "Karski Bench" is unveiled at Tel Aviv University by then-marshal of the Sejm, Bronisław Komorowski.

The Taube Foundation establishes the Irena Sendler Award "For Repairing the World" to honor teachers who foster the spirit of dialogue and tolerance.

2010   JANUARY 27: On International Holocaust Remembrance Day, Rafał Betlejewski begins his initiative "I Miss You, Jew" (*Tęsknię za Tobą, Żydzie*) and paints the first graffito as a part of his project under the same title.

MARCH 28: Betlejewski organizes a happening at the University of Warsaw attended by about two hundred people who chant "I miss you, *Jew!*"

MARCH: Founding of the Polish Association for Yiddish Studies (*Polskie Towarzystwo Jidyszystyczne*) whose goal "is to preserve Yiddish language and culture as a living part of our common culture." It counts approximately sixty members.

APRIL 10: Death of President Lech Kaczyński in a plane crash in Smolensk, Ukraine. Several days of national mourning are declared.

JUNE: Oskar Schindler's Enamel Factory Museum in Kraków (*Fabryka Emalia Oskara Schindlera*) inaugurates its permanent exhibition *Kraków Under Nazi Occupation 1939–1945*.

JUNE 20: Bronisław Komorowski, of Civic Platform, is elected president of Poland.

JULY 10: Controversial commemorative performance "Burning Barn" (*Płonie Stodoła*) by Rafał Betljewski in the village of Zawady in central Poland, on the sixty-ninth anniversary of the Jedwabne pogrom.

Creation of "My Jewish Warsaw" (*Moja Żydowska Warszawa*), an initiative of ethnographer and Yiddishist Anna Ciałowicz, administered by the Warsaw Jewish Religious Community. The web-based project (http://varshe.org.pl) documents and translates primary sources related to people, places, institutions, and events in Jewish Warsaw.

Taube Jewish Heritage Tour Programs are launched by the Taube Center offering various tours for groups, families, and students.

2011 JANUARY 1: Official opening of the Marek Edelman Dialogue Center in Łódź (*Centrum Dialogu im. Marka Edelmana*).

MARCH: Publication of *Złote żniwa: Rzecz o tym, co się działo na obrzeżach zagłady Żydów* by Jan Tomasz Gross and Irena Grudzińska-Gross. The book is widely debated in the press, on television, and on social media. Its English translation, *Golden Harvest: Events at the Periphery of the Holocaust* (Oxford University Press), appears in 2012.

JUNE–NOVEMBER: Israeli artist Yael Bartana becomes the first non-Polish citizen to represent Poland at the Venice Biennale with her trilogy *And Europe Will Be Stunned*. Her short film *Assassination* (*Zamach*), the third and final part of the trilogy, premieres in June.

JULY: The festival Following Isaac Bashevis Singer's Traces (*Festiwal "Śladami Singera"*) is organized for the first time in Lublin and the Lubelskie Region.

SEPTEMBER 9: Polish premiere of *In Darkness* (*W ciemności*) directed by Agnieszka Holland. The film is based on the true story of a sewer worker who hid a group of Jews in the Lvi'v (Lwów, Lemberg) sewer system during World War II. It was nominated for an Academy Award the following year.

OCTOBER 9: Parliamentary elections result in a coalition government of Civic Platform and the Polish People's Party (*Polskie Stronnictwo Ludowe*).

2012 Year of Janusz Korczak, nominated by the Jewish Historical Institute and adopted by the parliament via resolution in September 2011. Korczak (pen name of Henryk Goldszmit) was a renowned Polish Jewish educator and author of children's books. He was deported with children from his orphanage in August 1942 and murdered in Treblinka.

FEBRUARY: Beit Polska organizes its first monthly Shabbat meeting, called Sabaton (*Szabaton*), in Łódź.

MAY 10: The European Parliament declares March 6 the day of Remembrance of the Righteous Among the Nations.

JULY 22: On the seventieth anniversary of the liquidation of the Warsaw Ghetto, the Jewish Historical Institute organizes its first March of Remembrance (*Marsz Pamięci*) in Warsaw. It is a resounding success and is held annually since.

AUGUST 3: The Polish Senate passes a resolution naming November 2012 the Month of Bruno Schulz. Schulz, killed by a Gestapo officer in 1942, was a Polish Jewish writer and artist, renowned for his unique prose style.

NOVEMBER: Premiere of Władysław Pasikowski's film *Aftermath* (*Pokłosie*), a fictional thriller loosely based on the 1941 Jedwabne pogrom. A debate ensues in the media, and many conservative groups boycott the film and protest in front of cinemas screening it.

NOVEMBER 28: Following a campaign by animal rights activists, the Constitutional Tribunal rules that the ritual slaughter of animals is illegal. The Union of Jewish Religious Communities challenges the ban claiming it violates the constitutional right of freedom of religious practice.

2013   JANUARY 1: The ban on ritual slaughter takes effect.

Year of Julian Tuwim, commemorating the renowned and widely read Polish Jewish poet. In contemporary Poland, Tuwim is known for his mastery of the Polish language as well as playful children's poems. His oeuvre also includes writings on Polish Jewish identity and interwar antisemitism.

MARCH 16: The City of Kraków's Eagle Pharmacy Museum (*Apteka pod Orłem*) inaugurates its permanent exhibition on the seventieth anniversary of the ghetto's liquidation. During the war, the pharmacy served as a medical, informational, and conspiratorial hub. It was led by pharmacist Tadeusz Pankiewicz, the only non-Jewish Pole living in the Jewish ghetto, who was recognized as a Righteous Among the Nations by Yad Vashem in 1983.

MARCH: Opening of the Museum of Mazovian Jews in Płock (*Muzeum Żydów Mazowieckich*), a city of over three hundred thousand inhabitants in central Poland.

APRIL 19: Opening of the Polin Museum of the History of Polish Jews' building on the seventieth anniversary of the Warsaw Ghetto Uprising. Poles wait in long queues snaking around the museum to visit the empty building.

MAY 15: Unveiling of the Irena Sendler honorary alley on the lawn area leading to the Monument to the Ghetto Heroes and the Polin Museum.

JUNE 11: Sixth "Karski Bench" unveiled in Warsaw, in the lawn area leading to the Monument to the Ghetto Heroes and the Polin Museum.

JUNE 15-16: Official opening of the renovated synagogue in Chmielnik, now converted into a museum and cultural center, the

Świętokrzyski Shtetl (*Ośrodek Edukacyjno-Muzealny "Świętokrzyski Sztetl"*). The opening takes place together with the 11th Meetings with Jewish Culture and an academic conference on the Everyday Life of the Jewish Community in Poland until 1942.

AUGUST 30: World premiere of Paweł Pawlikowski's film *Ida* at the Telluride Film Festival in Colorado. The Polish premiere takes place two weeks later, on September 11 at the Gdynia Film Festival. The film received that festival's Golden Lion Award but was denounced as anti-Polish in right-wing media.

OCTOBER 27: Founding of Warsaw's Jewish Community Center (JCC-Warsaw).

NOVEMBER: Inaugural edition of the Leopold Kozłowski National Jewish Song Competition (*Ogólnopolski Konkurs Piosenki Żydowskiej imienia Leopolda Kozłowskiego*) for high school students. The event has been held annually since then. Leopold Kozłowski-Kleinman (1918–2019), known as "the last klezmer of Galicia," popularized klezmer music among Poles.

NOVEMBER 11: The Polish Council of Christians and Jews initiates a one-day conference, Close Encounters of Christians and Jews (*Bliskie Spotkania Chrześcijan i Żydów*), to promote dialogue.

2014 The parliament proclaims 2014 the Year of Jan Karski to commemorate the hundredth anniversary of his birth. A series of events are organized in Kraków, Warsaw, and Sopot.

JUNE 9: JCC-Kraków's inaugural Ride for the Living, from the gate of Birkenau to Kazimierz. The event is held annually since.

OCTOBER 28: Ceremonial opening of the core exhibition of the Polin Museum of the History of Polish Jews in Warsaw. The presidents of Poland and Israel are present, as well as many ambassadors, politicians, prominent public figures, members of Poland's Jewish communities, and hundreds of journalists. Several VIP tours are organized, and a gala takes place at the Teatr Wielki.

OCTOBER: Publication of *Księgi Jakubowe* (*The Books of Jacob*) by Olga Tokarczuk, based on the historical figure of Jacob Frank, the leader of a heretical Jewish group in the fifteenth-century Polish-Lithuanian Commonwealth. In the months following the book's publication, Tokarczuk came to public prominence for her statement that Poles committed abhorrent crimes "as colonizers, slave owners, and murderers of Jews."

DECEMBER 10: The ritual-slaughter ban is repealed by the Constitutional Tribunal so as to conform to the protection of religious freedom.

2015 Paweł Pawlikowski's *Ida* wins the Academy Award for Best Foreign-Language Film, sparking a significant debate in Poland. Polish conservatives deem the film "anti-Polish" because of its treatment of Poles' role in the Holocaust. Over fifty thousand people sign a petition to the Polish Film Institute demanding that it specify that the film was a work of fiction. Prominent liberal film critics also find fault, but primarily for the way the film addresses postwar Polish-Jewish issues, and especially for its portrayal of one Jewish character as a prominent member of the Communist Party.

MAY 24: **Andrzej Duda, of Law and Justice, wins the presidential election.**

OCTOBER 25: **Law and Justice wins the parliamentary elections, forming the first single-party government since 1989.**

NOVEMBER 18: Far-right activist Piotr Rybak burns the effigy of an Orthodox Jew (purportedly representing George Soros) during an anti-immigrant and antirefugee manifestation organized by the neofascist National Radical Camp (*Obóz Narodowo-Radykalny*) in Wrocław's Old Square. On November 16, 2016, Rybak is sentenced to ten months' imprisonment, but a year later his sentence is reduced to three months.

2016 JANUARY 2: Seventh "Karski Bench" unveiled in Kraków, in front of the Remu Synagogue in Kazimierz.

2017   Year of Bolesław Leśmian is celebrated unofficially by various cultural, artistic, and intellectual circles after the Polish Senate does not pass the official resolution to name 2017 after the Polish Jewish poet on the eightieth anniversary of his death.

Founding of Hillel Polska. Chapters open in Warsaw and Kraków.

2018   Year of Irena Sendler. Various commemorative activities are organized throughout the year across the country, including a temporary exhibition on Sendler at the Polin Museum.

JANUARY 26: On the eve of International Holocaust Remembrance Day and the seventy-third anniversary of Auschwitz's liberation, the Polish parliament approves a bill to amend its Institute of National Remembrance Law. Most controversial is the article threatening up to three years in prison for those blaming the Polish state or the nation for participating in the Holocaust. The bill provokes an international outcry.

FEBRUARY 6: President Andrzej Duda signs the bill into law.

JUNE 27: The Institute of National Remembrance Law is amended under international pressure. Polish and Israeli prime ministers Mateusz Morawiecki and Benjamin Netanyahu make the announcement in a joint statement. The revision removes the possibility of criminal prosecution, but also removes the exemption of scholarship and arts from the law; charges may still be made in a civil court. In their joint statement, Morawiecki and Netanyahu also condemn "all forms of antisemitism" and reject "anti-Polonism." The statement is in turn denounced by Yad Vashem.

2019   Łódź celebrates the Year of Marek Edelman (*Rok Marka Edelmana*), leader of the Warsaw Ghetto Uprising. The celebrations were initially meant to be nationwide, but because of delays in the parliamentary ratification process they were ultimately limited to Łódź, where Edelman worked as a cardiac surgeon after the war, and were organized by the Marek Edelman Dialogue Center.

MAY 11: Right-wing demonstrators march in Warsaw, chanting antisemitic and anti-American slogans to protest the Justice for

Uncompensated Survivors Today (JUST) resolution adopted by the US Senate in 2018. Protesters claim that the resolution involved the payment of $300 million by Poland to international Jewish associations as a compensation for property lost during the Holocaust.

OCTOBER 10: Olga Tokarczuk wins the Nobel Prize in Literature. In an interview she openly criticizes how the history of violence against Jews is taught in Poland. Right-wing circles call her "anti-Polish and anti-Catholic."

OCTOBER 13: Law and Justice retains its parliamentary majority in the election with 43.6 percent of the popular vote.

DECEMBER 4: Rafał Betlejewski is found guilty for attaching "I Miss You, Jew" posters to trees in Węgrów, a small town in Eastern Poland, earlier that year.

2020 FEBRUARY 12: The Lauder Foundation announces the planned opening of a Jewish high school (as part of the Lauder-Morasha School Team) in Warsaw in September 2020. The last Jewish high school in Poland was closed in 1968. The tuition cost, high for Polish standards at about $400 a month, is criticized in the Warsaw press.

FEBRUARY 27: The Institute of National Remembrance's Commission for the Prosecution of Crimes against the Polish Nation opens a new Hall of Remembrance (*Sala Pamięci*) near 8 Strzelecka Street in Warsaw, where the Soviet NKWD headquarters were located.

APRIL: Rafał Betlejewski paints "I Miss You, Jew" on the Jewish cemetery wall in Tykocin in northeastern Poland. The regional court of Białystok punishes him with a fine on January 21 the following year.

JULY 12: After a contentious campaign, Andrzej Duda of Law and Justice is reelected president of Poland.

OCTOBER: Opening of Landau's House (*Dom Landaua*), a small museum commemorating Jewish history in Bobowa, a town in

Southern Poland where a yeshiva led by the Bobov dynasty was located before the war.

2021 FEBRUARY 9: In a highly publicized libel case, Holocaust scholars Barbara Engelking and Jan Grabowski are ordered to apologize for having offended the memory of the defendant's deceased uncle in their study of Poles' collaboration with the Nazis. The appeals court in Warsaw overturns the ruling on August 16 , stating that "it is not the court's task to interfere in academic research."

JUNE 26: Celebration of the inaugural Holocaust Survivor Day instituted by JCC-Kraków along with its global partners to celebrate the lives of survivors. June 26th was chosen to honor renowned historian and journalist Marian Turski, who survived the Łódź ghetto and Auschwitz, and was born on that day in 1926.

AUGUST 13: President Andrzej Duda signs an amendment to Poland's restitution law, which now sets a thirty-year time limit to appeal administrative decisions resulting in property seizure. This in effect prevents the descendants of Jews whose property was seized during the Second World War and retained during the communist era from receiving restitution. The signing of the law creates sharp tensions between Poland and Israel, which recalls its envoy in protest. Poland's ambassador to Israel is also recalled. On November 25, Poland's Ministry of Foreign Affairs announced it was not sending back an ambassador to Israel, bringing its mission level in that country down to that of Israel's mission in Poland.

NOVEMBER 11: On the occasion of Poland's Independence Day, a far-Right group marches in Kalisz, in west-central Poland, carrying antisemitic banners and chanting, "This is Poland, Jews to Israel!" The group and their followers gather in the town's main square, where leaders make violent speeches and rouse a small crowd. Piotr Rybak, who had burned an effigy of a Jew in Wrocław in 2015, is among the speakers. The event culminates with the burning of a copy of the Statute of Kalisz. Issued in that town on September 8, 1264, by Prince Bolesław the Pious, the statute granted exclusive jurisdiction over Jewish matters to Jewish courts, established rules under which Jews were allowed to engage in trade and lending, and instituted norms concerning their relations with Christians. In addition, the statute specified penalties for the desecration of Jewish cemeteries and synagogues and contained provisions on blood libel directed against Jews. It was ratified by King Kazimierz the Great in 1334 and became the symbol of safe living for Jews in Poland. Following the antisemitic event, several public figures, organizations, and the chair of the Polish Episcopate's Committee on Dialogue with Judaism issue statements condemning the event and antisemitism more generally. Representatives of the Roman Catholic Church, along with six other Christian denominations in Kalisz, do so as well. The chief rabbi of Poland and the Union of Religious Communities conclude their statement with "Poland is our Fatherland. We are both Polish and Jewish. We wonder, however, why our right to consider Poland our home is increasingly questioned." On November 12, the organizers of the march are charged with public incitement to ethnic and religious hatred; insulting a group of persons on the basis of their ethnic and religious identities; and public incitement to commit criminal acts against individuals on the basis of their ethnic and religious identities. The three defendants face up to five years in prison.

Jewish Festivals in Poland, 1988–2019

NAME	LOCATION	YEARS ACTIVE	SIZE*
Jewish Culture Festival	Kraków	1988~	Extra-large
Days of Remembrance of the Jews of Galicia—"Galicjaner Sztetl" (*Dni Pamięci Żydów Galicyjskich "Galicjaner Sztetl"*)	Tarnów	1996~	Medium
Meetings with Jewish Culture "Bajit Chadasz" (*Spotkania z Kulturą Żydowską "Bajit Chadasz"*)	Kraków	1996~	Large
Havdalah Concerts (*Koncerty Hawdałowe*)	Wrocław	1996~	Small
Baltic Days of Jewish Culture (*Bałtyckie Dni Kultury Żydowskiej*)	Gdańsk	1999–2016	Small
Festival of Jewish Culture "Simcha" (*Festiwal Kultury Żydowskiej "Simcha"*)	Wrocław	1999~	Large
Festival of Three Cultures (*Festiwal Trzech Kultur*)	Włodawa	1999~	Medium
Days of Jewish and Israeli Culture and in Wielkopolska (*Dni Kultury Żydowskiej i Izraelskiej w Wielkopolsce*)	Wielkopolska	2001–14	Medium
Days of Jewish Culture (*Dni Kultury Żydowskiej*)	Słupsk	2002~	Medium
Łódź of Four Cultures Festival (*Festiwal Łódź Czterech Kultur*, originally *Dialog Czterech Kultur*)	Łódź	2002~	Large

NAME	LOCATION	YEARS ACTIVE	SIZE*
Festival of Polish and Jewish Culture: Celebration of Ciulim-Cholent (*Festiwal Kultury Polskiej i Żydowskiej: Święto Ciulimu-Czulentu*)	Lelów	2003~	Large
Jewish Film Festival of Warsaw (*Warszawski Festiwal Filmów o Tematyce Żydowskiej*)	Warsaw	2003~	Large
Meetings with Jewish Culture (*Spotkania z Kulturą Żydowską*, renamed *Festiwal Dni Kultur* in 2016)	Chmielnik	2003~	Small
Festival of Jewish Culture—"Singer's Warsaw" (*Festiwal Kultury Żydowskiej "Warszawa Singera"*)	Warsaw	2004~	Large
International Film Festival "Jewish Motifs" (*Międzynarodowy Festiwal Filmowy "Żydowskie Motywy"*)	Warsaw	2004~	Large
Students' Days of Israel (*Studenckie Dni Izraela*)	Kraków	2004~	Medium
Meetings with Jewish Culture (*Spotkania z Kulturą Żydowską*)	Pszczyna	2004~	Small
International Meetings with Jewish Culture (*Międzynarodowe Spotkania z Kulturą Żydowską*)	Sopot	2005~	Large
Festival of Klezmer Music and Tradition (*Festiwal Muzyki i Tradycji Klezmerskiej*)	Kazimierz Dolny	2006~	Medium
Days of Jewish Culture (*Dni Kultury Żydowskiej*)	Zielona Góra	2006–13	Medium
Szczekociny Jewish Culture Festival "Yahad-Together" (*Szczekociński Festiwal Kultury Żydowskiej "Yahad-Razem"*)	Szczekociny	2008–17	Small
Days of Remembrance of the Rymanów Jewish Community (*Dni Pamięci o Żydowskiej Społeczności Rymanowa*)	Rymanów	2009~	Small

NAME	LOCATION	YEARS ACTIVE	SIZE*
Meetings with Jewish Culture "Trace" (*Spotkania z Kulturą Żydowską "Ślad"*)	Radom	2009~	Small
Open Twarda Street (*Otwarta Twarda*)	Warsaw	2009–17	Medium
Life Festival	Oświęcim	2010–18	Large
Festival "New Jewish Music" (*Festiwal "Nowa Muzyka Żydowska"*)	Warsaw	2010–16	Small
Festival "Following I. B. Singer's Traces" (*Festiwal "Śladami Singera"*)	Lublin	2011~	Medium
Nationwide Festival of Jewish and Israeli Songs "Shalom" (*Ogólnopolski Festiwal Pieśni i Piosenki Żydowskiej i Izraelskiej "Shalom"*)	Kalisz	2011~	Small
Days of Jewish Culture—Chrzanów Shtetl (*Dni Kultury Żydowskiej—Sztetl Chrzanów*)	Chrzanów	2012~	Small
Silesian Jewish Culture Festival (*Śląski Festiwal Kultury Żydowskiej*)	Bielsko Biała, Gliwice, Katowice, Będzin, Zabrze	2012–13	Small
Shabatton (*Szabaton*)	Łódź	2012~	Medium
Jewish Culture Days "Adlojada" (*Dni Kultury Żydowskiej "Adlojada"*)	Szczecin	2012~	Small
Simchat Chajim Festival	Poznań, Buk, Jarocin, Koźmin Wielkopolski	2012~	Medium
Meetings with Jewish Holidays (*Spotkania z Żydowskimi Świętami*)	Nowy Sącz	2013–14	Small
Bobowa Days with Jewish Culture SHALOM (*Dni Bobowej z Kulturą Żydowską SZALOM*)	Bobowa	2013~	Small

NAME	LOCATION	YEARS ACTIVE	SIZE*
Meetings with Jewish Culture—"Pardes Festival" (*"Pardes Festival"—Spotkania z Kulturą Żydowską*)	Kazimierz Dolny	2013~	Medium
Festival of the Jewish Street (*Święto Ulicy Żydowskiej*)	Poznań	2013–14	Medium
Jewish Culture Festival "Zachor—Color and Sound" (*Festiwal Kultury Żydowskiej Zachor—Kolor i Dźwięk*)	Białystok	2013~	Medium
Festival of Three Cultures "3K" (*Festiwal Trzech Kultur "3K"*)	Zduńska Wola	2013–14	Small
Jewish Culture Festival "Rapprochements" (*Festiwal Kultury Żydowskiej "Zbliżenia"*)	Gdańsk	2013~	Large
Days of Jewish Culture in Nowy Żmigród (*Dni Kultury Żydowskiej w Nowym Żmigrodzie*)	Nowy Żmigród	2014	Small
Four Cultures, One Żelów (*Cztery Kultury, Jeden Żelów*)	Żelów	2014	Small
"Day of Jewish Culture" (*Dzień Kultury Żydowskiej*)	Cieszyn	2015~	Small
"Day of Jewish Culture" (*Dzień Kultury Żydowskiej*)	Brzeg	2015~	Small
Days of Jewish Culture in Dzierżoniów (*Dni Kultury Żydowskiej w Dzierżoniowie*)	Dzierżoniów	2017~	Small
Polin Music Festival	Warsaw	2018~	Small

*Size takes into account festival attendance, duration, and program offerings.

Interviews with Public Figures

Bartana, Yael (visual artist, director of the film trilogy *And Europe Will Be Stunned*, cofounder of the Jewish Renaissance Movement in Poland). Audio recording, Berlin, January 17, 2013.

Betlejewski, Rafał (performing artist, initiator of "I Miss You, Jew"). Audio recording, Warsaw, March 24, 2011.

Czernek, Helena (designer, cofounder and CEO of Mi Polin). Audio recording, Warsaw, October 25, 2015.

Czubak, Irek (religious activist, organizer of "Christian seders" throughout Poland). Audio recording, Kraków, March 27, 2013.

Czubak, Maryla (religious activist, organizer of "Christian seders" throughout Poland). Audio recording, Kraków, March 27, 2013.

Dodziuk, Anna (Jewish activist, author). Audio recordings, Warsaw, May 2004; March 28, 2013.

Dorosz, Magda (executive director, Hillel-Warsaw). Audio recording, Warsaw, March 12, 2017.

Elliott, Monika (program director, Joint Distribution Committee Poland). Warsaw, March 22, 2013.

Folwarczny, Andrzej (president, Forum for Dialogue). Audio recording, Warsaw, May 19, 2016.

Gądek, Robert (deputy director, grant manager, Jewish Culture Festival in Kraków). Audio recordings, Kraków, March 6, 2012; March 27, 2013.

Gebert, Konstanty (public intellectual, frequent contributor to *Gazeta Wyborcza*, founder and former editor-in-chief of the Polish Jewish monthly *Midrasz*). Audio recordings, Warsaw, May 25, 2004; March 8, 2012.

Gembala, Grzegorz (genealogist). Audio recording, Kraków, March 23, 2011.

Herberger, Tyson (rabbi in Warsaw, 2010–13, Wrocław 2013–15). Warsaw, September 27, 2012.

Horovitz, Itzchak (*mashgiach* and cantor). Audio recording, Kraków, February 29, 2012.

Jakubowicz, Tadeusz (president of the Jewish Religious Community in Kraków, 1997–present). Audio recording, Kraków, March 5, 2012.

Jonas-Kowalik, Matylda (program coordinator, Hillel-Warsaw). Audio recording, Warsaw, March 12, 2017.

Kadlčik, Piotr (president, Union of Jewish Religious Communities in Poland, 2003–14). Audio recording, Warsaw, May 12, 2004.

Kahan, Bente (artist, community activist, and founder of the Bente Kahan Foundation). Audio recording, Wrocław, May 23, 2016.

Kolek, Anna (visual artist). Phone interview, December 11, 2020.

Kowalewski, Paweł (program manager, Jewish Culture Festival in Kraków). Audio recording, Kraków, March 6, 2012; March 27, 2013.

Krajewski, Stanisław (co-chair of the Committee on Christian-Jewish Dialogue, member of the International Council of the Auschwitz-Birkenau State Museum, and consultant for the American Jewish Committee). Audio recordings, Warsaw, 2001; May 24, 2004.

Krawczyk, Monika (CEO, Foundation for the Preservation of Jewish Heritage in Poland, 2004–19). Audio recording, Warsaw, May 25, 2016.

Krawczyk, Piotr (author, deputy director, Świętokrzyski Shtetl Museum). Chmielnik, June 26, 2014.

Makuch, Janusz (cofounder and director, Jewish Culture Festival in Kraków). Audio recordings, Kraków, March 19, 2011; March 1, 2012; March 27, 2013.

Nawrocki, Piotr (board member, Jewish Religious Community in Kraków; board member, Jewish Culture Festival in Kraków). Audio recording, Kraków, March 21, 2011.

Nizio, Mirosław (architect and designer, specialized in museum exhibitions). Audio recording, Warsaw, June 2, 2011.

Ornstein, Jonathan (director, Kraków Jewish Community Centre). Audio recordings, Kraków, March 2011, 2012, 2013, 2021.

Pash, Boaz (chief rabbi of Kraków, 2006–12). Audio recording, Kraków, March 6, 2012.

Prugar, Aleksander (photographer, cofounder and CEO of Mi Polin). Audio recording, Warsaw, October 25, 2015.

Schudrich, Michael (chief rabbi of Poland). Audio recording, Warsaw, September 28, 2012.

Segal, Tanya (rabbi, Beit Kraków). Audio recording, Kraków, March 7, 2012.

Sierakowski, Sławomir (public intellectual, cofounder of *Krytyka Polityczna*, author and actor in Yael Bartana's *And Europe Will Be Stunned*, cofounder of the Jewish Renaissance Movement in Poland). Audio recording, Warsaw, September 26, 2012.

Sokołowska, Karina (director, Joint Distribution Committee Poland). Audio recording, Warsaw, May 19, 2016.

Primary Sources

Białystok City Hall. 2018. *The Many Cultures of Białystok: A Cultural Guide to the Capital of Podlasie.*

Bikont, Anna. 2016. *The Crime and the Silence: Confronting the Massacre of Jews in Wartime Jedwabne.* New York: Farrar, Straus & Giroux.

——. 2017. *Sendlerowa: W ukryciu.* Wołowiec: Wydawnictwo Czarne.

Błoński, Jan. 1990. "The Poor Poles Look at the Ghetto." In *My Brother's Keeper? Recent Polish Debates about the Holocaust,* edited by Antony Polonsky, 34–48. London: Routledge.

Centrum Badania Opinii Społecznej. 2008. *Słuchacze Radia Maryja.* Warsaw: Centrum Badania Opinii Społecznej.

——. 2018. *Religijność Polaków i ocena sytuacji Kościoła katolickiego.* Warsaw: Centrum Badania Opinii Społecznej.

——. 2021. *Religijność młodych na tle ogółu społeczeństwa.* Warsaw: Centrum Badania Opinii Społecznej.

Cichocki, Sebastian, and Galit Eilat, eds. 2011. *A Cookbook for Political Imagination.* Warsaw: Zachęta National Gallery.

Dodziuk, Anna. 2010. *Druga dusza: O dwudziestu Festiwalach Kultury Żydowskiej w Krakowie.* Warsaw: Czarna Owca.

Engelberg, Stephen. 1990. "Polish Jewish Festival Elicits Mixed Emotions." *New York Times,* April 30.

Fishman, Chuck. 2019. *A Portrait of Polish Jews, 1975–2018.* Kraków: Galicia Jewish Museum.

Gebert, Konstanty. 2008. *Living in the Land of Ashes.* Kraków: Austeria.

Gebert, Konstanty, and Helena Datner. 2001. *Jewish in Poland: Achievements, Challenges and Priorities since the Collapse of Communism.* London: Institute for Jewish Policy Research.

Główny Urząd Statystyczny. 2015. "Struktura narodowo-etniczna, językowa i wyznaniowa ludności Polski." https://stat.gov.pl/spisy-powszechne/nsp-2011/nsp-2011-wyniki/struktura -narodowo-etniczna-jezykowa-i-wyznaniowa-ludnosci-polski-nsp-2011,22,1.html.

——. 2016. *1050 lat chrześcijaństwa w Polsce.* Warsaw: Główny Urząd Statystyczny.

Hałkowski, Henryk. 2003. *Żydowskie życie.* Kraków: Wydawnictwo Austeria.

Hoffman, Eva. 1989. *Lost in Translation: A Life in a New Language.* New York: E. P. Dutton.

——. 2004. *After Such Knowledge: Memory, History, and the Legacy of the Holocaust.* New York: Public Affairs.

Jankowska, Agata. 2011. "I Love koszer." *Przekrój,* October 24.

Jewish Culture Festival in Kraków. *Annual Reports*. 1991–2019.

Kirshenblatt-Gimblett, Barbara, and Antony Polonsky, eds. 2014. *Polin: 1000 lat Żydów polskich*. Warsaw: Muzeum Historii Żydów Polskich.

Krajewski, Stanisław. 2005. *Poland and the Jews: Reflections of a Polish Jew*. Kraków: Austeria.

Lipman, Steve. 1996. "Notes from a New Poland: A Half-Century after the Jews of Poland Were Wiped Out in the Holocaust, a New Generation of Non-Jews Is Breathing Life into Jewish Culture: Scenes from a Philo-Semitic Revival." *New York Jewish Week*, September 20.

Machcewicz, Paweł, and Krzysztof Persak. 2002a. *Wokół Jedwabnego*. Vol. 1. *Studia*. Warsaw: Instytut Pamięci Narodowej.

———. 2002b. *Wokół Jedwabnego*. Vol. 2. *Dokumenty*. Warsaw: Instytut Pamięci Narodowej.

Magdziak-Misewska, Agnieszka. 2001. "The Most Serious Test." In *Thou Shalt Not Kill: Poles on Jedwabne*, edited by William Brand, 307–11. Warsaw: Więź.

Niezabitowska, Małgorzata. 2015. *In the Beginning Was a Dream: The Origins of the Museum of the History of Polish Jews, 1993–2014*. Warsaw: Polin Museum of the History of Polish Jews and the Association of the Jewish Historical Institute in Poland.

Niezabitowski, Michał, and Bartosz Piłat. 2010. "Tramwaj historii." *Gazeta Wyborcza*, June 24.

Osicka, Rita. 2010. "Kocham Żydów." *Glamour*, February 19.

Ostachowicz, Igor. 2012. *Noc żywych Żydów*. Warsaw: Wyd. WAB.

Penn, Shana, ed. 2014. *Deep Roots, New Branches: Personal Essays on the Rebirth of Jewish Life in Poland since 1989*. Warsaw: Taube Foundation for Jewish Life and Culture.

Penn, Shana, Konstanty Gebert, and Anna Goldstein, eds. 2009. *The Fall of the Wall and the Rebirth of Jewish Life in Poland: 1989–2009*. Warsaw: Taube Foundation.

Sadłoń, Wojciech. 2021. "Religijność Polaków." In *Kościół w Polsce: Raport*, 13–20. Warsaw: Katolicka Agencja Informacyjna.

Tuszyńska, Agata. 2005. *Rodzinna historia lęku*. Kraków: Wydawnictwo Literackie.

Winiewski, Mikołaj, Karolina Hansen, Michał Bilewicz, Wiktor Soral, Aleksandra Świderska, and Dominika Bulska. 2017. *Contempt Speech, Hate Speech: Report from Research on Verbal Violence against Minority Groups*. Warsaw: Center for Research on Prejudice at the University of Warsaw.

Wiszniewska, Irena. 2014. *My, Żydzi z Polski*. Warsaw: Czarna Owca.

Zieliński, Jarosław, and Jerzy S. Majewski. 2014. *Spacerownik po żydowskiej Warszawie*. Warsaw: Biblioteka Gazety Wyborczej and Polin Muzeum Historii Żydów Polskich.

Filmography

Bartana, Yael. 2007. *And Europe Will Be Stunned / Mary koszmary (Nightmares)*.

———. 2009. *And Europe Will Be Stunned / Mur i wieża (Wall and Tower)*.

———. 2011. *And Europe Will Be Stunned / Zamach (Assassination)*.

Cywińska, Izabella. 2000. *Cud Purymowy*.

Dylewska, Jolanta. 2008. *Po-Lin: Okruchy Pamięci*.

Fedorenko, Eugene, and Rose Newlove. 1999. *A Village of Idiots*.

Fissel, Curt, and Ellen Friedland. 2001. *From Kristallnacht to Crystal Day: A Synagogue in Wrocław Glows Again*.

Kertsner, Ronit. 2011. *Torn*.

———. 2013. *H.I. Jew Positive*.

Lanzman, Claude. 1985. *Shoah*.

Pasikowski, Władysław. 2012. *Aftermath*.

Pawlikowski, Paweł. 2013. *Ida*.

Strom, Yale. 2004. *Klezmer on Fish Street*.

Wolinsky, Yari, and Cary Wolinsky. 2015. *Raise the Roof*.

Zucker, Adam. 2014. *The Return*.

Zuckerman, Francine. 2013. *We Are Here*.

Secondary Literature

Alba, Richard. 2005. "Bright vs. Blurred Boundaries: Second-Generation Assimilation and Exclusion in France, Germany, and the United States." *Ethnic and Racial Studies* 28: 20–49.

Aleksiun, Natalia. 2003. "Jewish Response to Antisemitism in Poland, 1944–1947." In *Contested Memories: Poles and Jews during the Holocaust and Its Aftermath*, edited by Joshua D. Zimmerman, 249–56. New Brunswick, NJ: Rutgers University Press.

Alexander, Jeffrey, Ron Eyerman, Bernhard Giesen, Neil Smelser, and Piotr Sztompka, eds. 2004. *Cultural Trauma and Collective Identity*. Berkeley: University of California Press.

Alexander, Jeffrey, Bernhard Giesen, and Jason Mast, eds. 2006. *Social Performance: Symbolic Action, Cultural Pragmatics, and Ritual*. New York: Cambridge University Press.

Alteflix, Thomas. 2000. "The 'Post-Holocaust Jew' and the Instrumentalization of Philosemitism." *Patterns of Prejudice* 34(2): 41–56.

Altglas, Véronique. 2014. *From Yoga to Kabbalah: Religious Exoticism and the Logics of Bricolage*. New York: Oxford University Press.

Anderson, Benedict. 1991 [1983]. *Imagined Communities: Reflections on the Origins and Spread of Nationalism*. London: Verso.

Appiah, Kwame Anthony, and Amy Gutmann. 1996. *Color Conscious*. Princeton, NJ: Princeton University Press.

Arkin, Kimberly. 2013. *Rhinestones, Religion, and the Republic: Fashioning Jewishness in France*. Palo Alto, CA: Stanford University Press.

Austin, John Langshaw. 1975. *How to Do Things with Words*. Oxford: Oxford University Press.

Bach, Jonathan. 2017. *What Remains: Everyday Encounters with the Socialist Past in Germany*. New York: Columbia University Press.

Baksik, Łukasz. 2013. *Macewy codziennego użytku / Matzevot for Everyday Use*. Wołowiec, Poland: Wydawnictwo Czarne.

Barth, Fredrik. 1969. "Introduction." In *Ethnic Groups and Boundaries: The Social Organization of Culture Difference*, edited by Fredrik Barth, 9–38. London: George Allen & Unwin.

Barthes, Roland. 1957. *Mythologies*. Paris: Éditions du Seuil.

Bartoszewski, Władysław T. 1991. *The Convent at Auschwitz*. New York: George Braziller.

Baudrillard, Jean. 1996. *The System of Objects*. London: Verso.

Bauman, Zygmunt. 1998. "Allosemitism: Premodern, Modern, Postmodern." In *Modernity, Culture, and "the Jew,"* edited by Bryan Cheyette and Laura Marcus, 143–56. Cambridge, UK: Polity.

Belavusau, Uladzislau, and Aleksandra Gliszczyńska-Grabias, eds. 2017. *Law and Memory: Towards Legal Governance of History*. Cambridge: Cambridge University Press.

Berdhal, Daphne. 2010. *On the Social Life of Postsocialism: Memory, Consumption, Germany*. Bloomington: Indiana University Press.

Bernhard, Michael, and Jan Kubik, eds. 2014. *Twenty Years after Communism: The Politics of Memory and Commemoration*. Oxford: Oxford University Press.

Bilewicz, Michał, Mikołaj Winiewski, and Zuzanna Radzik. 2012. "Antisemitism in Poland: Economic, Religious, and Historical Aspects." *Journal for the Study of Antisemitism* 4: 2801–20.

Bilewicz, Michał, and Mikołaj Winiewski. 2013. "Harmful Ideas: The Structure and Consequences of Antisemitic Beliefs in Poland." *Political Psychology* 34(6): 821–39.

Billig, Michael. 1995. *Banal Nationalism*. London: Sage.

Bjork, James E. 2008. *Neither German nor Pole: Catholicism and National Indifference in a Central European Borderland*. Ann Arbor: University of Michigan Press.

Blobaum, Robert, ed. 2005. *Antisemitism and Its Opponents in Modern Poland*. Ithaca, NY: Cornell University Press.

Bodemann, Michal. 1996. *Jews, Germans, Memory: Reconstructions of Jewish Life in Germany*. Ann Arbor: University of Michigan Press.

Borowik, Irena. 2017. "Religion in Poland between Tradition and Modernity, or Religious Continuity and Change in Conditions of Transformation." In *Religion, Politics, and Values in Poland*, edited by Sabrina Ramet and Irena Borowik, 185–207. New York: Palgrave Macmillan.

Bourdieu, Pierre. 1984. *Distinction: A Social Critique of the Judgement of Taste*. Cambridge, MA: Harvard University Press.

———. 1991. *Language and Symbolic Power*. Cambridge, MA: Harvard University Press.

Bowen, John. 2007. *Why the French Don't Like Headscarves: Islam, the State, and Public Space*. Princeton, NJ: Princeton University Press.

Boym, Svetlana. 2002. *The Future of Nostalgia*. New York: Basic Books.

Brand, William, ed. 2001. *Thou Shalt Not Kill: Poles on Jedwabne*. Warsaw: Więź.

Bratcher, Ian. 2020. "Ideological Others and National Identifications in Contemporary Poland." *Nations and Nationalism* 26(3): 677–91.

Brown, Tamara, and Baruti Kopano, eds. 2014. *Soul Thieves: The Appropriation and Misrepresentation of African American Popular Culture*. New York: Palgrave Macmillan.

Brubaker, Rogers. 1992. *Citizenship and Nationhood in France and Germany*. Cambridge, MA: Harvard University Press.

———. 2004. *Ethnicity without Groups*. Cambridge, MA: Harvard University Press.

———. 2016. *Trans: Gender and Race in an Age of Unsettled Identities*. Princeton, NJ: Princeton University Press.

Brubaker, Rogers, Margit Feischmidt, Jon Fox, and Linnea Grancea. 2006. *Nationalist Politics and Everyday Ethnicity in a Transylvanian Town*. Princeton, NJ: Princeton University Press.

Brykczynski, Paul. 2016. *Primed for Violence: Murder, Antisemitism, and Democratic Politics in Interwar Poland*. Madison: University of Wisconsin Press.

Buber, Martin. 1937. *I and Thou*. Translated by Ronald Gregor Smith. Edinburgh: T. & T. Clark.

Bunzl, Matti. 2004. *Symptoms of Modernity: Jews and Queers in Late-Twentieth-Century Vienna*. Berkeley: University of California Press.

Cała, Alina. 1995. *The Image of the Jew in Polish Folk Culture*. Jerusalem: Magnes.

Casanova, José. 1994. *Public Religions in the Modern World*. Chicago: University of Chicago Press.

Chmielewska-Szlajfer, Helena. 2010. "The Plastic Palm and Memories in the Making: Conceptual Art Work on Warsaw's Jerusalem Avenue." *International Journal of Politics, Culture, and Society* 23: 201–11.

Chomątowska, Beata. 2012. *Stacja Muranów*. Sękowa, Poland: Wydawnictwo Czarne.

Chwiejda, Ewelina. 2017. "Juif, tu me manques! La culture polonaise contemporaine face aux relations entre Juifs et non-Juifs dans la Pologne de l'après-guerre." In *Juifs d'Europe: Identités plurielles et mixité*, edited by Ewa Tartakowsky and Marcelo Dimentstein, 179–90. Tours, France: Presses Universitaires François Rabelais.

Cichopek-Gajraj, Anna. 2014. *Beyond Violence: Jewish Survivors in Poland and Slovakia, 1944–48*. Cambridge: Cambridge University Press.

Cohen, Daniel. 2017. "Towards a History of 'Philosemitic' Europe since 1945." *Europe Now: A Journal of Research & Art* 12. https://www.europenowjournal.org/2017/11/01/towards-a -history-of-philosemitic-europe-since-1945/#_edn15 (accessed December 10, 2021).

Cohen, Judith. 1999. "Constructing a Spanish Jewish Festival: Music and the Appropriation of Tradition." *The World of Music* 41(3): 85–113.

Connerton, Paul. 1989. *How Societies Remember*. New York: Cambridge University Press.

———. 2009. *How Modernity Forgets*. New York: Cambridge University Press.

Cukras-Stelągowska, Joanna. 2016. "Identity and Negotiation of Boundaries among Young Polish Jews." In *Boundaries, Identity and Belonging in Modern Judaism*, edited by Maria Diemling and Larry Ray, 48–62. New York: Routledge.

Davidman, Lynn. 1991. *Tradition in a Rootless World: Women Turn to Orthodox Judaism*. Berkeley: University of California Press.

Davidman, Lynn, and Wendy Cadge. 2006. "Ascription, Choice, and the Construction of Religious Identities in the Contemporary United States." *Journal for the Scientific Study of Religion* 45(1): 23–38.

Davis, Fred. 1979. *Yearning for Yesterday: A Sociology of Nostalgia*. New York: Free Press.

De Brito, Alexandra Barahona, Carmen Gonzalez Enríquez, and Paloma Aguilar, eds. 2001. *The Politics of Memory and Democratization*. Oxford: Oxford University Press.

De Certeau, Michel. 1984. *The Practice of Everyday Life*. Translated by Steven Rendall. Berkeley: University of California Press.

DellaPergola, Sergio. 2020. "World Jewish Population, 2019." In *American Jewish Year Book 2020: An Annual Record of the North American Jewish Communities since 1899*, vol. 119, edited by Arnold Dashefsky and Ira M. Sheskin, 263–353. New York: American Jewish Committee.

DellaPergola, Sergio, and L. Daniel Staetsky. 2020. *Jews in Europe at the Turn of the Millennium: Population Trends and Estimates*. London: Institute for Jewish Policy Research, European Jewish Demography Unit.

Deloria, Philip Joseph. 1998. *Playing Indian*. New Haven, CT: Yale University Press.

Deme, Katalin. 2015. "From Restored Past to Unsettled Present: New Challenges for Jewish Museums in East Central Europe." *East European Jewish Affairs* 45(2–3): 252–60.

Di Trani, Antonella. 2020. "The Venitian Ghetto: In Search of an Authentic Jewish Space." In *Jewish Europe Today: Between Memory and Everyday Life*, edited by Ewa Tartakowsky and Marcelo Dimentstein, 215–28. Kraków: Austeria.

Dobrosielski, Paweł. 2015. "Żyd z pieniążkiem jako praktyka polskiej kultury wernakularnej: Wstępny raport z badań." *Kultura Współczesna* 3: 61–75.

——. 2017a. "Pierzyna." In *Ślady Holokaustu w imaginarium kultury polskiej*, edited by Justyna Kowalska-Leder, Paweł Dobrosielski, Iwona Kurz, and Małgorzata Szpakowska, 341–64. Warsaw: Wydawnictwo Krytyki Politycznej.

——. 2017b. "Stodoła." In *Ślady Holokaustu w imaginarium kultury polskiej*, edited by Justyna Kowalska-Leder, Paweł Dobrosielski, Iwona Kurz, and Małgorzata Szpakowska, 365–82. Warsaw: Wydawnictwo Krytyki Politycznej.

——. 2017c. *Spory o Grossa: Polskie problemy z pamięcią o Żydach*. Warsaw: Instytut Badań Literackich PAN.

Doniger, Wendy. 1988. *Other Peoples' Myths: The Cave of Echoes*. New York: Macmillan; London: Collier Macmillan.

Durkheim, Émile. 1995 [1912]. *The Elementary Forms of Religious Life*. Translated by K. Fields. New York: Free Press.

Edensor, Tim. 2002. *National Identity, Popular Culture and Everyday Life*. Oxford: Berg.

Edgell, Penny, Joseph Gerteis, and Douglas Hartmann. 2006. "Atheists as 'Other': Moral Boundaries and Cultural Membership in American Society." *American Sociological Review* 71(2): 211–34.

Edgell, Penny, Douglas Hartmann, Evan Stewart, and Joseph Gerteis. 2016. "Atheists and Other Cultural Outsiders: Moral Boundaries and the Non-Religious in the United States." *Social Forces* 95(2): 607–38.

Elżanowski, Jerzy. 2018. "Manufacturing Ruins: Architecture and Representation in Post-Catastrophic Warsaw." *Journal of Architecture* 23(5): 740–55.

Engelking, Barbara, and Jan Grabowski, eds. 2018. *Dalej jest noc: Losy Żydów w wybranych powiatach okupowanej Polski*. Vols. 1–2. Warsaw: Centrum Badań nad Zagładą Żydów.

Engelking, Barbara, and Jacek Leociak. 2001. *Getto Warszawskie: Przewodnik po nieistniejącym mieście*. Warsaw: Wydawnictwo IFiS PAN.

Etkind, Alexander, Rory Finnin, Uilleam Blacker, Julie Fedor, Simon Lewis, Maria Mälksoo, and Matilda Mroz. 2012. *Remembering Katyń*. Cambridge, UK: Polity.

Forecki, Piotr. 2010. *Od Shoah do Strachu: Spory o polsko-żydowską przeszłość i pamięć w debatach publicznych*. Poznań, Poland: Wydawnictwo Poznańskie.

Forecki, Piotr, and Anna Zawadzka. 2016. "The Rule of the Golden Mean." In *Poland and Polin: New Interpretations in Polish-Jewish Studies*, edited by Irena Grudzińska-Gross and Iwa Nawrocki, 99–120. New York: Peter Lang.

Fox, Jon, and Cynthia Miller-Idriss. 2008. "Everyday Nationhood." *Ethnicities* 8(4): 536–63.

Gell, Alfred. 1998. *Art and Agency*. London: Oxford University Press.

Gensburger, Sarah, and S. Lefranc. 2017. *À quoi servent les politiques de mémoire?* Paris: Presses de Sciences Po.

Gerrits, André. 2008. *The Myth of Jewish Communism: A Historical Interpretation.* New York: Peter Lang.

Gershenson, Olga, and Barbara Kirshenblatt-Gimblett. 2015. "New Jewish Museums in Post-Communist Europe." *East European Jewish Affairs* 45(2-3): 153-57.

Gilman, Sander L., and Karen Remmler, eds. 1994. *Reemerging Jewish Culture in Germany: Life and Literature since 1989.* New York: NYU Press.

Gitelman, Zvi. 1990. "Eastern European Countries." In *American Jewish Year Book 1990: A Record of Events and Trends in American and World Jewish Life*, vol. 90, edited by David Singer and Ruth R. Seldin, 378-92. New York: American Jewish Committee.

———. 2003. "Collective Memory and Contemporary Polish-Jewish Relations." In *Contested Memories: Poles and Jews during the Holocaust and Its Aftermath*, edited by Joshua Zimmerman, 271-90. New Brunswick, NJ: Rutgers University Press.

———. 2011. "The Phoenix? Jewish Studies in Post-Communist Europe." *Journal of Modern Jewish Studies* 10(1): 65-69.

Głownia, Marek, and Stefan Wilkanowicz, eds. 1998. *Auschwitz: Konflikty i dialog.* Kraków: Wydawnictwo Św. Stanisława.

Golonka-Czajkowska, Monika. 2018. "In the Shadow of the Sacred Bodies: The Monthly Smoleńsk Commemorations in Kraków." *Ethnologia Polona* 38: 107-23.

Gowin, Jarosław. 1995. *Kościół po komunizmie.* Kraków: Znak.

———. 2000. *Kościół w czasach wolności 1989-1999.* Kraków: Znak.

Grabowksa, Mirosława. 2018. *Bóg a sprawa polska: Poza granicami teorii sekularyzacji.* Warsaw: Wydawnictwo Naukowe Scholar.

Grabowski, Jan. 2013. *Hunt for the Jews: Betrayal and Murder in German-Occupied Poland.* Bloomington: Indiana University Press.

———. 2016. "The Holocaust as a Polish Problem." In *Poland and Polin: New Interpretations in Polish-Jewish Studies*, edited by Irena Grudzińska-Gross and Iwa Nawrocki, 17-27. New York: Peter Lang.

———. 2020. *Na Posterunku: Udział polskiej policji granatowej i kryminalnej w zagładzie Żydów.* Wołowiec, Poland: Wydawnictwo Czarne.

Grabowski, Jan, and Dariusz Libionka, eds. 2014. *Klucze i kasa: O mieniu żydowskim w Polsce pod okupacją niemiecką i we wczesnych latach powojennych 1939-1950.* Warsaw: Stowarzeszenie Centrum Badań nad Zagładą Żydów.

Graff, Agnieszka. 2008. *Rikoszetem: Rzecz o płci, seksualności i narodzie.* Warsaw: WAB.

Gross, Jan Tomasz. 2000. *Sąsiedzi: Historia zagłady żydowskiego miasteczka.* Sejny, Poland: Pogranicze.

———. 2001. *Neighbors: The Destruction of the Jewish Community in Jedwabne, Poland.* Princeton, NJ: Princeton University Press

———. 2006. *Fear: Anti-Semitism in Poland after Auschwitz.* New York: Random House.

Gross, Jan Tomasz, and Irena Grudzińska-Gross. 2011. *Złote żniwa: Rzecz o tym, co się działo na obrzeżach zagłady Żydów.* Kraków: Znak.

Gruber, Ruth Ellen. 2000. "East Central Europe." In *American Jewish Year Book 2000: A Record of Events and Trends in American and World Jewish Life*, vol. 100, edited by David Singer and Lawrence Grossman, 373-95. New York: American Jewish Committee.

———. 2002. *Virtually Jewish: Reinventing Jewish Culture in Europe.* Los Angeles: University of California Press.

Grudzińska-Gross, Irena. 2014. "Peryskop." In *My, Żydzi z Polski*, edited by Irena Wiszniewska, 7-13. Warsaw: Czarna Owca.

Gurian, Elaine Heumann. 2002. "Choosing among the Options: An Opinion about Museum Definitions." *Curator: The Museum Journal* 45(2):75-88.

Gryta, Janek. 2020. "Creating a Cosmopolitan Past." *History & Memory* 32(1): 34-68.

Hanebrink, Paul. 2018. *A Specter Haunting Europe: The Myth of Judeo-Bolshevism.* Cambridge, MA: Harvard University Press, 2018.

Hertz, Aleksander. 1988 [1961]. *The Jews in Polish Culture*. Translated by Richard Lourie. Evanston, IL: Northwestern University Press.

Hobsbawm, Eric J. 1983a. "Introduction: Inventing Traditions." In *The Invention of Tradition*, edited by Eric J. Hobsbawm and Terence Ranger, 1–14. Cambridge: Cambridge University Press.

——. 1983b. "Mass-Producing Traditions: Europe, 1870–1914." In *The Invention of Tradition*, edited by Eric J. Hobsbawm and Terence Ranger, 263–307. Cambridge: Cambridge University Press.

hooks, bell. 1992. *Black Looks: Race and Representation*. Brooklyn, NY: South End Press.

Huener, Jonathan. 2003. *Auschwitz, Poland, and the Politics of Commemoration, 1945–1979*. Athens: Ohio University Press.

Ingall, Andrew. 2003. "Making a Tsimes, Distilling a Performance: Vodka and Jewish Culture in Poland Today." *Gastronomica: The Journal of Food and Culture* 3(1): 22–27.

Iordachi, Constantin, and Pétr Apor, eds. 2021. *Occupation and Communism in Eastern European Museums: Re-Visualizing the Recent Past*. New York: Bloomsbury.

Irwin-Zarecka, Iwona. 1989. *Neutralizing Memory: The Jew in Contemporary Poland*. New Brunswick, NJ: Transaction.

Janicka, Elżbieta. 2011. *Festung Warschau*. Warsaw: Wydawnictwo Krytyki Politycznej.

——. 2015. "The Square of Polish Innocence: POLIN Museum of the History of Polish Jews in Warsaw and Its Symbolic Topography." *East European Jewish Affairs* 45(2–3): 200–214.

——. 2016. "The Embassy of Poland in Poland: The Polin Myth in the Museum of the History of Polish Jews as Narrative Pattern and Model of Minority-Majority Relations." In *Poland and Polin: New Interpretations in Polish-Jewish Studies*, edited by Irena Grudzińska-Gross and Iwa Nawrocki, 121–71. Frankfurt: Peter Lang.

Janicka, Elżbieta, and Tomasz Żukowski. 2021. *Philo-Semitic Violence: Poland's Jewish Past in New Polish Narratives*. Lanham, MD: Lexington Books.

Jankowski, Robert, ed. 2002. *Jedwabne: Spór historyków wokół książki Jana T. Grossa "Sąsiedzi."* Warsaw: Biblioteka Frondy.

Jochnowitz, Eve. 1998. "Flavors of Memory: Jewish Food as Culinary Tourism in Poland." *Southern Folklore* 55(3): 224–37.

Judaken, Jonathan. 2008. "Between Philosemitism and Antisemitism: The Frankfurt School's Anti-Antisemitism." In *Antisemitism and Philosemitism in the Twentieth and Twenty-First Centuries: Representing Jews, Jewishness, and Modern Culture*, edited by Phillys Lassner and Lara Trubowitz, 23–46. Newark: University of Delaware Press.

Kącki, Marcin. 2015. *Białystok: Biała siła, czarna pamięć*. Wołowiec, Poland: Wydawnictwo Czarne.

Kaczmarek, Olga. 2017. "Las." In *Ślady Holokaustu w imaginarium kultury polskiej*, edited by Justyna Kowalska-Leder, Paweł Dobrosielski, Iwona Kurz, and Małgorzata Szpakowska, 219–44. Warsaw: Wydawnictwo Krytyki Politycznej.

Kapralski, Sławomir. 2001. "Battlefields of Memory: Landscape and Identity in Polish-Jewish Relations." *History & Memory* 13(2): 35–58.

——. 2015. "Amnesia, Nostalgia, and Reconstruction: Shifting Modes of Memory in Poland's Jewish Spaces." In *Jewish Space in Contemporary Poland*, edited by Erica Lehrer and Michael Meng, 149–69. Bloomington: Indiana University Press

Karp, Jonathan, and Adam Sutcliff, eds. 2011. *Philosemitism in History*. New York: Cambridge University Press.

Keane, Webb. 2006. "Subjects and Objects." In *Handbook of Material Culture*, edited by Chris Tilley, Webb Keane, Susanne Küchler, Mike Rowlands, and Patricia Spyer, 197–202. London: Sage.

Keff, Bożena. 2013. *Antysemityzm: Niezamknięta historia*. Warsaw: Czarna Owca.

Kelman, Ari Y. 2018. "Learning History through Culture: The Krakow Jewish Festival." In *Teaching and Learning the Difficult Past: Comparative Perspectives*, edited by Magdalena Gross and Luke Terra, 274–89. New York: Routledge.

Kelner, Shaul. 2010. *Tours That Bind: Diaspora, Pilgrimage, and Israeli Birthright Tourism*. New York: NYU Press.

Kertzer, David I. 1988. *Ritual, Politics, and Power*. New Haven, CT: Yale University Press.

Kidron, Carol. 2016. "Breathing Life into Iconic Numbers: Yad Vashem's Shoah Victims' Names Recovery Project and the Constitution of a Posthumous Census of Six Million Holocaust Dead." In *Taking Stock: Cultures of Enumeration in Contemporary Jewish Life*, edited by Deborah Dash Moore and Michal Kravel-Tovi, 47–68. Bloomington: Indiana University Press.

Kijek, Kamil. 2017. "For Whom and about What? The Polin Museum, Jewish Historiography and Jews as a 'Polish Cause.'" *Studia Litteraria et Historica* 6: 1–21.

Kirshenblatt-Gimblett, Barbara. 2015. "The Museum of the History of Polish Jews: A Postwar, Post-Holocaust, Post-Communist Story." In *Jewish Space in Contemporary Poland*, edited by Erica Lehrer and Michael Meng, 264–79. Bloomington: Indiana University Press.

Kirshenblatt-Gimblett, Barbara, and Ewa Klekot. 2016. "Muzeum, przedmiot, doświadczenie." *Zbiór Wiadomości do Antropologii Muzealnej* 1: 47–54.

Klein, Théo. 1991. *L'affaire du Carmel d'Auschwitz*. Paris: Éditions Jacques Bertoin.

Klekot, Ewa. 2012. "Constructing a 'Monument of National History and Culture' in Poland: The Case of the Royal Castle in Warsaw." *International Journal of Heritage Studies* 8(5): 459–78.

———. 2015. "Memory and Oblivion in the Cityscape: Commemorations in the Warsaw Districts of Muranów and Mirów." *Ethnologia Europaea* 45(1): 58–79.

Kosicki, Piotr. 2015. "Forests, Families, and Films: Polish Memory of Katyń, 1943–2015." *East European Politics and Societies* 29(4): 730–60.

Kovács, András. 2010. "Jews and Jewishness in Post-War Hungary." *Quest: Issues in Contemporary Jewish History* 1: 34–57.

Kowalska-Leder, Justyna. 2017. "Szafa." In *Ślady Holokaustu w imaginarium kultury polskiej*, edited by Justyna Kowalska-Leder, Paweł Dobrosielski, Iwona Kurz, and Małgorzata Szpakowska, 383–412. Warsaw: Wydawnictwo Krytyki Politycznej.

Kowalski, Sergiusz, and Magdalena Tulli. 2003. *Zamiast procesu: Raport o mowie nienawiści*. Warsaw: Instytut Studiów Politycznych PAN.

Krzemiński, Ireneusz, ed. 1996. *Czy Polacy są antysemitami? Wyniki badania sondażowego*. Warsaw: Oficyna Naukowa.

———. 2001. "Polacy i Żydzi. Wizja wzajemnych stosunków, tożsamość narodowa i antysemityzm." In *Trudne sąsiedztwa: Z socjologii konfliktów narodowościowych*, edited by Aleksandra Kania, 171–200. Warsaw: Wydawnictwo Narodowe Scholar.

———, ed. 2009. *Czego nas uczy Radio Maryja?* Warsaw: WAiP.

———, ed. 2015. *Żydzi——Problem prawdziwego Polaka: Antysemityzm, ksenofobia i stereotypy narodowe po raz trzeci*. Warsaw: Wydawnictwa Uniwersytetu Warszawskiego.

———. 2017. "Radio Maryja and Fr. Rydzyk as a Creator of the National-Catholic Ideology." In *Religion, Politics, and Values in Poland: Continuity and Change since 1989*, edited by Sabrina Ramet and Irena Borowik, 85–112. New York: Palgrave Macmillan.

Krzyżanowski, Michał. 2018. "Discursive Shifts in Ethno-Nationalist Politics: On Politicization and Mediatization of the 'Refugee Crisis' in Poland." *Journal of Immigrant & Refugee Studies* 16(1–2): 76–96.

Kubica, Aleksandra, and Thomas Van de Putte. 2019. "Remembering Jews in Poland: The Encounter between Warsaw's POLIN Museum and Rural Memories of Jewish Absence——Divergent Aims and Needs." *Holocaust Studies* 25(3): 422–39.

Kubik, Jan. 1994. *The Power of Symbols against the Symbols of Power: The Rise of Solidarity and the Fall of State Socialism in Poland*. University Park: Pennsylvania State University Press.

Kugelmass, Jack, and Anna-Maria Orla-Bukowska. 2008. "If You Build It They Will Come: Recreating a Jewish District in Post-Communist Kraków." *City & Society* 10(1): 315–53.

Lamont, Michèle. 1992. *Money, Morals, and Manners: The Culture of the French and American Upper-Middle Class*. Chicago: University of Chicago Press.

Lamont, Michèle, and Christopher Bail. 2005. "Sur les frontières de la reconnaissance: Les catégories internes et externes de l'identité collective." *Revue européenne des migrations internationales* 21: 61–90.

Lamont, Michèle, and Virág Molnár. 2002. "The Study of Boundaries in the Social Sciences." *Annual Review of Sociology* 28: 167–95.

Lamont, Michèle, Sabrina Pendergrass, and Mark C. Pachucki. 2015. "Symbolic Boundaries." In *International Encyclopedia of Social and Behavioral Sciences*, edited by James Wright, 850–55. Oxford: Elsevier.

Lassner, Phillys, and Lara Trubowitz, eds. 2008. *Antisemitism and Philosemitism in the Twentieth and Twenty-First Centuries: Representing Jews, Jewishness, and Modern Culture*. Newark: University of Delaware Press.

Leder, Andrzej. 2014. *Prześniona rewolucja: Ćwiczenia z logiki historycznej*. Warsaw: Krytyka Polityczna.

Lehrer, Erica. 2003. "Repopulating Jewish Poland—in Wood." *Polin: Studies in Polish Jewry* 16: 335–55.

———. 2013. *Jewish Poland Revisited: Heritage Tourism in Unquiet Places*. Bloomington: Indiana University Press.

———, ed. 2014. *Lucky Jews: Poland's Jewish Figurines*. Kraków: Korporacja Ha!art.

Lehrer, Erica, and Magdalena Waligórska. 2013. "Cur(at)ing History: New Genre Art Interventions and the Polish-Jewish Past." *East European Politics and Societies and Cultures* 27(3): 510–44.

Leociak, Jacek. 2017. "The Holocaust in a 'Museum of Life' (the Polin Museum and Its Trouble with the *Genius Loci* of the Muranów District)." *Holocaust Studies and Materials (Warsaw)* 4: 538–48.

Levy, Daniel, and Natan Sznaider. 2006. *The Holocaust and Memory in the Global Age*. Philadelphia: Temple University Press.

Lofton, Kathryn. 2017. *Consuming Religion*. Chicago: University of Chicago Press.

Lorenz, Jan. 2016. "Shades of Closeness: Belonging and Becoming in a Contemporary Polish-Jewish Community." In *Boundaries, Identity and Belonging in Modern Judaism*, edited by Maria Diemling and Larry Ray, 63–75. New York: Routledge.

Loveman, Mara. 2014. *National Colors: Racial Classification and the State in Latin America*. Oxford: Oxford University Press.

Loveman, Mara, and Jeronimo O. Muniz. 2007. "How Puerto Rico Became White: Boundary Dynamics and Intercensus Racial Reclassification." *American Sociological Review* 72(6): 915–39.

Małkowska-Bieniek, Ewa. 2014. *Warszawa, Warsze: Jewish Warsaw, Warsaw's Jews*. Warsaw: Polin Museum of the History of Polish Jews.

Manchin, Anna. 2015. "Staging Traumatic Memory: Competing Narratives of State Violence in Post-Communist Hungarian Museums." *East European Jewish Affairs* 45(2–3): 236–51.

Marks, Lawrence. 2014. *The Unity of the Senses: Interrelations among the Modalities*. New York: Academic Press.

Marody, Mirosława, and Sławomir Mandes. 2017. "Polish Religious Values as Reflected in the European Values Study." In *Religion, Politics, and Values in Poland*, edited by Sabrina Ramet and Irena Borowik, 231–55. New York: Palgrave Macmillan.

Martyn, Peter. 2001. "The Brave New-Old Capital City: Questions Relating to the Rebuilding and Remodelling of Warsaw's Architectural Profile from the Late 1940s until 1956." In *Falsifications in Polish Collections and Abroad*, edited by Jerzy Miziołek, 193–233. Warsaw: Instytut Archeologii, Uniwersytet Warszawski.

Matyjaszek, Konrad. 2014. "Przestrzeń pożydowska." *Studia Litteraria et Historica* 2: 130–47.

———. 2016. "Wall and Window: The Rubble of the Warsaw Ghetto as the Narrative Space of the POLIN Museum of the History of Polish Jews." In *Poland and Polin: New Interpretations in Polish-Jewish Studies*, edited by Irena Grudzińska-Gross and Iwa Nawrocki, 59–98. Frankfurt: Peter Lang.

———. 2019. "Not Your House, not Your Flat: Jewish Ghosts in Poland and the Stolen Jewish Properties." In *The "Spectral Turn": Jewish Ghosts in the Polish Post-Holocaust Imaginaire*, edited by Zuzanna Dziuban, 185–208. Bielefeld: Transcript.

McDonald, Charles A. 2021. "Rancor: Sephardi Jews, Spanish Citizenship, and the Politics of Sentiment." *Comparative Studies in Society and History* 63(3): 722–51.

Meng, Michael. 2012. *Shattered Spaces: Encountering Jewish Ruins in Postwar Germany and Poland*. Cambridge, MA: Harvard University Press.

———. 2017. "Monuments of Ruination in Postwar Berlin and Warsaw: The Architectural Projects of Bohdan Lachert and Daniel Libeskind." *Comparative Studies in Society and History* 59(3): 550–73.

Michlic, Joanna. 2006. *Poland's Threatening Other: The Image of the Jew from 1880 to the Present.* Lincoln: University of Nebraska Press.

Michnik, Adam. 1999. "Wystąpienie." In *Kościół polski wobec antysemityzmu, 1989–1999: Rachunek sumienia,* edited by Bohdan Oppenheim, 69–76. Kraków: WAM.

———. 2010. "Wstęp." In *Przeciw antysemitizmowi 1936–2009,* vol. 1, edited by Adam Michnik, iii–xiii. Kraków: Universitas.

Michowicz, Waldemar. 1988. "Problemy mniejszości narodowych." In *Polska Odrodzona, 1918–1939,* edited by Jan Tomicki, 285–321. Warsaw: Wiedza Powszechna.

Monterescu, Daniel, and Sára Zorándy. 2020. "Reviving Judapest: Improvising Community in Central Europe." In *Jewish Europe Today: Between Memory and Everyday Life,* edited by Ewa Tartakowsky and Marcelo Dimentstein, 193–214. Kraków: Austeria.

Mosse, George. 1985. *Nationalism and Sexuality: Respectability and Abnormal Sexuality in Modern Europe.* New York: Fertig.

Murzyn, Monika. 2004. "From Neglected to Trendy: The Process of Urban Revitalization in the Kazimierz District in Cracow." In *Featuring the Quality of Urban Life of Contemporary Cities of Eastern and Western Europe,* edited by Iwona Sagan and Mariusz Czepczyński, 259–74. Gdańsk: Wydawnictwo Naukowe Bogucki.

———. 2006. *Kazimierz: The Central European Experience of Urban Regeneration.* Kraków: International Cultural Centre.

Murzyn-Kupisz, Monika. 2015. "Rediscovering the Jewish Past in the Polish Provinces: The Socioeconomics of Nostalgia." In *Jewish Space in Contemporary Poland,* edited by Erica Lehrer and Michael Meng, 115–48. Bloomington: Indiana University Press.

Mushkat, Marion. 1992. *Philo-Semitic and Anti-Jewish Attitudes in Post-Holocaust Poland.* Lewiston, NY: Edwin Mellon.

Napiórkowski, Marcin. 2016. *Powstanie umarłych: Historia pamięci 1944–2014.* Warsaw: Wydawnictwo Krytyki Politycznej.

Napiórkowski, Marcin, Artur Szarecki, Paweł Dobrosielski, Piotr Filipkowski, and Olga Kaczmarek. 2015. "Kultura wernakularna. Antropologia projektów nieudanych." *Kultura Współczesna* 3: 4–26.

Nielsen, Kai. 1999. "Cultural Nationalism, Neither Ethnic nor Civic." *Philosophical Forum: A Quarterly* 28(1–2): 42–52.

Nirenberg, David. 2013. *Anti-Judaism: The Western Tradition.* New York: W. W. Norton.

Noiriel, Gérard. 2012. "De l'histoire-mémoire aux 'lois mémorielles': Note sur les usages publics de l'histoire en France." *Revue Arménienne des questions contemporaines* 15: 35–49.

Nowakowski, Jakub. 2020. "Between Colonization and Revival: Polish-Jewish Relations in Contemporary Poland." In *Jewish Europe Today: Between Memory and Everyday Life,* edited by Ewa Tartakowsky and Marcelo Dimentstein, 241–54. Kraków: Austeria.

Nowicka-Franczak, Magdalena. 2017. *Niechciana debata: Spór o książki Jana Tomasza Grossa.* Warsaw: Wydawnictwo Sedno.

Olick, Jeffrey K. 2007. *The Politics of Regret: On Collective Memory and Historical Responsibility.* New York: Routledge.

Opalski, Magdalena, and Israel Bartal. 1992. *Poles and Jews: A Failed Brotherhood.* Hanover, NH: Brandeis University Press.

Pasieka, Agnieszka. 2014. "Neighbors: About the Multiculturalization of the Polish Past." *East European Politics and Societies* 28(1): 225–51.

———. 2015. *Hierarchy and Pluralism: Living Religious Difference in Poland.* New York: Palgrave Macmillan.

Persak, Krzysztof. 2011. "Jedwabne before the Court: Poland's Justice and the Jedwabne Massacre—Investigations and Court Proceedings, 1947–1974." *East European Politics and Societies* 25(3): 410–32.

Pinkser, Shachar. 2018. *A Rich Brew: How Cafés Created Modern Jewish Culture*. New York: NYU Press.

Pinto, Diana. 1996. "Fifty Years after the Holocaust: Building a New Jewish and Polish Memory." *East European Jewish Affairs* 26(2): 79–95.

Plocker, Anat. 2022. *The Expulsion of Jews from Communist Poland: Memory Wars and Homeland Anxieties*. Bloomington: Indiana University Press.

Polonsky, Antony. 2009. *Polish-Jewish Relations since 1984: Reflections of a Participant*. Kraków: Austeria.

Polonsky, Antony, and Joanna Beata Michlic, eds. 2004. *The Neighbors Respond: The Controversy over the Jedwabne Massacre in Poland*. Princeton, NJ: Princeton University Press.

Popescu, Diana. 2017. "The Aesthetics and Ethics of Performative Holocaust Memory in Poland." *Scandinavian Jewish Studies* 28(1): 22–37.

Porter-Szűcs, Brian. 2012. *Faith and Fatherland: Catholicism, Modernity, and Poland*. New York: Oxford University Press.

Potel, Jean-Yves. 2009. *La fin de l'Innocence: La Pologne face à son passé juif*. Paris: Autrement.

Renan, Ernest. [1882] 1996. "Qu'est-ce qu'une nation." In *Becoming National: A Reader*, edited by Geoff Eley and Ronald G. Suny, 41–55. New York: Oxford University Press.

Reszke, Katka. 2013. *Return of the Jew: Identity Narratives of the Third Post-Holocaust Generation of Jews in Poland*. Brighton, UK: Academic Studies Press.

Ricoeur, Paul. 2004. *Memory, History, Forgetting*. Chicago: University of Chicago Press.

Rittner, Carol, and John K. Roth, eds. 1991. *Memory Offended: The Auschwitz Convent Controversy*. New York: Praeger.

Rogozińska, Renata. 2002. *W stronę Golgoty: Inspiracje pasyjne w sztuce polskiej w latach 1970–1999*. Poznań, Poland: Księgarnia Św. Wojciecha.

Rohr, Isabelle. 2007. *The Spanish Right and the Jews, 1898–1945: Antisemitism and Opportunism*. Portland, OR: Sussex Academic Press.

Rothberg, Michael. 2009. *Multidirectional Memory: Remembering the Holocaust in the Age of Decolonization*. Palo Alto, CA: Stanford University Press.

———. 2019. *The Implicated Subject: Beyond Victims and Perpetrators*. Stanford, CA: Stanford University Press.

Rothstein, Rachel. 2015. "'Am I Jewish?' and 'What Does It Mean?': The Jewish Flying University and the Creation of a Polish-Jewish Counterculture in Late 1970s Warsaw." *Journal of Jewish Identities* 8(2): 85–111.

Said, Edward. W. 1979. *Orientalism*. New York: Vintage Books.

Sarkisova, Oksana, and Peter Apor. 2013. *Past for the Eyes: East European Representations of Communism in Cinema and Museums after 1989*. Budapest: Central European University Press.

Sartre, Jean-Paul. 1986. *Anti-Semite and Jew*. New York: Schocken Books.

Sawicki, Zygmunt. 2005. *Bitwa o prawdę: Historia zmagań o pamięć Powstania Warszawskiego 1944–1989*. Warsaw: Wydawnictwo DiG.

Saxe, Leonard, and Barry Chazan. 2008. *Ten Days of Birthright Israel*. Hanover, NH: Brandeis University Press.

Schnapper, Dominique. 1994. *Sur l'idée moderne de la nation: La communauté des citoyens*. Paris: Gallimard.

Schöpflin, George. 1997. "The Function of Myth and a Taxonomy of Myths." In *Myths and Nationhood*, edited by Geoffrey Hosking and George Schöpflin, 19–35. London: Hurst.

Scott, Joan Wallach. 2007. *The Politics of the Veil*. Princeton, NJ: Princeton University Press.

Sekerdej, Kinga, and Agnieszka Pasieka. 2013. "Researching the Dominant Religion: Anthropology at Home and Methodological Catholicism." *Method and Theory in the Study of Religion* 25: 53–77.

Sendyka, Roma. 2016. "Sites That Haunt: Affects and Non-Sites of Memory." *East European Politics and Societies and Cultures* 30(4): 687–702.

Shapiro, Eleanor. 2020. "The Sound of Change: Performing 'Jewishness' in Small Polish Towns." *Polin: Studies in Polish Jewry* 32: 477–97.

Skórzyńska, Izabela. 2014. "Commemorating the Past through Performance: 'Brama Grodzka-NN Theatre' Centre in Lublin." In *Performing the Past: Post-Communist Poland and Romania*, edited by Izabela Skórzyńska and Christine Lavrence, 171–91. Poznań, Poland: Adam Mickiewicz University Press.

Smilde, David. 2007. *Reason to Believe: Cultural Agency in Latin American Evangelicalism*. Berkeley: University of California Press.

Smith, Anthony D. 1986. *The Ethnic Origins of Nations*. New York: Blackwell.

Snyder, Tymothy. 2010. *Bloodlands: Europe between Hitler and Stalin*. New York: Random House.

Śpiewak, Paweł. 2012. *Żydokomuna*. Warsaw: Czerwone i Czarne.

Środa, Magdalena. 2014. "Nowi Żydzi." *Wprost*. https://www.wprost.pl/tygodnik/432887/nowi -zydzi.html.

Stefaniak, Anna, Michał Bilewicz, and Mikołaj Winiewski, eds. 2015. *Uprzedzenia w Polsce*. Warsaw: Liberi Libri.

Steinlauf, Michael. 1997. *Bondage to the Dead: Poland and the Memory of the Holocaust*. New York: Syracuse University Press.

Stern, Frank. 1991. *The Whitewashing of the Yellow Badge: Antisemitism and Philosemitism in Postwar Germany*. Oxford: Pergamon.

Stier, Oren Baruch. 2016. "Six Million: The Numerical Icon of the Holocaust." In *Taking Stock: Cultures of Enumeration in Contemporary Jewish Life*, edited by Deborah Dash Moore and Michal Kravel-Tovi, 29–46. Bloomington: Indiana University Press.

Stola, Dariusz. 2000. *Kampania antysyjonistyczna w Polsce 1967–1968*. Warsaw: Instytut Studiów Politycznych Polskiej Akademii Nauk.

——. 2003. "Jedwabne: Revisiting the Evidence and Nature of the Crime." *Holocaust and Genocide Studies* 17(1): 139–52.

——. 2005. "Fighting against the Shadows: The Anti-Zionist Campaign of 1968." In *Antisemitism and Its Opponents in Modern Poland*, edited by Robert Blobaum, 175–201. Ithaca, NY: Cornell University Press.

——. 2008. "The Polish Debates on the Holocaust and the Restitution of Property." In *Robbery and Restitution: The Conflict over Jewish Property in Europe*, edited by Martin Dean, Constantin Goshler, and Philip Ther, 240–55. New York: Berghahn Books.

——. 2010. *Kraj bez wyjścia? Migracje z Polski 1949–1989*. Warsaw: Instytut Pamięci Narodowej, Komisja Ścigania Zbrodni przeciwko Narodowi Polskiemu and Instytut Studiów Politycznych PAN.

Sztop-Rutkowska, Katarzyna. 2011. "Niepamiętane historie miasta: Żydowska przeszłość Białegostoku i Lublina w (nie)pamięci obecnych mieszkańców." *Pogranicze. Studia Społeczne* 18: 67–83.

Tartakowsky, Ewa. 2017. "Le Juif à la piece d'argent." *La vie des Idées*. https://laviedesidees.fr /Le-Juif-a-la-piece-d-argent.html (accessed June 23, 2019).

Taylor, Judith, Ron Levi, and Ronit Dinovitzer. 2012. "Homeland Tourism, Emotion, and Identity Labor." *Du Bois Review: Social Science Research on Race* 9(1):167–85.

Tenenbaum, Shelley, and Lynn Davidman. 2007. "It's in My Genes: Biological Discourse and Essentialist Views of Identity among Contemporary American Jews." *Sociological Quarterly* 48(3): 435–50.

Till, Karen. 2005. *The New Berlin: Memory, Politics, Place*. Minneapolis: University of Minnesota Press.

——. 2008. "Artistic and Activist Memorywork: Approaching Place-Based Practice." *Memory Studies* 1(1): 99–113.

Todorova, Maria, and Zsuzsa Gille, eds. 2010. *Postcommunist Nostalgia*. New York: Berghahn Books.

Tokarska-Bakir, Joanna. 2008. *Legendy o krwi: Antropologia przesądu*. Warsaw: W.A.B.

——. 2012. *Okrzyki pogromowe*. Wołowiec, Poland: Wydawnictwo Czarne.

——. 2013. "Żyd z pieniążkiem." In *PL: Tożsamość wyobrażona*, edited by Joanna Tokarska-Bakir, 6–31. Warsaw: Wydawnictwo Czarna Owca.

——. 2016. "Polin: 'Ultimate Lost Object.'" In *Poland and Polin: New Interpretations in Polish-Jewish Studies*, edited by Irena Grudzińska-Gross and Iwa Nawrocki, 49–58. New York: Peter Lang.

Tomaszewski, Jerzy. 1993. "The National Question in Poland in the Twentieth Century." In *The National Question in Europe in Historical Context*, edited by Mikulas Teich and Roy Porter, 293–316. Cambridge: Cambridge University Press.

Traverso, Enzo. 1997. *L'Histoire déchirée: Essai sur Auschwitz et les intellectuels*. Paris: Éditions du Cerf.

Tych, Feliks, and Monika Adamczyk-Garbowska, eds. 2014. *Jewish Presence in Absence: The Aftermath of the Holocaust in Poland, 1944–2010*. Jerusalem: Yad Vashem.

Waligórska, Magdalena. 2013. *Klezmer's Afterlife: An Ethnography of the Jewish Music Revival in Poland and Germany*. New York: Oxford University Press.

Waślicka, Zofia, Artur Żmijewski, and Jacek Leociak. 2015. "Leociak: Gruz z papier mâché. Pytają Zofia Waślicka i Artur Żmijewski." http://www.krytykapolityczna.pl/artykuly/kultura/20150331/leociak-gruz-z-papier-mache-rozmowa (accessed December 10, 2021).

Waślicka, Zofia, Artur Żmijewski, and Dariusz Stola. 2015. "Muzeum Tożsamości: Z Dariuszem Stolą rozmawiają Zofia Waślicka i Artur Żmijewski." *Krytyka Polityczna* 40–41: 276–91.

Wawrzyniak Joanna. 2015. *Veterans, Victims, and Memory: The Politics of the Second World War in Communist Poland*. Frankfurt: Peter Lang.

Weber, Donald. 1991. "Reconsidering the Hansen Thesis: Generational Metaphors and American Ethnic Studies." *American Quarterly* 43(2): 320–32.

Weber, Max. 1978. *Economy and Society: An Outline of Interpretive Sociology*. Berkeley: University of California Press.

Weinberg, Jeshajahu. 1994. "A Narrative History Museum." *Curator: The Museum Journal* 37(4): 231–39.

White, Hayden V. 1973. *Metahistory: The Historical Imagination in Nineteenth-Century Europe*. Baltimore: Johns Hopkins University Press.

Wilczyk, Wojciech. 2009. *There's No Such Thing as an Innocent Eye*. Kraków: Atlas Sztuki.

Wimmer, Andreas. 2008a. "Elementary Strategies of Ethnic Boundary Making." *Ethnic and Racial Studies* 31(6): 1025–55.

——. 2008b. "The Making and Unmaking of Ethnic Boundaries: A Multilevel Process Theory." *American Journal of Sociology* 113(4): 970–1022.

Wodziński, Marcin. 2011. "Jewish Studies in Poland." *Journal of Modern Jewish Studies* 10(1): 101–18.

——. In press. "Prospects for Jewish Studies in Poland: An Update for a New Decade." *Studies in Contemporary Jewry* 32.

Wolska-Pabian, Karolina, and Paweł Kowal, eds. 2019. *Muzeum i zmiana: Losy muzeów narracyjnych*. Kraków: Universitas.

Wóycicka, Zofia. 2019. "Global Patterns, Local Interpretations: New Polish Museums Dedicated to the Rescue of Jews during the Holocaust." *Holocaust Studies* 25(3): 248–72.

Yack, Bernard. 1996. "The Myth of the Civic Nation." *Critical Review* 10(2): 193–211.

Young, James Edward. 1993. *The Texture of Memory: Holocaust Memorials and Meaning*. New Haven, CT: Yale University Press.

Young, James O. 2010. *Cultural Appropriation and the Arts*. Oxford: Wiley-Blackwell.

Zarycki, Tomasz. 2014. *Ideologies of Eastness in Central and Eastern Europe*. London: Routledge.

Zerubavel, Eviatar. 1982. "Easter and Passover: On Calendars and Group Identity." *American Sociological Review* 47(2): 284–89.

——. 1991. *The Fine Line: Making Distinctions in Everyday Life*. New York: Free Press.

——. 2003. *Time Maps: Collective Memory and the Social Shape of the Past*. Chicago: University of Chicago Press.

——. 2012. *Ancestors and Relatives: Genealogy, Identity, and Community*. New York: Oxford University Press.

Zerubavel, Yael. 2014. "'Numerical Commemoration' and the Challenges of Collective Remembrance in Israel." *History & Memory* 26(1): 5–38.

Ziarek, Ewa Płonowska. 2007. "Melancholic Nationalism and the Pathologies of Commemorating the Holocaust in Poland." In *Imaginary Neighbors: Mediating Polish-Jewish Relations after the Holocaust*, edited by Dorota Glowacka and Joanna Zylinska, 301–26. Lincoln: University of Nebraska Press.

Ziff, Bruce, and Pratima V. Rao. 1997. "Introduction to Cultural Appropriation: A Framework for Analysis." In *Borrowed Power: Essays on Cultural Appropriation*, edited by Bruce Ziff and Pratima V. Rao, 1–30. New Brunswick, NJ: Rutgers University Press.

Zimmerman, Joshua D. 2003. *Contested Memories: Poles and Jews during the Holocaust and Its Aftermath*. New Brunswick, NJ: Rutgers University Press.

Zubrzycki, Geneviève. 2001. "'We, the Polish Nation': Ethnic and Civic Visions of Nationhood in Post-Communist Constitutional Debates." *Theory and Society* 30(5): 629–69.

——. 2005. "'Poles-Catholics' and 'Symbolic Jews': Jewishness as Social Closure in Poland." *Studies in Contemporary Jewry* 21: 65–87.

——. 2006. *The Crosses of Auschwitz: Nationalism and Religion in Post-Communist Poland*. Chicago: University of Chicago Press.

——. 2010. "What Is Pluralism in a 'Monocultural' Society? Considerations from Post-Communist Poland." In *After Pluralism: Reimagining Models of Interreligious Engagement*, edited by Courtney Bender and Pamela Klassen, 277–95. New York: Columbia University Press.

——. 2011. "History and the National Sensorium: Making Sense of Polish Mythology." *Qualitative Sociology* 34: 21–57.

——. 2013a. "Polish Mythology and the Traps of Messianic Martyrology." In *National Myths: Constructed Pasts, Contested Presents*, edited by Gérard Bouchard, 110–32. London: Routledge.

——. 2013b. "Narrative Shock and (Re)Making Polish Memory in the Twenty-First Century." In *Memory and Postwar Memorials: Confronting the Violence of the Past*, edited by Florence Vatan and Marc Silberman, 95–115. New York: Palgrave.

——. 2020. "Quo Vadis, Polonia? On Religious Loyalty, Voice, and Exit." *Social Compass* 67(2): 267–81.

Zubrzycki, Geneviève, and Anna Woźny. 2020. "The Comparative Politics of Collective Memory." *Annual Review of Sociology* 46: 175–94.

Żukowski, Tomasz. 2021. "The Object and Subject of Nostalgia: 'I Miss You, Jew' and 'The Burning Barn' by Rafał Betlejewski (2010)." In Elżbieta Janicka and Tomasz Żukowski, *Philo-Semitic Violence: Poland's Jewish Past in New Polish Narratives*, 93–124. Lanham, MD: Lexington Books.

INDEX